WAR AND PEACE IN THE
BALTIC 1560–1790

WAR IN CONTEXT
Series Editor: Jeremy Black

WAR AND SOCIETY IN EARLY-MODERN EUROPE, 1495–1715
Frank Tallett

WAR AND PEACE IN THE BALTIC
1560–1790

Stewart P. Oakley

Routledge
Taylor & Francis Group

LONDON AND NEW YORK

First published 1992
by Routledge
11 New Fetter Lane, London EC4P 4EE

Simultaneously published in the USA and Canada
by Routledge
29 West 35th Street, New York, NY 10001

Reprinted 2001, 2002

Transferred to Digital Printing 2003

Routledge is an imprint of the Taylor & Francis Group

© 1992 Stewart P. Oakley

Phototypeset in 10 on 12 point Bembo by
Intype, London
Printed in Great Britain by
Biddles Short Run Books

British Library Cataloguing in Publication Data

Oakley, Stewart P.
War and Peace in the Baltic, 1560–1790.
(War in Context Series)
I. Title II. Series
947

Library of Congress Cataloging in Publication Data

Oakley, Stewart P.
War and Peace in the Baltic, 1560–1790 / Stewart P. Oakley.
p.   cm. — (War in context)
Includes bibliography references and index.
1. Baltic States—History. 2. Europe, Eastern—History.
3. Europe—History—17th century. 4. Europe, Eastern—History—18th
century.
I. Title. II. Title: War and Peace in the Baltic, 1560–1790.
III. Series.
DK502.7.025   1993
947.4—dc20   92–6571

ISBN 0–415–02472–2

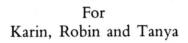

For
Karin, Robin and Tanya

CONTENTS

CONTENTS

MAPS

PREFACE

The immediate origins of this book lie in an essay on the Baltic
area contributed to a volume on the theme of the causes of war
in early modern Europe.[1] Its roots, however, lie much deeper,
indeed in my earliest forays into historical research, which
resulted in a doctoral dissertation on Anglo–Dutch relations with
Denmark and Sweden in the later seventeenth century.[2] Since
then I have been tempted to stray from the discipline of diplomatic history into the rather more fashionable one of social
history and forward in time into the eighteenth century. Never,
however, have I wandered very far from the Baltic world, and
in teaching Scandinavian history for many years in both Britain
and the United States I have constantly returned with pleasure to
the age when the Baltic was a centre of European attention as it
had not been since the Viking Age and which it was not to be
again. While my principal interest has remained the countries
which make up Scandinavia in its broadest meaning, I have been
made increasingly aware that these must always be seen in a
broader context and in particular in that of the part of Europe
adjacent to them. I trust, however, that the fact that my experience of this part of Europe is still less than that of Scandinavia
itself will not be too glaringly apparent in the subsequent
study.

For enlivening my early interest in the diplomatic history of
the Baltic as well as for launching me on my academic career I
have above all to thank professor Ragnhild Hatton. To her I owe
most of what I know in the field. For keeping alive my enthusiasm for the Scandinavian past I have to thank innumerable friends
in Scandinavia and those of my colleagues in Britain who form
the Nordic History Group. Finally to my publisher I owe thanks

for patience in response to my requests for yet another extension of the deadline for delivery of the manuscript.

Stewart Oakley
Norwich
November 1991

THE HOUSE OF VASA

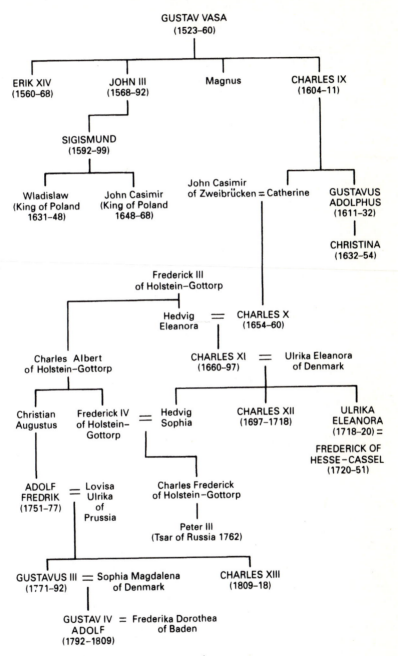

RULERS OF THE BALTIC LANDS 1560–1790

Denmark–Norway	Sweden–Finland	Poland–Lithuania	Muscovy/Russia
		Sigismund II Augustus 1548–72	Ivan IV ('the Terrible') 1533–84 (regency to 1547)
Frederik II 1559–88	Erik XIV 1560–8		
	John III 1568–92	Henry of Valois 1573–4	
Christian IV 1588–1648 (regency to 1596)		Stephen Bathory 1575–86	Fedor I 1584–98
		Sigismund III Vasa 1587–1632	
	Sigismund 1592–9		Boris Godonov 1598–1605
	Charles IX (regent 1599–1604; king 1604–11)		Basil (Vasili) Shuisky 1606–10
			Władysław (Vasa) 1610–12
			Michael Romanov 1613–45
	Gustavus II Adolphus 1611–32		
			Alexis 1645–76
	Christina 1632–54 (regency to 1644)	Władysław IV Vasa 1632–48	
		John II Casimir 1648–68	
Frederik III 1648–70	Charles X 1654–60		
		Michael Wisniowiecki 1669–73	

RULERS OF THE BALTIC LANDS 1560–1790

Denmark–Norway	Sweden–Finland	Poland–Lithuania	Muscovy/Russia
Christian V 1670–99	Charles XI 1660–97 (regency to 1672)		Fedor II 1676–82
		John III Sobieski 1674–96	Ivan V and Peter I 1682–96
Frederik IV 1699–1730	Charles XII 1697–1718	Augustus II 1697–1704	Peter I ('the Great') 1696–1725
	Ulrika Eleanora 1719–20	Stanislav Leszczyński 1704–9	Catherine I 1725–7
	Fredrik I 1720–51	Augustus II (restored) 1709–33	Peter III 1727–30
			Anna 1730–40
Christian VI 1730–46		Augustus III 1733–63	Ivan VI 1740–1
Frederik V 1746–66	Adolf Fredrik 1751–71		Elizabeth 1741–61
Christian VII 1766–1808		Stanislas II Augustus Poniatowski 1764–95	Peter III 1761–2
	Gustavus III 1771–92		Catherine II ('the Great') 1762–96

Margraves of Brandenburg	Grand Masters of the Livonian Order
Joachim II 1535–71	Heinrich von Galen to 1557
Johan George 1571–98	
Joachim Frederick 1598–1608	Wilhelm von Fürstenberg 1557–8 (abdicated)
John Sigismund 1608–19 (duke of Prussia from 1618)	Gotthard Kettler 1558–61 (last Grand Master)
Margraves of Brandenburg and dukes of Prussia George William 1619–40	*Dukes of Kurland* Gotthard (Kettler) 1561–87
Frederick William (the 'Great Elector') 1640–88	Friedrich and Wilhelm (Kettler) 1587–1616 Wilhelm (Kettler) 1616–40
Frederick III 1688–1701	Jakob (Kettler) 1640–82

RULERS OF THE BALTIC LANDS 1560–1790

Kings of Prussia	*Dukes of Kurland*
Frederick I 1701–13	Friedrich Kasimir 1682–98
	Friedrich Wilhelm 1698–11
Frederick William I 1713–40	
	(vacant 1711–26)
	Maurice de Saxe 1726
	(vacant 1726–31)
	Ferdinand (Kettler) 1731–7
Frederick II ('the Great') 1740–86	Ernst Johann (Biron) 1737–49
	Charles (of Saxony) 1758–62
	Ernst Johann (Biron) 1763–9
	Peter (Biron) 1769–95
Frederick William II 1786–97	

THE BALTIC 1558–1790:
A CHRONICLE

1621   Swedes capture Riga

1625   Denmark enters the Thirty Years War
1626   Battle of Lütter (defeat of Denmark by Catholic League)
        Battle of Wallhof (defeat of Poles by Swedes). Swedes transfer war against Poland to Prussia

1629   Peace of Lübeck (Denmark withdraws from Thirty Years War)
        Truce of Altmark (between Sweden and Poland)
1630   Gustavus Adolphus lands in Germany
1631   Battle of Breitenfeld (victory by Swedes over Catholic League)
1632   Battle of Lützen (death of Gustavus Adolphus)

1635   Truce of Stuhsmdorf (Poland and Sweden)

1643   Sweden attacks Denmark
1645   Peace of Brömsebro (Denmark and Sweden)

1648   Peace of Westphalia and end of Thirty Years War

1655   Sweden invades Poland
1656   Treaties of Marienburg and Labiau (Brandenburg–Prussia and Sweden)
1657   Treaty of Wehlau (Brandenburg–Prussia and Poland; Brandenburg wins sovereignty of East Prussia)
1658   Peace of Roskilde (Denmark and Sweden)

1660   Peace of Copenhagen (Denmark and Sweden) and Oliva (Sweden, Poland and Brandenburg–Prussia)
1661   Peace of Kardis (Russia and Sweden)

1667   Truce of Andrussovo (Poland and Russia)

1672   Franco–Swedish alliance

1675   Sweden invades Brandenburg
        Battle of Fehrbellin (defeat of Sweden)

1679   Peace of St Germain (Brandenburg and Sweden)
        Peace of Fontainebleau and Lund (Denmark and Sweden)

1683   Baltic crisis (threat of attack on Sweden by Denmark and Brandenburg–Prussia)

1686	'Eternal Peace' between Poland and Russia
1689	Peace of Altona (Restoration of duke of Holstein–Gottorp)
1691	First League of Armed Neutrality (Denmark and Sweden)
1698	Treaty between Saxony and Denmark (against Sweden)
1699	Treaties between Denmark and Russia and between Russia and Saxony (against Sweden)
1700	Opening of Great Northern War Treaty of Travendal (Denmark leaves war) Battle of Narva (Swedish victory over Russia)
1702	Battle of Kliszów (Swedish victory over Saxons)
1706	Peace of Altranstädt (Sweden and Saxony)
1709	Battle of Poltava (Sweden defeated by Russia)
1719	Peace between Sweden and Hanover
1720	Peace between Sweden and Brandenburg–Prussia/Denmark
1721	Peace of Nystad (Sweden and Russia)
1733–8	War of the Polish Succession
1741	Sweden attacks Russia
1743	Peace of Åbo (Russia and Sweden)
1757	Sweden attacks Brandenburg–Prussia (the 'Pomeranian War')
1762	Sweden makes peace with Brandenburg–Prussia
1764	Prusso–Russian alliance
1767	'Mageskifte' agreement between Denmark and Russia
1772	Coup d'etat by Gustavus III of Sweden
1773	First Partition of Poland
1788	Sweden attacks Russia
1790	Naval battle of Svensksund (Swedish victory over Russians) Peace of Fredrikshamn (Russia and Sweden)

INTRODUCTION

This book is an attempt to describe and make sense of the conflicts which occurred in the area of the Baltic Sea between the middle of the sixteenth and the end of the eighteenth century.

These conflicts formed part of a longer struggle for dominance in the area which can be traced back to the advance of the Germanic peoples into eastern Europe in the early Middle Ages, driving the Slavic inhabitants further and further along the southern coastline until they were largely cut off from the sea. Colonization was accompanied by the establishment of trading posts to tap the rich hinterlands. Such towns came together under the lead of Lübeck to form the eastern branch of the great Hanseatic League which dominated the region's economy from the end of the thirteenth century.[1] Against such German dominance the Scandinavian kingdoms of Denmark, Norway and Sweden formed the Union of Kalmar at the end of the fourteenth century. Of this Denmark, with its command of the entrance to the Sea, its wealth and its strong fleet, was the leader and the prime contender to enforce the doctrine of *mare clausum* or the right to exclude the ships of all nations which lay beyond it. It was also Denmark who first asserted the principle (if not in so many words) of *dominium maris Baltici*, an assertion of sovereignty over at least the Baltic between the Danish islands and the eastern coast of the Sea.[2] The clash between the League and the Union was complicated by rivalries within the latter which led to its eventual break-up in the 1520s, leaving Denmark and Norway united and a suspicious Sweden–Finland fearing the forced reimposition of control from Copenhagen.

A new stage in the struggle began in the middle of the sixteenth century with the collapse of political authority in the area of the

1

south-eastern Baltic, which now makes up the republics of Estonia and Latvia, and the efforts made by the expanding state of Muscovy under Tsar Ivan IV ('the Terrible' or 'the Dread') to exploit the situation in order to reach the sea on a broad front. By the end of the century Muscovy had, however, once more been pushed back from the coastline and the area divided between Sweden and Poland, who were in fact to struggle for its possession for another half century. Out of this conflict, and its participation in the Thirty Years War in central Europe, Sweden emerged as the leading power in the Baltic with control of a string of territories around the sea's southern and eastern rim, toppling Denmark from its earlier eminence. This was the position until the early eighteenth century when, as a result of the so-called Great Northern War, Sweden was forced to surrender most of the territories it had gained earlier and Russia took its place. The conflicts of the eighteenth century largely represent Sweden's attempts to recover at least some of the ground which it had lost.

In less detail and in the form of a briefer epilogue and a post-lude, I have also recounted the developments which led up to the further strengthening of Russia's position in the area with its acquisition of Finland during the Napoleonic Wars and the challenges to Russia's pre-eminence which came with the emergence of a Germany united under Prussia in the later nineteenth century and the ebb and flow of fortunes in the twentieth century. The reunification of Germany and the apparent break-up of the Soviet Union have changed the balance in the Baltic yet again in ways which at the time of writing are difficult to assess but which have cast the spotlight on a part of Europe which has been comparatively neglected by historians living beyond its bounds.

Struggles begun in the Baltic often spread into central and eastern Europe; Gustavus Adolphus's campaigns in Germany which began as a bid to push back the allies of his Polish enemies from the Baltic carried him almost to the gates of Vienna, and the turning point in his successor Charles XII's fight to preserve intact the kingdom which he had inherited against its jealous neighbours came in the Ukraine. I have, however, tried to resist the temptation to trace either campaign so far in any detail and thus to make the book a history of eastern and central Europe in the period. The accent is always on the Baltic and the countries surrounding it.

But the story is still a complex one, involving as it does the aims and ambitions not only of the leading protagonists in the region – Denmark, Sweden, Russia, Poland, Lithuania – but also of the smaller states of the area like the duchy of Kurland. The great powers of Europe outside the area, in particular Britain, France and the United Provinces of the Netherlands, also had their own interests to protect and the power – particularly the naval power – often to intervene quite decisively in Baltic conflicts. I have, however, attempted to deal with the latters' policies only when they are necessary to understand the struggles between the Baltic powers themselves.

Foreign policies and military achievements cannot be understood in isolation. They are strongly influenced by the internal political systems and economic resources of the countries involved. These I have analysed as seemed necessary.

I have generally used proper names in the forms in which they are most likely to be familiar to the English-speaking reader (e.g. Cracow rather than Kraków and the German Danzig rather than the Polish Gdańsk) or in which they were usually referred to in the period (thus the Swedish and German Reval rather than the Estonian Tallinn) while noting the native form of place-names and occasionally also of personal names when first mentioned. Thus I have preferred Charles to Karl, Gustavus Adolphus to Gustav Adolf and George Frederick to Georg Friedrich. I do not, however, pretend to have been consistent in this. Thus I have used the Danish form Frederik and the Swedish form Fredrik in Danish and Swedish names respectively.

1

SETTING THE SCENE

The Baltic, like the much larger Mediterranean,[1] of which it is in many ways northern Europe's equivalent,[2] is almost an inland sea. Access to the world's oceans is provided only by three narrow outlets: the Sound between the most easterly and largest Danish island of Zealand (Sjælland) and the southernmost part of the west coast of what is now Sweden, only 5 km wide at its northern end; the Great Belt between Zealand and the second largest Danish island of Fyn;[3] and the Little Belt between Fyn and the Danish mainland (Jutland or Jylland). The Mediterranean is divided into western and eastern basins between Sicily and Tunisia. The Baltic is similarly divided into two well-defined main areas: a larger southern basin between the Danish islands and the coasts of 'Balticum';[4] and a smaller northern arm – the Gulf of Bothnia. These are separated from each other by an almost continuous string of islands between the Swedish capital of Stockholm and the ancient Finnish capital of Turku (Åbo),[5] of which the Åland islands (now Finnish) form the central core.

The struggle for power in the Baltic in the early modern period, which will be examined in the succeeding chapters, was in effect a struggle for power in the southern Baltic, which takes up well over half its total area.[6] Around this lie the most densely populated land, the main ports of the region and the most productive agricultural areas. But, as will be seen, for long periods the struggle centred even more narrowly on the Baltic's eastern inlet of the Gulf of Finland, at the extreme eastern end of which Tsar Peter I (the Great) of Russia founded at the beginning of the eighteenth century his new capital of St Petersburg to be his 'window on the west'.

In the middle of the southern Baltic basin lies the Sea's largest

5

island of Gotland. By the sixteenth century this had lost its earlier importance as a commercial centre for trade between eastern and western Europe, but it was still of considerable strategic significance, lying as it does close to the main channels of communication by sea between central Sweden and the north coast of Germany. Of the other Baltic islands, that of Öland, lying like a long cigar off the east coast of Sweden south-west of Gotland and sheltering the port of Kalmar, has played only a minor role in the region's history, but those of Ösel (Saaremaa), which blocks access to the Gulf of Riga and the mouth of the River Dvina (Düna), of Bornholm between the north German coast and southern Sweden, and of Rügen and Usedom at the mouth of the river Oder in Pomerania have all been the subject of dispute because of their value as bases.

The main rivers flowing northward or north-westward into the Baltic from the heart of the European landmass have provided access to a large and potentially rich hinterland.[7] The Oder, Vistula (Wisla) and Dvina each has at or near its mouth an important port, respectively Stettin (Szczecin), Danzig (Gdańsk) and Riga. Also of some significance is the river Neva flowing into the Gulf of Finland and linking the Russian interior with the Baltic via lakes Ladoga and Pskov.[8] The rivers flowing from the interior of the Scandinavian peninsula into the Gulf of Bothnia became of significance only with the opening up of northern Sweden in the nineteenth century. The whole coast of the Baltic is low-lying and provides few good natural harbours, although the southern coast offers comparatively frequent sheltering river mouths such as that of the Oder and inlets such as the Bay of Pucka (Putzig) north of Danzig.[9] The Sea itself is comparatively shallow, especially at its outlets; the Sound and the Belts have saddle depths of only about 35 m. The paucity of deep channels and the plenitude of small islands in coastal waters have strongly influenced the character of naval warfare in the area and distinguished it from that of the open waters beyond; large deep-draught vessels have been unable to penetrate extensive strategic stretches of water.

The climate of the region is continental, modified by maritime influences. The Sea's considerable length north to south (over ten degrees of latitude) means that there are appreciable differences in winter temperatures. Ice usually forms along the whole coast in winter and in normal years in the twentieth century the northern part of the Gulf of Bothnia, the narrow channels through the archipelago at its southern end and the Gulf of Finland are frozen over during the winter months. In particularly severe winters the narrower channels in the southern Baltic can also be ice-bound for brief periods, while drift ice can hinder navigation for longer. During the so-called 'Little Ice Age', a period which began before and extended beyond our period, severe winters were more frequent and freezing could be more extensive. This could have serious effects on communications, particularly across the Gulf of Bothnia. The Sound and the Belts might on occasion freeze over to a considerable depth, and naval actions and sea-borne trade were largely limited to the spring, summer and early autumn.[10]

In the north of the region the severity of the climate as well as the short growing season have discouraged settlement. In the south nature has been more generous. The plains bordering the southern and south-eastern coasts and the Danish islands provide potentially rich grain-growing areas. Further north mixed farming has been the rule; only in exceptional years was there a surplus of grain with which to trade. But other resources have provided some compensation. An almost continuous belt of forests stretching from southern Sweden to southern Finland and eastward into Russia has not only offered plentiful timber for building and other domestic purposes but also provided tar for preserving ships' timber and charcoal for the smelting of iron. The latter was of particular significance for the area of Bergslagen north-west of Stockholm, rich not only in good quality iron but also other metals in demand like copper and even small quantities of silver. The harvest of the sea has, since the sixteenth century, when the herring migrated into the North Sea, been rather meagre, and fishing as an occupation has been of only local significance.

Traditionally water in pre-industrial Europe bound people together rather than kept them apart. Transport by sea was generally easier and swifter than travel by land over roads which were often impassable, and the Baltic from Viking times acted as the main channel along which flowed goods between western and north-eastern Europe.[11] The earliest nation state and for long the most important power in the Baltic grew up around the Sea's exits and entrances. By the end of the Viking period in the eleventh century, the kingdom of Denmark, centring on the island of Zealand, embraced not only the surrounding islands and the Jutish peninsula but also the southern part of what is now Sweden (the provinces of Scania (Skåne), Halland and Blekinge). This encouraged its kings to claim the right to control all shipping sailing into and out of the Baltic, a symbol of which was the toll exacted from all merchantmen passing the castle of Elsinore (Helsingør) from 1429. In the course of the early Middle Ages Danish power spread along the southern coast of the Baltic as far as the river Oder and for a time established itself on the southern coast of the Gulf of Finland, where the Estonian capital of Tallinn (literally Danish fort) commemorates these activities. Of its medieval conquests only the island of Gotland remained in the middle of the sixteenth century, but the kingdom's historical associations with both the north coast of Germany and with the south-eastern Baltic were never forgotten and were to play some part in Danish foreign policy in the sixteenth and seventeenth centuries.

To the north of Denmark, the effective power of the Swedish monarchy was confined to what is now south-central Sweden and south-western and southern Finland as far as the eastern end of the Gulf of Finland.[12] The country's only access to the west lay through a narrow strip of coastline around the mouth of the river Göta, squeezed between the Norwegian province of Bohuslän to the north and the Danish province of Halland to the south and far from the heartland of the monarchy around lake Mälar.[13] To the north, the Norwegian provinces of Jämtland and Härjedalen reached out towards the Gulf of Bothnia and further north still Sweden's frontier with Norway, whose crown had been united with that of Denmark since 1380, was ill defined, a fact which was liable to lead to disputes between the two monarchies. The frontier between eastern Finland and Muscovy had in theory been delimited by the treaty of Nöteborg (Orechovets) in 1323, but this was liable to more than one interpretation, and disputes over it also caused friction, especially as the inhabitants on either side of it often moved about as if it did not exist, and the Swedish government actually encouraged settlement beyond it.[14]

Muscovy touched the Baltic only where the river Neva flowed into the easternmost end of the Gulf of Bothnia. This limit had been reached as the result of the absorption of the republic of Novgorod between 1471 and 1478, and in 1492 Tsar Ivan III had built there the fortress of Ivangorod opposite the Estonian port of Narva, to which he hoped it would become a commercial rival. It never did.[15]

8

To the south of the Gulf lay the most complex of the Baltic's political units – an area referred to loosely as Livonia and occupying roughly the territory of the modern republics of Estonia and Latvia (the most northerly part was after the middle of the sixteenth century usually treated separately as Estonia (Estland), while the term 'Livonia' was confined to the area to the south). It consisted of a loose confederation of trading cities, most of whom were members of the Hanseatic League, ecclesiastical territories dominated by the archbishopric of Riga, and the estates of the Knights of the Sword or Livonian Order under their Grand Master, isolated in the eastern Baltic since the secularization of the parent Order of Teutonic Knights in 1525 as a result of the Protestant Reformation. All had since 1526 owed a vague allegiance to the Holy Roman Emperor in Vienna, who, however, took only an occasional interest in Baltic affairs. The original inhabitants of these lands, many of them still only nominally Christian, had long played a minor role in Livonian affairs; both political and economic life were dominated by German-speakers.[16]

South of the river Dvina began the sprawling grand duchy of Lithuania, united with the 'Republic' of Poland under the same king reigning in Cracow but retaining its own laws and institutions. Both Lithuania and Poland had only small coastlines, but between them lay that of the duchy of Prussia. This was ruled over by the successors of the last Grand Master of the Teutonic Knights, who had received it from the king of Poland when the Order was secularized and who still ruled it as a Polish vassal from his seat of power in the city of Königsberg (Kaliningrad). The king of Poland also exercised a claim to sovereignty over Danzig, the busiest of the Baltic's ports, through which flowed the bulk of Poland's grain and timber exports. The city, however, jealously guarded its privileges granted in the fifteenth century as reward for backing Poland against the Teutonic Order and which included freedom from taxation and a wide degree of autonomy.[17] Further west the boundary of the Holy Roman Empire reached the Baltic. The two duchies of Pomerania and Mecklenburg which lay between this border and Danish territory were poor and backward. Pomerania's main significance was as a barrier between the Baltic and the rising margravate of Brandenburg, whose ruling house of Hohenzollern had strong family ties with both Livonia and Prussia.

On the coast of Mecklenburg also lay the Hanseatic cities of Wismar and Lübeck, the former enjoying an uneasy relationship with its overlord, the duke of Mecklenburg, the latter an Imperial city owing allegiance only to the Emperor in Vienna and recognized as the leader of the League in the Baltic. The circle was completed by the two duchies of Holstein and Schleswig. The former lay within and the latter outside the Empire. Together they formed a jigsaw of lands, some ruled by the king of Denmark as duke of Schleswig–Holstein, some by various members of the Danish royal house of Oldenborg, and some administered jointly by king and dukes. On the Baltic coast of Holstein, the port of Kiel offered potential as a naval base.

2

THE BALTIC WORLD IN THE MIDDLE OF THE SIXTEENTH CENTURY

In the middle of the sixteenth century the Baltic was thus surrounded by three independent kingdoms – Denmark–Norway,
Sweden–Finland and Poland–Lithuania; a number of secular prin-
cipalities owing allegiance to the Holy Roman Empire – the
duchies of Holstein, Mecklenburg and Pomerania and the lands
of the Livonian Order; ecclesiastical territories in Livonia headed
by the archbishopric of Riga; and surrounding the Sea in an arc
from east to south-west, self-governing towns and cities, most
of them members of the Hanseatic League – Narva, Reval, Riga,
Elbing (Elbląg), Danzig, Stralsund, Lübeck and Wismar.

Of the kingdoms, only Sweden was an hereditary monarchy
and had become one as recently as 1544. Since finally breaking
away from the Danish-dominated Kalmar Union in the early
1520s, King Gustav, the first of the house of Vasa, had built up
a powerful position by his own personality and energy. For by
western European standards his system of government was still
rather primitive, relying as it did on the king's close personal
supervision with only a rudimentary civil service to carry out
decisions. Central government headed by the Chancery lay within
an itinerant court, travelling from royal castle to royal castle
throughout the year in medieval fashion. While Stockholm was
the largest town and the most important commercial centre of
the realm, it was not to be a centre of administration for nearly
a century. Local control was exercised through royal bailiffs in
charge of estates which had grown considerably as a result of the
Reformation settlement and from which much of the king's regular income was drawn, and through the royal castellans. The
system was financed largely by assigning the revenues (largely in
kind) of royal farms for the support of specific offices. The

11

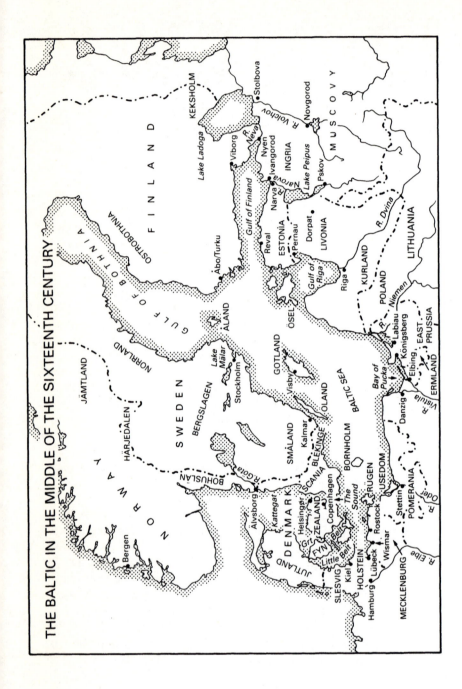

THE BALTIC IN THE MIDDLE OF THE SIXTEENTH CENTURY

considerable mineral deposits in central Sweden, in particular iron and copper, had been exploited since the early Middle Ages, but, in spite of Gustav's valiant efforts and his success in building up a store of silver, the economy in general was backward, overseas trade small scale and largely in foreign hands, ready money in short supply, the land thinly peopled and the crown's resources consequently limited.[1]

Royal power was restricted in theory by the terms of the medieval Land Law of King Magnus Eriksson. This bound the king to rule with the advice of his Council of great nobles (*med råds råde* as the phrase went) and by his coronation oath, and in practice by dependence on a nobility which monopolized all the great offices of state and, conscious of its own power, was jealous of any attempts by the king to increase his. The Diet (*Riksdag*), consisting of the Estates of nobles, clergy, burghers and peasants was not yet firmly established as an organ of government, but, as with Henry VIII and the English parliament, the king's use of it to drive through the new religious settlement since 1527 had helped to strengthen its power. Its claim to approve significant changes in the law and to grant new taxes was already becoming accepted. The monarch, however, could – and did – still call together representatives of only one or two of the Estates to deal with matters he deemed relevant to them alone, or summon provincial meetings to discuss local issues. The limitations on the king's powers were thus both in theory and practice quite considerable. But in matters of foreign policy, he had the final say.[2]

Denmark and Poland were elective monarchies. In both the crown had in practice passed for some time from father to son, but in Denmark the right of rebellion against an unpopular monarch had been exercised by the nobility as recently as the 1520s, when Christian II had been forced to make way for his uncle Frederik I, and the Council was able to force on each new monarch a Charter (*håndfæstning*) which obliged him to consult it on all matters of peace and war, on relations with foreign powers, and on the raising of taxes and troops.

In Poland the king was also expected to consult his noble Council on all important matters and to call regular meetings of the national Diet or *Sejm*. This consisted of two houses: a Senate of bishops, the chief officers of state and provincial governors; and a House of Representatives made up of all other members of the nobility (*szlachta*) able to attend, together with representatives of the city of Cracow. To this body the monarchy had to submit proposals for new laws and taxes. The royal bureaucracy was pitifully small, and the king's need to rely on the *Sejm* for much of his war expenditure made it difficult for him to act decisively in foreign affairs and to take advantage of opportunities which were offered. Many of the great nobles in fact felt free to conduct their own relations with foreign princes, and the nobility as a whole claimed the right to form armed 'confederations' to oppose a king who, they felt, had infringed upon their rights.[3]

In Denmark the Estates (*Stænder*) of nobles, clergy, burghers and peasants were called only when new taxes were needed and at irregular intervals. *Herredage* or afforced meetings of the Council were also at the king's disposal. Unlike Sweden, Denmark possessed a national centre of administration; by the middle of the sixteenth century Copenhagen was a capital city in every sense.

The kings of both Denmark and Poland–Lithuania ruled over territories with different traditions and semi-autonomous constitutions. Christian III of Denmark was also king of Norway by hereditary right. In his coronation oath, indeed, Norway had been referred to as if to a Danish province, but in practice the country maintained its own administration with a governor or viceroy in Åkershus castle. Norwegians were not represented in the Danish Estates. More significant for the future was the Danish king's position in the duchies of Schleswig and Holstein (Slesvig and Holsten respectively in Danish and often referred to simply as 'the Duchies' in Danish historiography). As duke of Schleswig–Holstein, he was in theory bound to consult the local nobility, but he was not tied down by any charter and had therefore a much freer hand than in the kingdom. As duke of the wholly German-speaking Holstein he was also a prince of the Holy Roman Empire owing allegiance to the Emperor and a member of the Lower Saxon Circle, one of the administrative and military divisions into which the Empire had been divided some fifty years earlier. Disputes between successive Danish kings and their cousins of the house of Holstein–Gottorp, with whom they shared the government of the duchies, were to play a prominent part in Danish foreign policy during the seventeenth and eighteenth centuries and, as with the responsibilities of the Danish crown in Norway, often to divert its attention away from the Baltic.[4]

The epicentre of the king of Poland's territories with his capital at Cracow also lay far from the Baltic. He was king only in Poland. In Lithuania, he was grand duke, while in Masovia, north of the river Vistula, and in western Prussia, at the mouth of the Vistula, he was no more than duke. Prussia east of the Vistula ('ducal' as distinct from 'royal' Prussia) was ruled by a duke of the Ansbach line of the house of Hohenzollern, the son of the last Grand Master of the Order of Teutonic Knights, but as a vassal of the king of Poland, to whom his subjects could appeal in case of dispute with him. Each of these areas had its separate administration. The nobility of Lithuania was particularly jealous of its privileges and, as will be seen, did not always see eye to eye with the king in Cracow on matters of foreign policy.[5]

The duchies of Pomerania and Mecklenburg, economically poor, were socially and politically dominated by a powerful land-owning nobility, which controlled the hereditary dukes through estates. Pomerania was to disappear as a political unit in the course of the next hundred years, by which time the south-east Baltic lands or 'Livonia' were to be carved up and shared out between their neighbours. Around 1550, however, they still consisted of a complex of competing jurisdictions, as already described (see above, p. 9).

The Hanseatic League was in the middle of the sixteenth century still an important naval power, and also able to use its wealth to raise troops to defend its interests; it could be a useful ally and a dangerous enemy. But, while the merchant marine which its members commanded in terms of number of ships remained considerable throughout the sixteenth century, and component cities like Riga, Danzig and Lübeck were flourishing trade centres, its commercial significance had waned rapidly in face of Dutch competition, and lack of a permanent central organization weakened its political effectiveness; since the crushing defeat of its fleet by Denmark and Sweden in the so-called Count's War in the 1530s, it was only a minor power in the Baltic, and never again was it to fight as a League.[6]

There was considerable rivalry between the Livonian cities, led by Riga but including also Reval, Dorpat (Tartu) and Pernau (Pärnu), who guarded jealously their control of trade with the interior of Muscovy, and the 'Prussian' or 'Wendish' cities led by

15

Lübeck, who were anxious to regain some share of this trade for themselves, were more strongly opposed to the growing activities of the Dutch merchants and were less inclined to take seriously the threat from Muscovy.[7]

In the middle of the sixteenth century Muscovy was not yet a Baltic power of any rank. It stood, however, as a brooding presence on the borders of Sweden (in Finland), Livonia and Lithuania. Its contacts with its neighbours were not intimate, and what little was known about its system of government and its military potential aroused a mixture of fear and contempt, with which was intermixed religious bigotry; some in the west even doubted whether Russian Orthodoxy was Christian at all. Its neighbours were particularly anxious that it should not be strengthened by gaining access to western technology and weaponry, while its more ambitious rulers were equally keen to secure such advantages.[8] In fact the way in which Muscovy was governed was not all that unlike that found elsewhere in eastern Europe. The Grand Prince of Muscovy (tsar only after 1546) inherited his title, but was advised by a number of high officials and a Council of noble boyars, intensely jealous of their privileges. The Council was afforced if necessary to create a form of Diet or *Zemsky Sobor*, containing representatives of the lesser nobility, towns and church, but its form and functions were ill defined and it never became an established institution. After a minority of fourteen years, during which the boyars had ruled unopposed, Ivan IV had to re-establish the authority of the crown and reform the administration so as to limit boyar influence; during the 1550s the powers of local governors were limited, the duties of the service nobility (*dvoryanstvo*) defined, government centralized through the creation of ministries (*izby*) with a variety of tasks and beginnings made with the creation of a standing army.[9]

The only navies regularly sailing the Baltic in the sixteenth century were those of Denmark, Sweden and Lübeck. Poland had only a small coastline in relation to its large total landmass and an insignificant merchant marine, and lacked a reliable base for a fleet. In any case its rulers generally were without the financial resources to maintain one; they required all they could husband to defend their extensive land frontiers, which marched not only with Muscovy in the east but also with the Turks in the south. In times of conflict in the 1560s and 1570s, however, large numbers of Polish privateers might be found sailing the eastern Baltic with royal blessing.[10] Denmark, which had succeeded the Hansa as the leading Baltic naval power after the Count's War, had the advantage over its Swedish rival both of a large pool of experienced seamen, especially from the seafaring Norwegians, and of its base on the Sound. Even Denmark, however, relied largely on the mobilization of large merchant ships for its sea defence in time of war. Gustav Vasa had succeeded in forming an equally large fleet, including some twenty large galleys for use in the archipelagos of central Sweden and southern Finland. But the main Swedish naval base in Stockholm was inconveniently far north for operations in the southern Baltic.[11]

Denmark had no form of standing army until the seventeenth century. Its nobles were expected to provide 'knight service' in time of war, which provided about 2,000 horses. Otherwise professional German mercenary or Scots units were raised as seemed necessary for the occasion. The Swedish kings were compelled to rely much more on native infantry, raised by regular conscription from the peasant population and armed with cross-bows or arquebuses, but in time of large-scale warfare they also had to employ mercenaries, which proved a serious drain on their treasury.[12]

The core of the tsar's military forces throughout the sixteenth and much of the seventeenth century was made up of the feudal levy of horse provided by the chief landowners as a condition for holding their estates. This was poorly armed and largely untrained. From the 1550s it was afforced by bodies of *streltsy*, hereditary infantrymen armed with arquebuses. The king of Poland and grand duke of Lithuania had at his disposal only a very small standing army, mainly stationed in the east of his realm. In time of war he could call on such enlisted foot soldiers as financial resources would allow and by a mounted feudal host provided by the nobility, brave and skilful fighters but resentful of discipline. The Livonian Knights had long ceased to be of any military significance.[13]

Since the Count's War had ended in 1536 with peace between a victorious Christian III of Denmark and the city of Lübeck, the Baltic had been spared a large-scale armed conflict. There were, however, a number of potential flash-points, and tension was not lacking. Danish rulers were far from reconciled to the break-up of the Kalmar Union, which Denmark had dominated, and peace between Christian and Gustav Vasa of Sweden (who remained on the throne until 1560) was maintained largely because of the common problems they faced, the solution of which might lead to a resumption of hostilities: a common threat from the heirs and supporters of King Christian II, who had been captive in Denmark since his abortive attempt to regain his throne in 1541; and the carrying through of a Protestant religious settlement, which had been introduced by King Christian only after his triumph in the Count's War and only partially implemented by Gustav Vasa. This latter in particular led to complications in relations with the Catholic Emperor during the religious war in Germany which was not brought to an end until 1555 with the peace of Augsburg, and an alliance between the two powers at Brömsebro in 1541 was, if nothing more, a reflection of their common concerns.[14]

But old subjects of dispute between the Scandinavian monarchies were always liable to erupt and new ones to emerge. King Gustav was very conscious of the weakness of his realm's strategic position should war break out with Denmark. Its only direct access to the west lay through the narrow strip of coast on either side of the Göta river protected by the fortress of Älvsborg. This was threatened in the north from the Norwegian province of Bohuslän and in the south from the Danish province of Halland. Communications with the southern Baltic were threatened by the island of Gotland, the ownership of which was still a bone of contention but was in Denmark's possession. An opportunity to break out of the ring which Denmark thus seemed to throw round the Swedish kingdom might tempt its king to take action which would lead to conflict, and in anticipation Gustav tried to establish contact with powers beyond the Baltic, in particular with England, whither he sent an embassy in 1557, and to build up a national army and to refound a naval force.[15]

Poland–Lithuania had since the end of the fifteenth century been struggling to halt the advance of Muscovy westward, but its attentions were divided between the Baltic and the expanding Turkish power to its south, and since 1532 there had been a truce in the struggle with Muscovy.[16]

The only military action which disturbed the peace of the Baltic in the 1550s was on the eastern border of Finland, where ancient disputes led to war between Sweden and Muscovy in 1554. The main cause of this was Swedish settlement to the east of the ill-defined frontier between the two powers in Karelia.[17]

How far the expansion of Muscovite/Russian power during the succeeding centuries can be interpreted as a conscious 'Drive to the Sea' is the subject of dispute. But ever since the days of Ivan III ('the Great') in the later fifteenth century, the princes of Muscovy had been extending their control outwards along the river system at the heart of which Moscow lay. As has been seen, Ivan's annexation of the republic of Novgorod had brought his principality to the extreme eastern end of the Gulf of Finland. He had also inherited Novgorod's traditional opposition to the eastward march of the Germanic peoples, which the republic had successfully halted in the middle of the thirteenth century. He had in fact himself clashed with both the Order of Knights in Livonia and with Sweden in Finland, but the acquisition of Novgorod had also given Muscovy a common frontier with Lithuania. The latter occupied a large area which had formed part of the Kievan state before its dissolution under the impact of the Mongol invasion in the thirteenth century (the 'patrimony of St Vladimir') and to which Muscovy would lay claim as Kiev's successor. This diverted Ivan away from the Baltic and created for his successors a dilemma in foreign policy: whether, with the limited resources at their disposal, to lay the emphasis on defence and expansion in the north, west or south of their dominions. A sixty-year truce with Sweden had been concluded in 1510, and there was thereafter no further incursion by Muscovy into the Baltic region until the end of the regency for Ivan IV.[18]

Ivan had, however, continued his predecessor's policy of expansion. Having secured his position on the lower Volga river in the south-east by 1557, he turned his attention to the north-west. There Sweden and Livonia blocked direct contact between Muscovy and a western world which offered the military and technical know-how of which Muscovite rulers had long felt the need, and from which the rulers of Sweden and Lithuania were determined they should not benefit. In addition Ivan could claim historical rights to Livonia and in particular to the see of Dorpat on its border with Muscovy, which had half a millennium before been ruled over by Yuriev of Kiev. A treaty in 1555, which renewed the truce between Muscovy and Livonia for fifteen years, in fact recognized Muscovite rights to tribute from the see, of which Ivan claimed fifty years' back payment. Religious differences also helped to create tension in the area in relations, for example,

19

between Orthodox Muscovy and both the Protestants of Livonia and the Catholics of Poland.[19]

The Lithuanians in their turn had a particular interest in preventing further Muscovite expansion in the area, where again Livonia occupied a key position; its acquisition would be highly desirable should conflict between the two powers again break out after the expiry of the truce in 1562. There was at the same time a strong desire for peace and even alliance with the tsar among the Lithuanian nobility.[20]

And Livonia in the 1550s was rapidly moving towards political dissolution. It was becoming a power vacuum into which its neighbours would almost inevitably be drawn. Fierce antagonisms had flared up between William (Wilhelm) of Brandenburg, archbishop of Riga, and Henry (Heinrich) von Galen, the Grand Master of the Order of Livonian Knights. The two men represented two opposing orientations in Livonian foreign policy. William, who was the brother of duke Albert, administrator of ducal or East Prussia and thus a vassal of the king of Poland, looked to Poland–Lithuania for protection against Muscovite pressure, while von Galen favoured accommodation with the power to the east, in which policy he enjoyed the support of a fair number of Livonian nobles. It was a rivalry which King Sigismund (Zygmunt) Augustus of Poland (1520–72), imperial protector of the archbishop and closely related to him, encouraged as a means of extending his influence in the region. In this he was encouraged by his Lithuanian advisers led by Michael Radziwiłł . In 1556 the archbishop was charged by the Livonian Diet with treasonable correspondence with Poland, and the new Grand Master William (Wilhelm) von Fürstenburg made him prisoner.[21]

In September 1557, King Sigismund, having gathered an overwhelming military force on the frontier, forced on von Furstenberg the so-called Agreement of Poswol. By this archbishop William was released and restored and an alliance concluded against Muscovy. This was undoubtedly in breach of the treaty of 1554 between Livonia and Muscovy, in which the former had engaged not to make any military agreements with either Poland or Sweden. Nor had the same treaty been fulfilled by Livonia in regard to the Dorpat tribute, which in 1557 the Livonians asked to be cancelled or at least reduced.[22]

At the same time alarmed and encouraged by the situation, Ivan in March 1557, having failed to capture the Finnish town of

Viborg (Viipuri), concluded a forty-year truce with Sweden in which King Gustav promised not to aid Livonia against Muscovy, and somewhat precipitously in January 1558 invaded Livonia with an army of 40,000 men. Its Estates asked to negotiate and offered the outstanding tribute. Ivan agreed to a brief armistice, but when this was violated renewed the struggle and in May succeeded in capturing the key port of Narva.[23] The modern struggle for Baltic dominance had begun.

While Ivan's involvement with the Baltic after taking Kazan in 1552 has usually been pictured as a logical and almost inevitable development, it is worth noting that a majority of his advisers, including Ivan Viskovaty and Aleksei Adashev, believed that Muscovite strength should be concentrated rather against the Crimean Tatars in the south and that for the time being at least Muscovite activity in Livonia should be strictly limited. But Ivan did not feel ready to face the Turks and in 1557 was won over to the idea of a full-scale Livonian campaign, thus committing himself to a fateful war on two fronts, for the Tatars continued to menace his territories from the south and thus divided his strength.[24] Before, however, examining further the consequences of Ivan's decision, it is necessary to look at a motive for the ensuing struggle which has not as yet been touched on but which was undoubtedly of considerable importance.

Since the fifteenth century the hinterland of the southern and south-eastern Baltic had acquired growing economic importance, not only for the littoral states but also for many beyond it. With the revival of the economy of Europe from the depression from which it had suffered for much of the later Middle Ages and the rise in population which accompanied this revival, the demand grew enormously for the increasing quantities of grain offered by the lands drained by the Oder, Vistula and Dvina rivers and for 'naval stores' like timber from Poland, hemp for ropes and flax for sails from Livonia and Muscovy, and tar from Finland. The slow spread of inflationary pressures towards eastern Europe also meant that the price differences between the produce of western and eastern Europe went far to cover the additional cost of transportation. The Baltic gradually took over from the Mediterranean as the main axis of European trade and, in the course of the early sixteenth century, more and more of such goods were loaded in ports like Reval, Riga, Königsberg and Danzig to be transported through the Sound largely on Dutch but also on French, Spanish and even English ships.[25]

The merchants of the old Hanseatic towns were pushed increasingly onto the sidelines, while none of the other Baltic powers had merchant fleets able to compete. The Hansa's trade had been based to a large extent on the herring fisheries off the Baltic coasts of Denmark and on Lüneberg salt for preservation of the catch, traded along the land route across the base of the Jutish peninsula between Lübeck and Hamburg. With the migration of the herring to the northern Kattegat in the later sixteenth century, the Dutch were able to break the Hanseatic monopoly and also to replace Lüneberg with the cheaper 'Bay salt' from the Bay of Bourgneuf on the Atlantic coast of France. The closing of the Hanse's *kontor* in Novgorod by Tsar Ivan III in 1494 had also considerably weakened the League's position in the eastern Baltic and opened up to western merchants the possibility of direct trade with Muscovy through the Livonian ports. For the Dutch, their Baltic trade, particularly in grain, was until the eighteenth century the basis of their economic prosperity, considerably more important indeed than their more spectacular and colourful activities in the Indies.[26]

For the rulers of the Baltic powers, at a time when costs of administration and in particular of military establishments were imposing greater and greater burdens on their exchequers, control of such trade could provide a highly desirable source of income in the form of customs dues, which, unlike the rents from their landed estates on which they still largely relied, would grow as the economy grew. In the case of the princes of Muscovy and Lithuania this meant the acquisition of direct control of the trade flowing to a large extent down their own rivers but to a port which was not under their control. In the case of Sweden, it meant the acquisition of ports on the southern Baltic from which the 'Russian' trade could be supervised and milked or the diversion of trade northward through the ports on the northern shore of the Gulf of Finland like Viborg and Helsinki. The latter was founded in 1550 for just this purpose, and in 1558 King Gustav tried without success to attract Russian merchants to Viborg.[27]

That such considerations played a part in the calculations of a number of rulers and of their advisers can hardly be doubted. Marxist historians in particular have, however, tended to assume that they were the be-all and end-all of Baltic policy in the sixteenth and seventeenth centuries and that the struggle for power in the Baltic in this epoch was a struggle for trade routes, ports and markets and little else. Ivan IV certainly tried to develop Ivangorod as a replacement for the nearby Narva as the staple for trade flowing down the Narova river, even though its harbour was not deep enough to accommodate large Dutch and English ships, and his contact with the English merchants on the White Sea was motivated by the need to provide an alternative outlet for Muscovite exports. But his war in Livonia was in fact launched without reference to the Muscovite merchants who might have been expected to support it, and is more likely to have begun as an assertion of treaty rights, which developed into something more when the weakness of the opposition became apparent. Muscovite merchants do, on the other hand, appear to have been influential in the decision to maintain the war in Livonia in 1566, when they attended the *Zemsky Sobor* for the first time.[28]

Ivan's attack led to renewed calls from both the Livonian Order and the ill-defended independent cities of Livonia for assistance from neighbouring powers: from Sweden on the other side of the Gulf of Finland and Poland–Lithuania to the south, both of which had recently been at war with Muscovy and could be expected to oppose any extension of its power; and further afield to Denmark, the strongest naval power in the Baltic with a traditional interest in the area and, indeed, certain claims in Estonia, which it had held in the thirteenth and early fourteenth centuries before selling it to the Order.[29] Even the Emperor and the Hanseatic League were approached. All responded, though some with more alacrity and effectiveness than others.

The Emperor did dispatch a delegation to Moscow in October 1559 to try to secure peace, and the Imperial Diet, where Duke John Albert (Johann Albrecht) of Mecklenburg, whose brother had been named coadjutor and thus his expected successor by the archbishop of Riga, spoke up strongly for the Livonians, voted 100,000 gulden to defend Livonia. But the delegation never reached Moscow, and the voted sum was never collected; the southern German princes favoured Muscovy as a possible ally against the Turks. Only Duke John sent some help to the Order on his own initiative. As for the Hanseatic Wendish towns, they tried to exploit the embarrassment of their Livonian brethren to wring concessions from them which would weaken their monopoly and actually welcomed the fall of Narva; through it they now hoped to secure direct access to the Russian trade which had been hitherto denied them by their Livonian rivals, who had kept the city out of the League. Only Danzig sent aid; led by Lübeck the other towns simply called on the Livonians to negotiate with the tsar under Danish mediation.[30]

In Denmark, Christian III, although already tempted by Albert (Albrecht) of Brandenburg with the prospect of recovering Reval and the neighbouring part of Estonia for the Danish crown, which he claimed had only been pawned to the Order since 1343, was extremely cautious. In July 1558 a pro-Danish faction in Reval, which looked to Denmark to hinder trade with the Russian-controlled Narva, seized the town's castle. From this they were not dislodged until the end of the year, and in 1558 Christoffer von Münchhausen, the brother of Johann, the bishop of Ösel and Kurland (Courland), offered to sell the island of Ösel and the district of Piltene in northern Kurland to Denmark in exchange for a pension.[31]

Christian, suspicious of the Muscovites but hoping to gain their support against Sweden, agreed to send an embassy to Moscow, which set off in October 1558 to negotiate peace. At the same time he demanded from the Order, in exchange for further help, the cession of the Estonian districts of Harrien and Wierland, terms which proved too high for it. To the Danish claims on Estonia, the Muscovites replied that the area had been theirs six hundred years even further back. The negotiations were interrupted by Christian's death the following year. But his son and successor Frederik II, anxious to find an appanage for his younger brother, the 18-year-old prince Magnus, and to avoid a further division of Schleswig–Holstein, as well as to acquire a further base from which to threaten Sweden's communications with the southern Baltic, accepted the offer of Ösel and Piltene on behalf of the young man at the cost of 30,000 daler. Magnus landed in Livonia in April 1560.[32] In June of the same year Lübeck also secured a trade treaty with Denmark. But even had the Danes wished to be drawn further into the struggle, distance made their direct participation difficult, and Magnus found himself forced into greater and greater isolation in his eastern outpost, and further opportunities for aggrandisement slipped from his grasp.[33]

Disappointed with Denmark, the Order turned to Poland–Lithuania, though in Riga and in Estonia there was fear of the effects of Polish intervention on trade and on the Protestant religious settlement. Sigismund himself agreed with some reluctance to accept the role of mediator and protector; the Lithuanian nobility opposed acceptance of the overlordship of Livonia, to which Poland also had an historical claim but which would bring Lithuania into conflict not only with Muscovy but also with the Scandinavian monarchies, and the king hesitated before committing himself to a full-scale war for which he could not count on the wholesale support of his subjects. Not until August 1559, after the resumption of the Muscovite assault, did he conclude the treaty of Vilna (Wilno) with the new Grand Master, Gotthard Kettler, and the archbishop of Riga. The treaty gave him approximately one-seventh of the Order's lands bordering on Lithuania and the right to instal garrisons in ten castles in exchange for his services as peace-maker.[34]

In Sweden, Gustav Vasa proved as cautious as Christian III. It was not in Sweden's interests to save the Order, reports about which were such as to make its cause seem a hopeless one. And the king was particularly unwilling to risk reopening hostilities with Muscovy at a time when his relations with Denmark were becoming strained. An embassy to Stockholm by the Order in April 1558 brought no response, and in the following July the king refused a request from Reval, temporarily under Danish control, to ban trade with Russia. The following February he offered the tsar his mediation. But his son and heir Prince Erik, and Erik's half-brother John (Johan) had their appetites whetted by the prospects opened up by the appeal. One of Erik's dreams was of attracting Baltic trade with the west through Sweden by means of a canal which could bypass the Danish-controlled Sound. And as grand duke of Finland since 1556, John had already begun to conduct his own foreign policy in the eastern Baltic, a policy which involved the extension of his influence south of the Gulf of Finland in collaboration with Poland–Lithuania and drawing Russian trade through a large area under his control. He offered Reval his protection.[35]

In July 1560 the Order was encouraged by Duke John to send a new delegation to Stockholm. This was followed the next month by one from the city of Reval, which had returned to its former allegiance to the Order but was now directly threatened by the Muscovite advance and wished for assistance in imposing an effective blockade on the Muscovite-controlled Narva. They found King Gustav on his deathbed.[36]

With Denmark having established a foothold in Livonia, Erik, once established on his throne, entered into negotiations with the delegates, who were offered help in exchange for their subjection to the Swedish crown. In May 1561 an agreement was reached in Reval by which Sweden would defend the city and the surrounding area of Estonia (Harrien, Wierland and Jerven) in exchange for the recognition of Swedish sovereignty. The expansion of the Swedish realm began with this act. But that this was not its intended result is suggested by the dispatch at the beginning of the year of a Swedish delegation to Moscow to seek an agreement with Ivan and in particular a renewal of the truce of 1557. Erik, while appreciating the strategic and economic danger of a Muscovite occupation of Livonia, did not desire war with Ivan if it could be avoided at a time when conflict with Denmark, Poland and Lübeck seemed likely. It is significant that he had not committed himself in the agreement he reached with Reval, in spite of the city's urgings, to enforce a blockade of Narva, whither merchants had begun to flock after it fell to the Muscovites, depriving Reval of much of its trade.[37]

3

THE STRUGGLE FOR
LIVONIA (1558–95)

The intervention of Denmark, Sweden and Poland in the war between Muscovy and the Order in Livonia marks the beginning of the early modern stage of the struggle for power in the Baltic (*dominium maris Baltici*, as it was first described in 1563 by King Sigismund of Poland, in disapproving of it) which was to continue with little interruption until the establishment of Russian supremacy in the early eighteenth century.[1]

By the middle of the 1580s the tsar had been expelled from Livonia and had lost his foothold on the Baltic; Denmark, while retaining a foothold in Balticum in the shape of the island of Ösel, had given up any serious attempt it may have entertained to establish control there; the Hanseatic League had ceased altogether to be a factor in Baltic politics; and the Emperor, although he did not entirely give up his Baltic interests, had had to acknowledge that the princes of the Empire were unwilling to support any pretensions he might have there. Only by bidding for the Polish crown for one of their number when it became vacant were the Austrian Habsburgs to intervene in the area for some time to come.

Livonia was effectively divided between Poland and Sweden. But not equally. Sweden, in fact, after twenty years of struggle held little more than the area which had sworn allegiance to Erik XIV in 1561. This first period can therefore be regarded as a victorious one for the Polish–Lithuanian Commonwealth as well as a serious setback for Muscovite hopes of securing a Baltic coastline and with it direct access to the west. And the election of the king of Sweden's son and heir as king of Poland in 1587 seemed to promise the complete domination of the Baltic by a great new power, or at least by a dual monarchy in which Poland

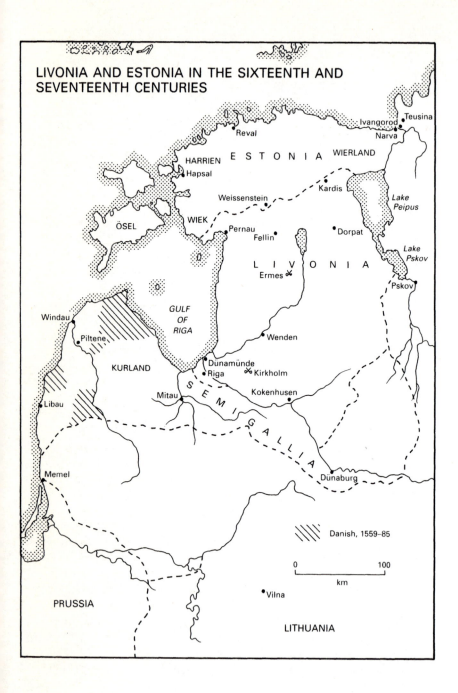

LIVONIA AND ESTONIA IN THE SIXTEENTH AND SEVENTEENTH CENTURIES

Reval

ESTONIA

WIERLAND

Ivangorod • Teusina
Narva

HARRIEN

Hapsal

Weissenstein

Kardis

Lake
Peipus

ÖSEL

WIEK

Pernau
Fellin

Dorpat

Lake
Pskov

LIVONIA

Ermes

Pskov

Windau

GULF
OF
RIGA

Piltene

Wenden

KURLAND

Dünamünde
Riga
Kirkholm

Libau

Mitau

S E M I G A L L I A

Kokenhusen

Danish, 1559–85

0   100

km

Memel

Dünaburg

PRUSSIA

Vilna

LITHUANIA

would be the senior partner. The reaction of the Swedish nobility to this development, however, brought about the rupture of the union only six years later, before it could become effective, and the commencement of over half a century of Swedo–Polish antagonism.

After his initial attack on Livonia the tsar lost the initiative. Dorpat fell to him in July 1558, and in the winter of 1558-9 his forces were raiding as far as Riga, helped by the widespread support he enjoyed among the Livonian peasants, who welcomed Muscovite aid against their oppressive German landlords. But Adashev was again advising his master to limit his demands to the eastern part of the country, including Dorpat and Narva, and to accept a Danish offer of mediation. Threatened by the Tatars in the south of his dominions, Ivan did in March 1559 agree to a six-month truce, negotiated by the Danish delegation in Moscow which had hoped to secure a permanent peace.[2]

But the pause in the fighting which resulted was exploited by the Order to secure a firm promise of Polish help in exchange for the occupation of south-eastern Livonia by Polish troops. This encouraged Kettler to break the truce by trying to recapture Dorpat at the end of 1559. He failed, and, inadequately supported by his Polish allies, the Order's main army in August 1560 suffered in the last battle it ever fought a serious defeat at Ermes which led to the capture of the key fortress of Fellin (Wiljandi), reputedly the strongest in Livonia.[3]

But the opportunity for a swift Muscovite occupation of Livonia had been missed. Adashev was blamed for the armistice which had caused this, was dismissed and thrown into prison, where he died at the end of 1560. Ivan attempted to secure peace with Lithuania on the basis of a marriage alliance involving himself and one of King Sigismund's sisters and the Lithuanian recognition of the Muscovite's possession of the city of Smolensk, but negotiations intending to lead to this failed.[4]

Erik XIV extended the area under his control in northern Estonia with the occupation of the fortresses of Weissenstein, Leal and Pernau, a move which antagonized the Order. And at the same time Poland's position in the area was strengthened in November 1561 at Vilna, where the archbishop and the Grand Master submitted to Sigismund Augustus. Kettler agreed to the secularization of the Order in exchange for Kurland and Semigallia as an hereditary grand duchy owing allegiance to the Polish crown.[5] A formal act of submission was concluded the following March. Only the city of Riga, in spite of being offered the privileges enjoyed by Danzig under the Polish crown, remained defiant. It had led the opposition to Poland during the negotiations and now would only agree to the settlement if the conditions were confirmed by the *Sejm*, which they were not. In fact the city was to withstand Polish blandishments and threats for a further twenty years. Ivan's reactions to these moves, which gave Sigismund a good claim to the whole of Livonia, was to renounce the truce with Lithuania and renew the war at the beginning of 1562. After some initial success, the tide of battle turned against him, but he was relieved by developments elsewhere in the Baltic.[6]

In October 1562 Erik XIV's half-brother John married King Sigismund's sister Catherine, whom the tsar himself had sought as his second wife with the object of weakening the war party in the Commonwealth. John continued to conduct an independent foreign policy in the area and acquired control of seven Livonian castles as security for a loan to his new brother-in-law. This ran counter to King Erik's policy, which favoured agreement with the tsar, who seemed less of a threat to Sweden's position in Estonia than did Poland after the treaty of Vilna. The Swedish king consequently proceeded to conclude a twenty-five-year truce with Ivan, to arrest his half-brother and to seize John's Livonian castles, which caused a breach with Sigismund.[7]

Ivan's position was further eased by the outbreak in 1563 of the so-called Seven Years War of the North between Sweden on one side and an alliance of Denmark, Poland and Lübeck on the other.

Denmark and Lübeck in particular had become increasingly irritated by King Erik's attempts finally to force all Russian trade to flow through the Swedish-controlled ports of Reval and Viborg and to blockade Narva. From the spring of 1562, when Muscovy and Poland were again in conflict, merchant ships attempting to trade with Narva found themselves constantly harrassed by Swedish naval vessels and by privateers fitted out by the burghers of Reval, and in June a large mixed merchant fleet was arrested, its crews harshly treated and the thirty-two Lübeck ships within it detained. But as far as Denmark was concerned, the ambitions of the brutal and irascible King Frederik II, who began to formulate claims to Danish sovereignty over the waters of the southern Baltic (*dominium maris septentrionalis*) and deeply resented Sweden's acquisition of Reval, and those of the vain and quixotic Erik XIV could not be reconciled; both dreamed of Baltic dominance, and an armed clash between the two, even if not desired, was eventually almost inevitable.[8]

In the middle of 1562 a Danish delegation arrived in Moscow to persuade the tsar to recognize Magnus's position and to propose an alliance against Sweden. The tsar refused to be drawn on the latter, but, on the eve of the resumption of hostilities with Poland–Lithuania, he did agree to recognize Denmark's right to the territories ruled by Prince Magnus and promised not to interfere with the young man. In August a trade agreement was concluded; both sides were to establish 'factories' on each other's territories and permit each other's merchants to trade freely. A further attempt by Frederik to gain a Russian alliance in 1564 ended, however, in a humiliating rebuff. Ivan was offended by Denmark's alliance with his main protagonist, the king of Poland.[9]

Both sides began mobilizing their forces at the beginning of 1563, and in May a Swedish naval detachment attacked Danish ships near Bornholm. Three Danish ships were lost and the Danish commander taken prisoner. Attempts to prevent the outbreak of war proved fruitless, and in August both Denmark and Lübeck, who had concluded an alliance in June, declared war on Sweden. Poland, who had sought an agreement with Erik but whose forces had already clashed with his in Livonia, joined the allies two months later with the professed aim of driving the Swedes from Estonia and freeing Duke John. A navy of fifteen ships was given a free hand to break the Swedish blockade of Narva, and King Frederik launched a successful attack on Älvsborg, thus cutting Sweden off from all direct communication with western Europe.[10]

The war was fought on three main fronts: in southern Scandinavia, in Livonia and at sea in the southern Baltic. On the latter the new Swedish navy, under the brilliant leadership from autumn 1564 of Klas Kristersson Horn, managed to keep open the vital sea lanes to the southern and south-eastern coasts of the Baltic against the threat of the numerically superior combined fleet of Denmark and Lübeck, so that essential supplies such as salt could continue to be imported and the troops in Estonia reinforced. Danish attempts to close the Sound in 1565 had to be abandoned after English and Dutch protests, and a large part of the Danish fleet was destroyed by a storm off Gotland the following year. The war ended with the Swedes masters of the Baltic waters, although Horn himself died of plague in September 1566.[11]

In southern Scandinavia, the Swedes managed in 1565 to counter the loss of Älvsborg by taking Varberg on the same coast to the south, but the Danish mercenary army led by the Holsteiner Daniel Rantzau succeeded the following year in penetrating deep into eastern Sweden. He was not, however, able to achieve a decisive victory, and had to retire when his supplies became depleted. Both sides caused widespread devastation in each other's border territories in their attempts to deny the enemies supplies and built up a fund of bitterness which was to sour relations between the two countries for many years. In Livonia the Poles managed to seize Pernau, but the Swedes held on to Reval and continued to enforce the blockade of Narva.[12]

By 1568 all the parties involved except Poland were ready for peace; King Sigismund, while he ordered a cessation of hostilities against his brother-in-law when John ascended the Swedish throne in that year and offered mediation between Sweden and Denmark, was unwilling to acknowledge Swedish claims in Livonia, which had in 1564 been formally incorporated into Lithuania as a duchy after being temporarily administered by the duke of Kurland. But Poland's relations with Denmark had been strained by clashes between the Danish fleet and Polish privateers, to which Sigismund had turned after failing to secure a fleet from Danzig or Prussia, and it found itself diplomatically isolated. Peace was finally concluded in Stettin at the end of 1570 under the mediation of the Emperor, the Elector of Saxony and the king of France.[13]

Of the Scandinavian contenders, Sweden had to pay a ransom of 150,000 daler for the return of Älvsborg, which had been occupied by the Danes throughout the war, and to raise the blockade of Narva. The contentious issue of Denmark's right to the three crowns, which it had incorporated in its coat of arms since 1546 but which Sweden claimed to be exclusively its emblem, was referred to arbitration, and arrangements were made for any future causes of dispute between the two countries to be discussed at frontier meetings. Lübeck's privileges in trading with Sweden were restored, but the war had exhausted the city, which ceased henceforth to play any significant role in the power struggles of the region. Formally Livonia, with the exception of the areas under Muscovite occupation and of Reval and Weissenstein, was declared an Imperial fief. The Emperor Maximilian II, after compensating the Swedes for their war expenses, was to grant Livonia to King Frederik of Denmark.[14]

Since, as the Swedes had anticipated, the Emperor was unable to pay the sum demanded and since Denmark in 1575 lost to the tsar all the territory it occupied in Livonia except the island of Ösel and consequently much of its interest in the area, this part of the treaty was never implemented. It was finally abrogated unilaterally by the Swedes in 1579. Only Riga, which had refused to recognize the overlordship of Poland, recognized that of the Emperor.[15]

By the time of the peace of Stettin Sweden's Baltic policy had undergone a striking change, not so much in its ends as in the means chosen to attain them. Erik XIV's attempts to strengthen royal power, his use of commoner secretaries as his instruments against the noble Council, his often quixotic behaviour, which culminated in the murder by his own hand of one of his supposed enemies in his prison cell and his marriage to his low-born mistress, united the nobility against him. In September 1568, led by Duke John, they rose in revolt. Erik was deposed and imprisoned. The following year John assumed the crown with the approval of the Estates.[16]

John III immediately set about turning Swedish foreign policy in a pro-Polish and anti-Muscovite direction. His attitude to the tsar had not been improved by the latter's demand to Erik when he was still on the throne to hand over John's wife as the price of ratifying a seven-year truce concluded in 1564. By this, Ivan offered to recognize Sweden's possession of Reval, Pernau and Weissenstein in exchange for Sweden's acceptance of the Muscovite claims to the rest of Livonia outside the areas ruled by prince Magnus and the lifting of the blockade of Narva. So anxious was the Swedish king for Muscovite support in securing vital supplies of salt and saltpetre that a new treaty between Sweden and Muscovy had in fact been concluded in Moscow at the beginning of 1567 on these terms, although its ratification was delayed so long as to be overtaken by Erik's deposition. The new reign in Sweden began with the humiliation of a Swedish delegation sent to Novgorod, after which a state of war existed *de facto* between the two countries.[17]

Ivan had renewed his truce with Sweden in May 1564 after

suffering a serious military defeat in Livonia and the defection of his own commander prince Andrey Kurbsky to Sigismund. He was under growing pressure to make peace also with Lithuania. Sigismund had succeeded in winning over a number of other boyars to his cause, and agreed to open negotiations with the tsar in 1565. But Muscovite demands, which included Riga, proved impossible to accept, and with the break-up of talks, Ivan found himself faced with a hostile Sweden as well as the Polish–Lithuanian Commonwealth. With the latter, however, he succeeded in concluding a three-year truce in June 1570, by which he retained Polotsk on the Dvina, which he had captured in 1562.[18]

Probably under the influence of his chancellor Viskovaty, he had evolved a plan to use the Danish prince Magnus to head a buffer vassal state in Livonia. Magnus, who favoured collaboration with Poland against the extension of Swedish power, had, in accordance with the agreement with Denmark, been left largely undisturbed by the tsar, who wished to remain on good terms with King Frederik.[19] According to the new plan, Magnus was to marry a Russian princess and be installed as puppet king in the area under Muscovite control. Magnus himself, after failing to win the hand of King Sigismund's sister Anna, agreed to the plan. He secured the approval of King Frederik, and travelled to Moscow to be invested with his new fief. He was created 'King of Livonia', engaged to Ivan's niece Eufemia and was given command of an army of 25,000 Muscovite troops, who opened the campaign in Livonia in August 1570 with an attack on the Swedes in Reval. He besieged the port until the following March. But his patron was unable to send him any reinforcements because of the growing Tatar threat to Moscow itself, and the Muscovites had no navy to prevent the Swedes provisioning the city. Magnus had finally to abandon the enterprise, and King John agreed to a brief truce.[20]

In the year of John's coronation, Poland and Lithuania were formally united in the so-called Union of Lublin, thus creating the largest political unit in Europe. The Lithuanian nobility, led by the Radziwiłł family, had long resisted such a move strongly, but were finally won over to the idea by their exposure to the Muscovite threat, to counter which they needed Polish support. By the terms of the Union they retained their own officials and their own laws, their own army and their own financial system, but the frontiers between the republic and the grand duchy were adjusted so as to make the two more equal in size: the provinces of Volnyia, Braslov and Kiev were transferred from Lithuania to Poland. A united *Sejm* was to meet at least every two years.[21]

The dynastic links between Sweden and Poland were temporarily broken by the death in July 1572 of Sigismund Augustus, the last of the Jagiełłon dynasty, who had ruled over both Poland and Lithuania for nearly two centuries, and the subsequent election by the Polish and Lithuanian nobility of the French prince Henry of Valois to be his successor. The ending of the Jagiełłon line in itself weakened the Polish monarchy and strengthened the position of the magnates who had revealed their power in the election charter or *pacta conventa* which they imposed on Henry and on every successive king. By it, he was obliged to consult the *Sejm* before imposing new taxes and raising troops. The *Sejm* appointed a committee of sixteen 'resident senators' to look after its interests between sessions.[22]

The seeds of Poland's decline may have been present in this settlement, but such decline was not immediately apparent. In June 1574 Henry returned to France to claim the French throne as Henry III after a reign of only 118 days. After a long interregnum, at the end of 1575 the 50-year-old prince of Transylvania Stephen (Istvan) Bathory was chosen to be the new king. One of the conditions of his election was that he marry Anna, the sister of Sigismund and of King John III's wife, thus re-establishing the Swedish connection.[23]

Stephen proved a strong and able ruler, who was determined to settle the long struggle with Muscovy and immediately to regain the line of the Dvina river and Polotsk. But before he could turn his attention to Livonia he became involved in a conflict with the city of Danzig. This had been defying the Polish crown since the beginning of the Seven Years War, when it had refused to comply with the king's ban on trade with Sweden, and was claiming far-ranging maritime rights. It had closed its gates to a royal commission sent to investigate its privileges in 1569 and rejected a constitution drawn up the following year which in effect abolished those privileges. It now sought help from Denmark, whose relations with Poland cooled as Poland's with Sweden warmed and which sent volunteers to the city's aid. In September 1576, after his coronation, Stephen ordered the city to be isolated. But the Danish navy came to its assistance, and although an army from the city was defeated in April 1577,

Danzig itself could not be taken. A settlement was not finally reached and the siege lifted until the end of the following year. The king's income from the city was consequently increased, but the question of maritime rights was not definitively resolved until 1585 after long negotiations. With this problem out of the way, however, the Polish king could hope to begin a vigorous campaign in Livonia with a reorganized army centred on German and Hungarian musketeers but also using Cossacks and Tatar cavalry and Livonian foot. The *Sejm* agreed to the formation of units of infantry based on the farms on royal estates and to the introduction of hussars.[24]

In Livonia the tsar had resumed the war against Sweden and Poland–Lithuania at the end of 1572 and taken advantage of the latter's weakness during the interregna (which he had attempted to lengthen by putting himself forward as a candidate for the throne on both occasions) and the following distraction of the campaign against Danzig to make considerable gains: Weissenstein fell to him at the beginning of 1573, Pernau in 1575 and Wiek the year after this. King John had trouble paying his German mercenary troops, who in 1574 handed the districts of Hapsal, Leal and Lode over to the Danes. In 1576 Ivan devastated them.[25] After these successes, however, the fortunes of war began to turn against him.

In 1565, partly because of the treachery of numbers of boyars during the Polish campaign, Ivan had instituted the so-called *oprichnina*. His realm was divided in two parts, one of which was ruled by officials hand-picked by the tsar and used as a base from which to launch a campaign of terror against the boyar class. It 'degenerated into little more than an instrument for squeezing resources for the long war . . . from an exhausted population' and caused confusion in both financial and military administration.[26] After his victory over the Tatars, the organization had been quietly abandoned, but the demoralization which had accompanied it remained; many leading boyars had been executed or driven to join the Poles. The war on the Baltic and southern fronts had imposed great strains on the Muscovite economy, and the tsar's treasury was nearly exhausted.

A new siege of Reval undertaken by him at the beginning of 1577 had soon to be abandoned, and the Livonian peasantry now became sickened by the cruelties of the Muscovites and turned against them; in 1579, under the leadership of Ivo Schenkenburg until his capture, they harried the occupying forces in the vicinity of Reval with Swedish encouragement.[27]

King Magnus also deserted Ivan. In 1577, having received little support from either the tsar or his brother, he called on the Livonian nobility to rally to him in a struggle against foreign occupation and took refuge in Wenden (Cēsis). There he was attacked by Ivan's forces and taken prisoner. On his release he renounced his royal title and in 1578 retired to Piltene. In October of that year the tsar's forces suffered a serious defeat at the hands of the Swedes and Poles and were driven from Wenden. The Swedes, having reorganized their army and navy and reached an agreement with the Poles, renewed the war in Livonia in 1578 and invaded Muscovy itself. In August 1579 Ivan was caught unawares by a successful Polish assault on Polotsk. Even Moscow itself was threatened. The tsar, who had since the execution of Viskovaty in 1570 been wholly responsible for his foreign policy, turned with a measure of desperation to both the Emperor and the Pope in the hope that they would put pressure on Poland to reach a settlement.[28]

The principal aim of John III's campaigns in Livonia was the capture of Narva, against which the considerable Swedish fleet in the Gulf of Finland could be used. But his reliance on German and Scots mercenaries caused financial problems, and disputes over rights to Estonia hindered any formal alliance with Poland. An initial assault on the city in 1579 failed. But two years later Swedish efforts were crowned with success. The new commander Magnus Pontus de la Gardie, a French mercenary formerly in Danish service, captured Narva in September 1581 by an assault from both land and sea and pushed on into Muscovy itself, threatening both Novgorod and Pskov. The Poles meanwhile took Dorpat.[29]

But Stephen Bathory also had problems. The revenues from his estates and tax yields had increased considerably under his able management, but income was still not sufficient to pay for the large bodies of mercenaries needed in the campaigns against Muscovy, and the *Sejm* had become more and more reluctant to vote the necessary additional funds. A siege of Pskov which the king began in August 1581 proved unsuccessful. He consequently agreed to open negotiations with the tsar at Iam Zapol'ski under papal mediation. These resulted in January 1582 in the conclusion of a ten-year truce and Ivan's recognition of Polish claims to southern and central Livonia, where Riga had finally submitted to King Stephen.[30]

The truce of Iam Zapol'ski provided some welcome relief for the tsar, but he could not concentrate his forces against the Swedes because of a serious revolt on the Volga. In August 1583 he agreed to a three-year truce which left the Swedes with Estonia, Narva and Keksholm (Käkisalmi) and cut off Muscovy's direct access to the Baltic.[31] Their possession of Narva provided them with control of the main trade routes to Novgorod and Pskov, which they dominated for over a century, though their attempts to make it the great Baltic staple for Russian trade were disappointed. Russian goods were diverted northwards through Archangel, founded three years after the loss of Narva, or from Pskov to Livonian and Polish ports further south. Narva became under Swedish rule a port of much less importance than hitherto. If Sweden were to acquire a dominant position in the Russian trade, it would have to continue its advance southward and also try to secure control of the northern route. When he died in March 1584, Ivan had, on the other hand, gained nothing and left his country exhausted and diplomatically isolated.[32]

Denmark played no direct part in the Baltic struggles of the last three decades of the sixteenth century. Its mercenary army had proved a heavy burden on a depleted treasury, and the years following Stettin were largely devoted to the reform of the state's financial system by the brilliant treasurer Peder Oxe, who had been recalled from disgrace in the middle of the war, and to the rebuilding of the navy. It did, however, continue to claim sovereignty over the southern Baltic and, as has been seen, clashed with Poland in 1577, when it sent aid to Danzig, and indeed Danish ships joined those of Danzig in an attack on Elbing. And at the same time relations with Russia deteriorated; a further attempt to secure an alliance in 1575 came to naught and a fifteen-year armistice concluded in 1578, which recognized Ivan's rights in Livonia and was meant to replace that of 1562, was not ratified in Copenhagen. In 1583 'King' Magnus died and his lands were immediately occupied by Polish troops, and two years later all the Danish possessions in Livonia, with the exception of the island of Ösel, were sold to a triumphant Poland, who had, however, to pawn Piltene to Brandenburg to raise the required sum.[33]

The truces concluded by Muscovy with its enemies in 1582 and 1583 were followed by an uneasy peace in the Baltic for the remainder of the decade. Muscovy, weakened by Ivan IV's efforts, still had to cope with Tatar raids from the south and was further distracted by a struggle for power at the court of Ivan's feeble-minded son and successor Fedor (Theodore), a struggle from which the boyar Boris Godonov finally emerged triumphant. Peace did bring economic recovery, but this was slow.[34]

In Poland–Lithuania Stephen Bathory, supported by his chancellor Jan Zamoyski, was anxious to defeat the Muscovites before launching a crusade against the Turks. The majority of his nobles were, however, opposed to further foreign adventures, and forced the king to renew the armistice when it expired. In 1586 he sought to win his ends by diplomatic means, proposing a dynastic agreement by which the rulers of the two countries would succeed each other to a united realm. The boyar council rejected the proposal but agreed to renew the armistice. King Stephen died at the end of the year.[35]

During the same period the links between Sweden and Poland, initiated at the accession of John III but threatened by the clash of interests in Livonia, were strengthened. They had been encouraged by the papacy, which had hopes of winning Sweden back to the fold through its king. John, who went so far as to initiate secret negotiations with Rome about such a return, himself dreamed not only of an alliance with Poland but even a political union between the two kingdoms, and he had his son Sigismund raised as a Catholic in anticipation of the boy's eventual election to the throne in Cracow. After the death of his Polish wife Catherine in 1583, he seems, however, to have temporarily abandoned such plans. His relations with his brother Charles were strained, and he feared that the power of the Swedish crown might be weakened by the absence of the king in Poland. For this very reason many Swedish nobles favoured the idea.[36]

As John's relations with his nobility improved again, the advantages of a union, however, once more gained the ascendancy; in particular, it was felt that Sweden's position in Livonia would be strengthened thereby and an agreement between Poland and Muscovy at Sweden's expense precluded. In Poland the idea of union was strongly backed by Stephen Bathory's childless widow Anna, who was devoted to the young Sigismund, and by a large body of the Polish nobility led by chancellor Zamoyski. They hoped not only for territorial gains in Livonia but also for Swedish naval support both against Muscovy and against the maritime pretensions of Denmark, whose backing of Danzig had been much resented. All in all, however, Sigismund's election seemed to promise reconciliation of the factions at home and peace and stability in the Baltic.[37]

The 21-year-old Prince Sigismund was elected to the Polish throne in August 1587. But the agreement reached between Sweden and Poland at the time (the first formal alliance between them) was shot through with misunderstandings about the fate of Estonia. While the Statutes of Kalmar, which were drawn up before Sigismund left Sweden to guarantee Sweden's independence, laid stress on the anti-Muscovite nature of the union and guaranteed Sweden's possession of Estonia, the more loosely worded *pacta conventa*, to which Sigismund submitted in Cracow as a condition of his election, obliged him to regain Estonia for Poland and made no mention of action against Muscovy; the Polish nobility did not wish to resume war against the tsar. Neither document envisaged a full union; the country's armies were to remain separate. It was finally agreed to postpone a settlement on Estonia until Sigismund ascended the Swedish throne.[38]

Sigismund succeeded his father in 1592. As a Catholic, he was treated from the beginning with suspicion by the Protestant Swedish nobility led by his unscrupulous uncle Charles, duke of Södermanland (Sudermania). In 1593 Charles finally persuaded the Diet to accept the Augsburg Confession, the main Lutheran creed, as the expression of faith of the Swedish church, and by 1598 Sigismund's authority in Sweden had been so undermined that he decided that he must reassert it by force. In August he sailed back to his northern kingdom with an army of 10,000 men, which was landed at Kalmar. Loyal troops from Finland, which had been landed north of Stockholm had, however, again been withdrawn and, defeated in battle and taken prisoner at Stångebro, Sigismund agreed to leave Sweden again. As it turned out, he did so for good.[39]

The following year his support in Finland and Estonia collapsed and he was formally deposed by the Diet. His uncle Charles was proclaimed regent. Sweden and Poland were as a result at war for the following sixty years. Indeed Sigismund's election can be regarded as the direct cause of Sweden's occupation of the south-eastern Baltic, which formed the basis of its seventeenth-century 'Empire'. For the latter was acquired in the course of the struggle to force Sigismund and his successors to surrender their claims to the Swedish crown.

The question of Estonia was thus to be settled by force of arms. And nothing came of the Swedo–Polish anti-Muscovite coalition. War had broken out again in Livonia in 1590. But only Swedish and Russian armies were now involved. In January Boris Godonov, having repelled a fresh Tatar assault and established himself as the tsar's chief minister, succeeded in taking the Swedes by surprise and occupying most of Ingria (Ingermanland) and taking Ivangorod, but he failed to take his chief objective, Narva. Like Adashev before him, he had only limited aims in Livonia and, threatened by unrest at home, wished to avoid a full-scale war with Poland–Lithuania. He renewed the truce with Sigismund in 1591 and concluded a two-year truce with Sweden in January 1593. Further tough negotiations with the latter brought about the peace of Teusina (Täyssinä; Isvos) in May 1595 with the help of an imperial mediator. By this, Sweden had to evacuate Ingria and Keksholm, thus restoring Muscovite access to the Baltic, but its possession of Narva and Estonia was confirmed.[40]

4

THE TIME OF TROUBLES
(1595–1617/21)

The expulsion of Sigismund Vasa from Sweden resulted in a sixty-year war between Poland–Lithuania and Sweden, broken only by truces of varying lengths. Not until Polish kings had lost all hope of recovering their position in the south-eastern Baltic, where they were still firmly entrenched at the end of the sixteenth century, let alone recover the throne of Sweden, to which they continued to lay claim while there was a Vasa in Warsaw,[1] did they withdraw from the struggle. The contest between Sweden and Poland–Lithuania also provided an opportunity for the Elector of Brandenburg, Poland's vassal for the duchy of East Prussia, to establish himself as an independent Baltic ruler; in 1605, in order to gain his support, the king of Poland granted elector Joachim Frederick the regency in the duchy, which would otherwise have reverted to the Polish crown.[2] The collapse of authority in Muscovy at the beginning of the seventeenth century and the ensuing 'Time of Troubles' extended the Baltic conflict as both Poland and Sweden sought to fill the vacuum in Moscow and each to use Muscovy's resources to win a decisive victory over the other. The revival of Muscovy under the first Romanov after 1613 enabled the country to rid itself of foreign invaders, but did not lead to an immediate resumption of the 'drive to the sea'.

The peace of Stolbova with Sweden in 1617 indeed cut Muscovy off from the Baltic as decisively as before its absorption of Novgorod over a century before. As Muscovy withdrew temporarily from the struggle to lick its wounds, Denmark under the young King Christian IV reappeared on the scene to challenge the growing influence of Sweden and to attempt to reassert the leadership in the Baltic which seemed in danger of slipping from its grasp. It enjoyed some initial successes, but as in Poland, the king's policy was not fully supported by the nobles on his Council, and Denmark had to watch its rival, under the brilliant leadership of the young King Gustavus Adolphus, rise inexorably in the course of its struggle against Poland to the ranks not only of a Baltic but even of a European power in a Europe more and more riven by confessional rivalries. Of this there was, however, still little sign around 1600.

The final departure of Sigismund from his northern kingdom after his defeat at Stångebro was soon followed by his attempts to impose a blockade on Sweden by the use of a hastily assembled fleet of eight ships and by the reopening of hostilities in Livonia. Lübeck agreed to stop trading with Sweden and sent out its own privateers against Charles, but Danzig was less compliant to the king's requests. Although Sigismund, encouraged by chancellor Zamoyski, was keen to drive the Swedes from Estonia, which he formally incorporated in his kingdom in March 1600, his *Sejm*, which controlled the purse strings, was distinctly lukewarm about the resumption of a war so obviously dynastic in character, and it was Duke Charles who, at the head of an army of 14,000, opened hostilities in August 1600.[3]

And with considerable initial success. His army, supported by most of the local nobility, swept forward to the river Dvina. Pernau and Dorpat fell to him. But the Swedish victory was illusory. The Poles had been caught unawares with far inferior local forces. In the spring of 1601 a large army, including 5,000 horse, under the Lithuanian hetman (marshal) Christian Radziwiłł, counter attacked and captured Wenden. Sigismund succeeded also in securing a truce with the tsar, persuaded the *Sejm* to vote supplies for two years and secured a loan from Danzig. In the autumn of 1601 a royal army of 11,000 forced Charles to abandon the siege of Riga, whose burghers had benefited from the association with Poland–Lithuania. Dorpat was regained in April 1603 by the new Polish commander Karl Chodkiewicz, and even Reval was threatened.[4]

The whole campaign revealed a Swedish army which was no match for the Poles. The reforms instituted but never fully implemented by Erik XIV, in particular his linear formations, the use of the pike as an aggressive weapon and the wearing of body armour, had been entirely abandoned under King John, who took little interest in military affairs and, in spite of Charles's efforts, he could not persuade his troops to resume them. Nor could he get his nobility to perform the cavalry service which was still a duty owed by them to the crown but more often commuted for a money payment. As a result, in 1603 he found himself hanging desperately onto small areas around Reval and Narva. In September of the following year, he was heavily defeated near Weissenstein, which was lost to the enemy. In 1605 a supreme effort enabled him again to reach the gates of Riga, only to be routed by a Polish force a third the strength of his at the battle of Kirkholm; in three hours the Swedes lost 9,000 men as against only 100 losses by the enemy. The Polish cavalry, the most aggressive in a Europe whose battlefields were still dominated by the foot soldier, swept away a Swedish cavalry still armed only with the pistol, leaving the infantry, unprotected by pikemen, at their mercy.[5]

But when all seemed lost, the Swedes were saved by a noble rebellion in Poland, itself caused by Sigismund's attempt to reform the Polish constitution. Until this was crushed in July 1607, no Polish initiative in Livonia was possible. In 1608 the Swedes retook Weissenstein and captured Dünamünde (Ust-Dvinsk), Kokenhausen (Koknese) and Fellin, but they failed in a further assault on Riga, and in the winter of 1609 even lost Pernau and Dünamünde to Chodkiewicz after the *Sejm* had approved fresh grants. The situation in Muscovy was diverting the attention of both rival powers away from the area.[6]

Boris Godonov, who had been elected tsar after the extinction of the line of Rurik with the death of Tsar Fedor in 1598, had immediately sought from Charles IX (as Duke Charles had finally become in 1604) revision of the Teusina agreement before he would recognize its validity and demanded the restoration of Narva as the price of an alliance. He welcomed the resumption of war in Livonia as promising a more compliant Swedish attitude and an opportunity to play off one combatant against the other.[7] He rejected an offer of an alliance from Lithuania, but did, as has been seen, welcome a long truce. But he himself was in 1603 faced with internal revolt by starving peasants and in the following year by a pretender to his throne in the shape of the first 'false Dmitri', who claimed to be the son of Ivan IV by that name, who had in fact died in 1591. 'Dmitri' had no official backing from Poland but was to be married to a Pole, arrived on the soil of Muscovy with Polish troops and was regarded as a Polish puppet. The struggle between the Vasas was thus spreading to Muscovy.[8]

No new settlement had been reached with Sweden when Boris died in April 1605. His son Fedor was deserted by his army and killed, and the pretender Dmitri succeeded in installing himself in the Moscow Kremlin. This was a dangerous situation for the Swedes, and King Charles even turned to the Turks for help. A year later, however, Dmitri was murdered. He had angered the boyars by trying to assert his authority against them, and the population of Moscow had turned against him because of the arrogant behaviour of his Polish supporters. He was finally trampled to death by an angry mob. To succeed him, the rebels chose the boyar Basil (Vasili) Shuisky, one of the leaders of the revolt against Dmitri. Shuisky, however, enjoyed little popular support. He was seen as a tool of the boyars, and was soon faced by a new pretender, who led a large army of Russians, Poles and Cossacks towards Moscow in the summer of 1608.[9]

In the face of this, the tsar finally accepted the offer of help which Charles, with his eyes on further territorial gains in the region of Narva, had been pressing on the Muscovites since 1606. By a preliminary agreement concluded in Novgorod in November 1608, the Swedes promised to send 5,000 troops to aid the tsar in exchange for a large subsidy. In the following February in Viborg the terms of Teusina were confirmed, and military aid was made dependent on the cession to the Swedes of the province of Keksholm, which would give them control of the northern Voldai river system.[10]

The 5,000 troops (very few of whom were Swedish) under Jakob de la Gardie, son of the conqueror of Narva, joined a force of 3,000 Muscovites and together defeated the new pretender at Tver, but most of them then deserted because they had not been paid. De la Gardie was compelled to return to Novgorod, but he there gathered a new force together, forced Dmitri to retreat and finally reached Moscow in March 1610. Sigismund had, however, decided to enter the struggle in Muscovy directly, using the excuse that the treaty between the tsar and the king of Sweden had violated the terms of the Russo–Polish armistice. He now himself claimed the throne of the tsars. In September 1609 he had laid siege to Smolensk, and in June of the following year crushed at Klushino a Swedo–Russian army which was attempting to relieve the city.[11]

A month later Shuisky was deposed by the pro-Polish faction in Moscow and dispatched to a monastery. The boyars, who had been suspicious of Sigismund, agreed in August 1610 through the intrigues of the Polish chancellor Stanislaw Zolkiewski rather to accept Sigismund's son Władisław (Ladislas) as their new ruler. De la Gardie, again deserted by most of his troops after Klushino, withdrew to the region of Novgorod, whose burghers in July 1611 he forced, on his own initiative, to accept one of King Charles's sons as their overlord when peace should return and to support his claims to the Russian throne. The pretender Dmitri was slain in his own camp at the end of the year, and Smolensk fell to the Poles in June 1611. But Sigismund hesitated to accept the offer to his son and was unable to follow up his military success. The crushing of the rebellion in 1607 had been followed by a general amnesty and had done nothing to strengthen royal powers. The *Sejm* again proved reluctant to vote him sufficient funds to pay his mercenaries, and at the end of the year he withdrew.[12]

All these developments had been watched closely in Copenhagen. King Christian IV had, almost since he took over the reins of government in 1596, been urging on a very reluctant Council, fearful of both the cost and increase in royal power war might bring, the need for a forward policy in the Baltic to counter the threat from Sweden. Denmark was in a better position to adopt one because of the financial reforms carried through by Peder Oxe since the Northern Seven Years War; the crown's land holdings had been made more compact by exchanges with the nobility, much land which had been alienated was resumed and holders of fiefs were made more accountable. In addition, the payment of the Sound Dues was reformed to make cargoes rather than ships the basis of payment and consequently income rose considerably.[13]

Though he rejected in 1598 a request for aid from Sigismund, rumours of whose negotiations with the Austrian and Spanish Habsburgs for a Baltic base had made him highly suspicious, Christian revived the ambition, which his father had in effect abandoned after the end of the Seven Years War, to reconstitute the Kalmar Union under his direction. And even a lesser success in foreign policy might strengthen the position of the crown vis-à-vis the Danish nobility.[14]

He devoted much energy in his early years to building up his border defences against Sweden (the entirely new fortress of Kristianopel in Blekinge was founded in 1609 and Kristianstad in Scamia the following year). In 1614 he introduced a peasant conscript army, largely recruited from the extensive crown estates,

46

but this was generally poorly trained and equipped. His principal objective was the building up of Danish naval power. This had been allowed to decline since his father's death; he inherited in 1597 a force of nine warships of twenty guns and thirteen smaller vessels. Not only did he set about adding to this number but encouraged his merchants to build for themselves 'defence ships' which could be converted readily into warships when needed and which enjoyed special customs privileges in time of peace.[15]

Christian had genuine causes for complaint against King Charles. The latter's blockade of the Polish ports, especially of Riga, and the activities of Swedish privateers in the southern Baltic threatened the Danish crown's revenue from Sound Dues. And even more irritating were Swedish activities outside the Baltic. Attempts to control Muscovite trade through the south-east Baltic ports had driven merchants to use the White Sea route through Archangel. King Charles sought to control this also not only by seeking, as had his brother John, to acquire direct control of the land route to Archangel from the south but also by pressing claims to part of the Atlantic coastline north of the Arctic circle past which the ships engaged in the trade sailed. His vigorous colonization policy in northern Scandinavia, which led to clashes along the ill-defined frontier between Sweden and Norway, his attempts to tax the Lapps who drove their reindeer herds through the region with little regard to national boundaries, his claims to sovereignty over part of the northernmost coast of Norway and his grant to the settlers in his new town of Gothenburg (Göteborg), founded at the mouth of the Göta river near Älvsborg five years previously, of the right to fish off the Norwegian coast – all were seen as provocative by the Danes, who claimed to control all trade around the North Cape.[16]

Negotiations on these and other matters in dispute, like the still unresolved question of the use of the three crowns, were conducted on the Dano–Swedish border in 1601–4 in accordance with the conditions laid down for the settlement of disputes between the two countries in the treaties of Brömsebro and Stettin. But these brought settlement no nearer. In fact Danish concessions only encouraged King Charles to raise his terms, and from 1603 Christian urged on his Council the necessity of reaching a conclusion on the field of battle. It demurred, while King Sigismund, who wished his war to be seen as one against the usurper Charles rather than against his misguided subjects the

Swedes, tried to dissuade the Danish king through Christian's brother-in-law the Elector of Brandenburg from opening hostilities.[17] The Swedish Council equally urged on King Charles the desirability of caution in view of Sweden's other commitments. But finally, in January 1611, the Swedish king's insulting reply to an appeal made by Christian, encouraged by news of the Swedish defeat at Klushino, to the Swedish Estates over their sovereign's head, enabled Christian to get his Council, after he had threatened to go to war as duke of Schleswig–Holstein rather than as king of Denmark, to give way. In April Denmark declared war.[18]

Charles was caught unawares. He had counted on the Danish Council's continuing constraint and on support from England and the United Provinces, to whom, however, he now appealed in vain for help. A large proportion of his troops was tied down in Russia and in Livonia, and his navy both in number and size of ships was much inferior to the one which Christian had at his disposal. Sweden was threatened with a complete blockade. In May a Danish force under the king's personal command appeared before the town of Kalmar, which fell at the end of the month. Though the Swedes took Kristianopel and successfully defended Älvsborg, Kalmar castle, the strongest in the kingdom, had to surrender at the beginning of September. At the end of the same month king Charles, who had never fully recovered from a stroke from which he had suffered two years previously, died in Nyköping.[19]

His 16-year-old son Gustavus Adolphus (Gustav II Adolf) was granted full powers by the Estates on conditions which appeared to place him under the control of his noble Council, led by the chancellor Axel Oxenstierna; he could neither promulgate a new law nor conclude a treaty nor make either peace or war without the consent of the Council and the Diet, and could raise no new taxes without the consent of the Council and 'those concerned'. These were conditions which, while certainly not obeyed scrupulously once the king was firmly in the saddle and had won the trust and respect of his nobles, never became dead letters.[20]

He was faced with an open conflict with Denmark being fought on Swedish soil, one with Poland in Livonia and with a threatening situation in Russia, where de la Gardie was hanging on to Novgorod but little else. The bulk of the Swedish army was tied down in the east, and the stronger Danish fleet had been able to cut off communications with the south. Oxenstierna himself described the gravity of the realm's position:

> Firstly it is generally known that all our neighbours are our enemies, the Poles, Russians and Danes, so that no place in Sweden, Finland or Livonia can say that it is safe from the enemy. Secondly we have absolutely no friends who are concerned about our difficulties. And thirdly there is not one of our enemies who is not or at least thinks it is not mightier and stronger than we.[21]

The striking military and diplomatic successes which Gustavus was to achieve during the following twenty years were all the more remarkable because of the limited resources with which he was presented at the beginning of his reign: a population of less than a million and a half, an army far from remarkable in either equipment or organization, indeed rather backward by European standards, and a treasury which still relied largely on taxes in kind and which could not even assess its assets by means of an annual budget. The financial situation was weakened by the considerable proportion of royal estates and tax revenues which had been alienated to members of the nobility in exchange for loans and cash grants since the days of King John.[22]

On the other hand, Sweden's economic assets were now able to be exploited as never before. The high quality iron deposits north of the central plain, which had been mined since the Middle Ages, had been greatly developed with the help of German and Walloon experts in the sixteenth century and were now not only in great demand in western Europe, but could be used as the basis of a native armaments industry. High prices could be demanded for the copper from the same region of which Sweden had a virtual European monopoly. And while the forests of central Sweden produced charcoal aplenty for the iron industry, those of southern Finland supplied the tar and pitch for the navies of the maritime nations. Foreign entrepreneurs led by the Fleming Louis de Geer brought much needed capital and expertise into the country.[23]

And the qualities of the king himself and of his chancellor must not be discounted. Imperious and impetuous as he often was, Gustavus was a born leader of men who managed to reconcile the factions within his realm and to inspire devotion in the field. His faults were balanced by the cool, calculating temperament of

Oxenstierna, his elder by ten years with whom, however, he worked harmoniously for twenty years in what has been called 'one of the great historic collaborations'.[24]

Gustavus on coming to the throne confirmed his commander's agreement with the citizens of Novgorod. He had at first put himself forward as a candidate for the princedom, but so hostile was the reaction to the idea in Novgorod that he transferred his claims to his younger brother Charles Philip (Karl Filip) who, after much procrastination, set off from Sweden on the road to Moscow. But he had waited too long. He got no further than Viborg, for in February 1613 Russia's 'Time of Troubles' came to an end with the election of the the first of the Romanovs to the throne.[25]

The revelation that the Polish king himself again aimed for the latter had led to a strong anti-Polish reaction in Muscovy, and in March 1611 to open revolt. The Polish garrison in Moscow was besieged in the Kremlin, and in October 1612 was forced to surrender. While there was considerable support among the boyars for Charles Philip, they grew impatient at his delay, and the common people and the Cossacks secured in February 1613 Michael Romanov's election. And having disposed of the Poles, the Muscovites turned on the Swedes. De la Gardie's position was parlous.[26]

King Gustavus had anticipated a rejection of Charles Philip's claims in Moscow, but he sought to bind Novgorod at least to Sweden. News of the election of Michael Romanov, however, caused growing unrest within the territories occupied by the Swedes, and the western powers had grown alarmed by the widespread disruption of trade in the Baltic since the beginning of the new century. Both the English and the Dutch offered their services as mediators to bring an end to hostilities.[27]

In May 1612 the Danes, led by Christian IV himself, managed to seize Älvsborg and destroyed the nascent city of Gothenburg. But another Danish army led by Gert Rantzau, having advanced from Kalmar into northern Småland, was driven back again to its base in some disarray. An assault on the fortress of Vaxholm in the Stockholm archipelago by a force of thirty-six Danish ships, also under the king's personal command in what appears to have been an attempt to destroy the Swedish fleet, failed. These setbacks and financial difficulties led Christian to give way to the urgings of his own Council and the Protestant princes of northern Germany, who desired Danish support in the threatening religious crisis there, and accept the mediation offered by England. Peace was consequently concluded near Knäred in Halland at the beginning of 1613.[28]

Christian had failed in his major objectives. But the price which Sweden had to pay for peace was a high one. Its blockade of Poland's ports had to be raised, its claims in Finnmark and to Sönnenburg on the island of Ösel abandoned and it had to promise to pay the enormous sum of one million rixdalers within six years to redeem Gothenburg, Älvsborg and the adjoining area at the mouth of the river Göta, which the Danes undoubtedly believed that they had won permanently. Christian had indeed wished to demand the area outright, but had been restrained by his Council. But with the help of Dutch loans and heavy taxation, the sum was raised, and in 1619 Gothenburg was refounded.[29]

A settlement with Muscovy proved even more difficult for the Swedes. De la Gardie managed, with reinforcements sent to him from Sweden, to drive back the Muscovite forces from Novgorod, and in 1615 Gustavus himself was even able to begin the siege of Pskov. The Muscovites, threatened as they were also by the Poles, who still hoped to dislodge Michael from the throne, agreed to English and Dutch mediation, and serious negotiations commenced soon after New Year in 1616. After delays caused by antagonism between the mediators, in December at Stolbova, in the house of the English mediator John Merrick of the Eastland Company, the tsar agreed to give up his claims to Livonia and to surrender the province of Ingria as well as that of Keksholm, thus cutting his realm off completely from the Baltic and giving Sweden control of the whole coast of the Gulf of Finland. Its claim to Novgorod and to any part of the Arctic coast had, however, to be surrendered. The final agreement was signed in February 1617.[30]

During the negotiations in Stolbova, Oxenstierna had warned the negotiators that: 'We have in Russia a false and at the same time a mighty neighbour, in whom . . . no faith is to be reposed, but who by reason of his power is terrible not only to us but to many of his neighbours.'[31] But in defending his policy in August 1617, the Swedish king was able to boast that: 'we may now live safe and secure in Finland and Estonia and be protected against Russian invasions not only in times of peace but also in time of war. . . . The trade of all Russia has to go through these countries.'[32] While he was oversanguine with regard to the last claim, for much Russian trade flowed through Livonian and Polish ports as well as a still small but growing amount through Archangel, he could be well pleased with Sweden's gains, and from now on his policy was once more one of friendship with Muscovy in the face of the common Polish enemy. Even an anti-Polish alliance between the two countries at first seemed a possibility.[33]

A local truce in Livonia in 1611 had been renewed until 1613, when the Elector of Brandenburg, who wished for Swedish support in his territorial claims on the Rhine, proposed to Sigismund a peace conference with England and the United Provinces as mediators. This never materialized, and a new meeting arranged to take place in Stettin in September 1615 also never got off the ground. In the middle of 1614 the truce had already been extended for two years. Negotiations to renew this once more in 1617 broke down. Sweden, as the royal Council recognized, could have benefited from a period of peace and recovery after the strains of the Muscovite campaigns, at least until the ransom for Älvsborg had been paid off. On the other hand the moment was in many ways propitious for a resumption of the war with Poland.[34]

In April 1616 the *Sejm* had voted funds for a campaign against Michael Romanov to put Wladisław on his throne, and the prince set off the following year with an army of 11,000 men. And in the south Tatars and Turks both threatened Poland's borders. In addition there was considerable tension between the Poles and the Livonian nobility; Duke William of Kurland, who had fallen out with his overlord King Sigismund over the execution of one of the king's agents, and the Livonian noble Volmar Farensbach were secretly negotiating with the Swedes for the surrender of the fortress of Dünamünde guarding the approaches to Riga in the event of a resumption of hostilities in Livonia. At the same time rumours were growing of preparations by the Poles for a seaborne assault on Sweden for which they had been seeking Imperial, Spanish and Hanseatic help. In 1615 Gustavus had sent a squadron to the Polish coast to discourage these. A victorious campaign in Livonia by the Swedes might be more successful.[35]

And when hostilities were resumed Sweden was in several respects stronger than it had been ten years before. Gustavus was maturing rapidly and establishing better relations with his nobility than any of his predecessors had enjoyed. With the help of his chancellor, he had already begun on those internal reforms which were to serve Sweden so well during the following half century and to build his army into one which was to be the envy of Europe (see below, pp. 68–9). In addition Sweden had gained an ally outside the Baltic, which Gustavus's predecessors had sought in vain. The Dutch, who had concluded an eleven-year truce in the struggle for independence from Spain in 1609, had become increasingly irritated by Denmark's policy at the Sound, by the disruption to Baltic trade caused by King Christian's attempted blockade of Sweden during the Kalmar War and were opposed to Christian's obvious ambitions in north-western Germany. In 1613 they consequently concluded with Lübeck, whose privileges had been cancelled by Christian IV and who had had many of its ships seized by the Danes in the Kalmar War, a pact in defence of navigation on the Baltic. They went on the following year to conclude a more ambitious fifteen-year defensive alliance with Sweden which broke that country's diplomatic isolation and was to become a cornerstone of its foreign policy for some time. Each side was to assist the other in the event of attack with 4,000 men or a money equivalent. Significantly in the treaty the Dutch promised to respect Sweden's *dominium maris Baltici*.[36]

While Denmark remained in the eyes of Europe the dominant power in the Baltic, the balance was beginning to move decisively in favour of Sweden.

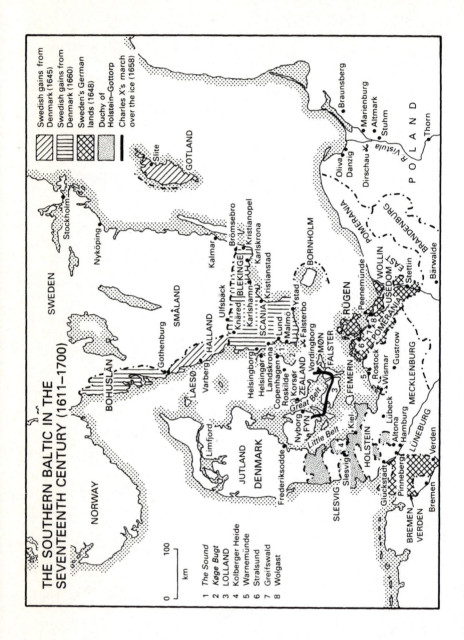

THE SOUTHERN BALTIC IN THE
SEVENTEENTH CENTURY (1611–1700)

Swedish gains from
Denmark (1645)

Swedish gains from
Denmark (1660)

Sweden's German
lands (1648)

Duchy of
Holstein–Gottorp

Charles X's march
over the ice (1658)

1 *The Sound*
2 *Køge Bugt*
3 LOLLAND
4 Kolberger Heide
5 Warnemünde
6 Stralsund
7 Greifswald
8 Wolgast

0   100
km

NORWAY

SWEDEN

Stockholm

Nyköping

BOHUSLÄN

Gothenburg

SMÅLAND

Kalmar

GOTLAND

Slite

Brömsebro

Kristianopel

Karlskrona

BLEKINGE

Karlshamn

Kristianstad

Ulfsbäck

Knäred

HALLAND

Varberg

LAESØ

SCANIA

Lund

Malmö

Helsingborg

Helsingør

Landskrona

Ystad

BORNHOLM

Falsterbo

Copenhagen

Roskilde

Korsør

ZEALAND

Vordingborg

MØN

Falster

FALSTER

Nyborg

FYN

Great Belt

Little Belt

Frederiksodde

JUTLAND

DENMARK

Limfjord

FEMERN

Kiel

SLESVIG

Slesvig

HOLSTEIN

Glückstadt

Pinneberg

Altona

Hamburg

Lübeck

Wismar

Rostock

MECKLENBURG

Gustrow

LÜNEBURG

Verden

Bremen

BREMEN
VERDEN

RÜGEN

Peenemünde

WOLLIN

USEDOM

POMERANIA

EAST
POMERANIA

Stettin

Bärwalde

BRANDENBURG

Oliva

Danzig

Dirschau

POLAND

Braunsberg

Marienburg

Altmark

Stuhm

Thorn

Vistula

5

THE BALTIC DURING THE
THIRTY YEARS WAR
(1618/21–48)

Gustavus Adolphus's campaigns in Livonia culminated in 1621 in the seizure of the great port of Riga, an event of European significance. Three years previously Bohemia had risen in revolt against its king, the Emperor's cousin Ferdinand, declared him deposed and chosen in his place the Calvinist Frederick V, Elector Palatine. This act precipitated a war which was to rage across central Europe for thirty years and which was to involve, in one way or another, all the powers around the Baltic. Denmark's entry into the struggle, motivated partly by jealousy of Sweden's growing power to the east, proved disastrous and left the field open for its rival. After nearly twenty years of campaigning, Sweden was in a position, when peace finally returned in 1648, to establish itself firmly on the southern shore of the Baltic as not only the leading Baltic power but as one of the leading European powers. In all these developments Muscovy played only a peripheral role.

Of the preoccupations of the Poles in Muscovy in 1617–18 the Swedes were not able to take the advantages they might have hoped for. The truce having finally run out, the main Swedish army took Pernau, and Farensbach did enable a smaller detachment under Nils Stiernsköld to seize Dünamünde as he had promised. But Stiernsköld failed to capture a poorly defended Riga and, disappointed with the lack of vigour with which the Swedes pursued the campaign in general, Farensbach went back to the Poles at the end of the year, Dünamünde had to be relinquished, and Swedish resources proved inadequate for a fresh attempt to take Riga. In the winter of 1617/18 Gustavus attempted to get Dutch, English and even Danish support against Poland, stressing the common interest of Protestants in the face of the Catholic threat. These attempts failed. Christian would participate only on condition of the permanent session of Älvsborg, and at the same time difficulties arose over the payment of the final instalment of the Älvsborg ransom so that until the Dutch came to the rescue with a loan at the last moment there was a distinct possiblity of hostilities between the two Scandinavian powers. In the circumstances Gustavus gave up the idea of a fresh campaign in 1618 and in September agreed to a two-year truce, leaving the Swedes in possession of Pernau.[1]

Marriage negotiations with Brandenburg–Prussia at this time must also be seen in the context of Sweden's efforts to secure allies against Poland. Charles IX had already proposed an alliance to Elector Joachim Frederick in 1601, but the latter, with his eye on securing East Prussia as a Polish fief, had determined to remain neutral in the struggle. As has been noted, the Elector had sought Swedish support in his Rhineland claims, and became alarmed when King Sigismund deprived Duke William of Kurland of his territories because of his links with Sweden, to replace him with his elder brother Frederick, who had ruled Semigallia since their father's death. A marriage between the Swedish king and Marie Eleonore, the second sister of the new Elector George William (Georg Wilhelm) had been on the cards since 1615. The proposal was, however, though championed by his mother, strongly opposed by the powerful Electress, while the Elector himself saw the negotiations only as a means of putting pressure on the king of Poland to allow him, in accordance with a family agreement made as far back as 1563 and a decision reached by the *Sejm* in 1615, to succeed in East Prussia his brother-in-law, the imbecile Duke Albert Frederick (Albrecht Friedrich), for whom he had acted as administrator since 1611. The agreement on the Swedish marriage was obtained, but soon afterwards Duke Albert Frederick died and further progress was delayed by the supposed illness of the princess. At the end of 1619, Elector John Sigismund, having been granted the duchy, was succeeded in Brandenburg by the weak and dilatory pro-Habsburg George William, who appointed the Catholic Adam von Schwartzenberg as his chancellor. Only when both men were absent from Berlin was the Dowager-Electress, who was on bad terms with her son, won over by the princess and King Gustavus himself on a personal visit in June 1620. George William claimed to the Polish Diet that his sister had acted without his consent, and refused to be drawn into the Swedo–Polish struggle, from which he had already been able to reap some profit from maintaining his neutrality.[2]

John Sigismund's succession to East Prussia established a ruler of Brandenburg firmly on the Baltic for the first time, though it was as a vassal of the Polish king, who had already ensured that his overlordship would be far from nominal; in 1611 King Sigismund secured promises from the duke of both men and money.[3]

In view of the threatening situation in the Empire, King Gustavus was willing to consider the surrender of Pernau in exchange for Sigismund's abandonment of his claim to the Swedish crown. But the Polish king was adamantly opposed to the latter. After a Cossack assault on Moscow had failed, he had secured at Deulino in December 1618 a fourteen-and-a-half-year truce with Tsar Michael by which the Poles gained Smolensk. But in 1620 war finally broke out between Poland and the Turks after nearly two hundred years of peace, and while Sigismund's forces were diverted to the south, the Swedes in the middle of 1621 renewed their campaign in Livonia with an army of some 18,000 men.[4]

This culminated in September in the capture of Riga, after a month's siege in which they used the most up-to-date methods against which the Poles had no answer. They had not believed that the Swedes would attack and had an army of only 3,000 to come to the city's relief. Against a besieging force of over 15,000, Riga was defended by no more than 300 regular troops and a town militia of 3,700 with an inadequate supply of powder and shot. After a six-day bombardment, it surrendered on terms which suggested Swedish plans to retain it permanently.[5] This success, which dealt a serious blow at trade from Lithuania, was followed by the occupation of Mitau (Jelgava), the chief town of the duchy of Kurland, after the pro-Polish Duke Frederick had refused to submit and his exiled brother William had rejected an offer of the title of Duke of Livonia. But further than this Gustavus's resources would not allow him to go; the conquest of Dorpat and the rest of Livonia was for the moment beyond him. Cossacks harried his troops, who were weakened by sickness, and financial resources were low. Only Sweden's copper, for the exploitation of which a special company had been set up in 1619, had enabled the campaign to be financed so far, and even so the Diet had been called upon to vote new taxes, crown lands were sold off and a large debt run up.[6]

In view of the threatening situation in the Empire, Gustavus appears at this stage to have been willing to use his new conquests, in spite of their strategic and economic importance, as bargaining counters in negotiations with the Poles to secure recognition of his right to the Swedish throne. In adopting this policy he was probably influenced by the urgings of his commander-in-chief Jakob de la Gardie who favoured conciliating the Polish nobility in the hope that they would put pressure on their king to make concessions. A part was also played by the financial strains to which Sweden was being subjected and which was causing expressions of discontent among the king's tax-paying subjects. A captured Polish senator was used in an attempt to win over the *szlachta* with an offer of a twenty-year armistice in exchange for the return of Livonia or the surrender of Sweden to Sigismund's sons should Gustavus die without heirs.[7]

Chancellor Oxenstierna, the most important figure in the formulation of Swedish foreign policy after the king himself, was less flexible than his master, and also attached rather more importance to reaching a satisfactory settlement with Poland before engaging Sweden in the problems further west. The king himself became less sanguine about reaching a solution of the Polish problem by negotiation. In November 1622, after a brief campaign in the course of which Mitau was lost, he agreed to a year's truce, which was eventually extended to 1625.[8] While negotiations continued with Sigismund for a permanent settlement, he discussed with the Protestant powers collaboration in the struggle in Germany.

King Sigismund, after suffering a crushing defeat at the hands of the Turks, had succeeded in concluding a truce with them in the autumn of 1621, but faced as he was by military confederacy, famine, plague and Cossack attacks and by the reluctance of his Diet, suspicious of his dynastic ambitions, to grant him the necessary taxes, he was not in a position to launch a decisive counterattack in Livonia. Renewed rumours in 1623 of Polish plans to launch a direct assault on Sweden in association with the Habsburgs did have some basis in fact; an army of 10,000 men was to be landed near Stockholm and a smaller force to be conveyed on Spanish ships to Gothenburg. Gustavus took the rumours seriously enough in June to visit Danzig, the only possible embarkation point for such an enterprise, with a small fleet.

He found Sigismund also on a visit there but no sign of preparations for invasion. The plans had proved much too ambitious for the latter.[9]

The fall of Riga certainly alarmed Christian IV of Denmark, already worried by the ties established between Sweden and Brandenburg. But he was most immediately concerned with developments in central and northern Germany. He had sent some financial aid to his nephew, King Frederick, in Prague at the instance of his brother-in-law King James VI and I, and had allowed some Danish officers to serve in the Bohemian army, but he was restrained from doing more by a Council which regarded Sweden as Denmark's main concern. In any case Christian was unhappy about Frederick's acceptance of a crown which had been offered to him by rebels against their legitimate sovereign.[10]

The Bohemian rebels had been defeated at the battle of the White Mountain outside Prague in 1620, and King Frederick had been forced to flee his kingdom. His lands on the Rhine were sequestrated by Emperor Ferdinand and occupied by troops provided by the Emperor's Spanish cousin and ally, while the army of the Catholic League, led by the duke of Bavaria's general, Jean 't Serclaes, count of Tilly, pursued the remnants of Frederick's forces into north-west Germany. The Dutch, whose truce with Spain was due to expire in 1621, were particularly alarmed by the presence of Spanish troops on the middle Rhine, and in England James I felt obliged to give his son-in-law, Frederick, some support, even if his parliament was singularly unwilling to grant him the necessary funds.[11]

Already in 1621 Maurice of Orange, the Dutch leader, sent an embassy to Copenhagen to try to persuade Denmark to head a Protestant league against the Habsburgs. Christian IV himself was anxious to accept the invitation, and in February, at a meeting of the Lower Saxon Circle in Segeberg, he had declared in favour of intervention with an army of 30,000 men if English support could be obtained. Even before the outbreak of the war in Bohemia he had been trying to extend Danish influence in north-western Germany. In 1616 he had founded the port of Glückstadt as a rival to Hamburg at the mouth of the river Elbe and was negotiating to get his younger son Frederik installed in the secularized bishoprics of Bremen, Verden and Halberstadt. The Swedish successes in Livonia made it even more imperative that he strengthen his position. Prince Frederick was finally elected as coadjutor-bishop (with the right of succession) in Bremen in 1621, in Verden the year following and in Halberstadt in 1624.[12]

Christian's council was, however, still strongly opposed to both a conflict with Sweden and intervention in Germany, fearing the economic burdens this would bring and the increased strength it might give to the crown. In 1624 they did consent to the strengthening of border garrisons in anticipation of an attack from Sweden but opposed the mobilization of the fleet and insisted on the disbanding of the mercenary army of 3,600 which had been gathered in the south but which they saw as a dangerous weapon in the hands of an ambitious sovereign. Three new fortresses were constructed and a permanent corps set up to man forts east of the Sound and form the core of a wartime army. This proved to be a first step in the creation in Denmark of a professional standing army as distinct from a peasant militia.[13]

In Stockholm Gustavus's brother-in-law John Casimir of Pfalz–Zweibrücken–Kleeberg[14] had been pleading the Bohemian cause since 1619, and before Frederick of Bohemia's defeat had urged the Swedish king to launch a direct attack on the Emperor's Polish ally. Gustavus in his turn now tried to persuade the Protestant powers that the best hope of relieving pressure on them in western Germany was to support his own renewed campaign against a Catholic king in the east. Oxenstierna and the rest of the Council did not favour direct involvement in the affairs of the Empire while Poland remained a threat or until Denmark had been dealt with.[15]

In November 1623 Frederick V's envoy Ludwig Camerarius visited Stockholm to try to persuade Gustavus to join an alliance to defend his master's rights, and the king did in fact propose to Maurice of Orange an alliance against Spain, the Emperor and Poland, which the German Protestant princes would be invited to join. To the latter he also suggested a league aimed at averting the threat posed by both the Emperor and Denmark in northern Germany. In pursuance of this aim he would transfer his operations against Poland from Livonia to the Vistula. At the same time Christian IV's renewed levying of dues on Swedish ships passing through the Sound in retaliation at a sales tax imposed by the Swedes on all exports led the Swedish Council and Estates reluctantly to agree to make war on Denmark unless these were abolished; in view of the strong defences built up by Christian in Scania, a direct Swedish attack on Zealand was planned. With the aim of keeping the Danish king in check, in the autumn of that year Gustavus did, after approaches from both England and Brandenburg, offer the latter to lead an army of 40,000 to the Rhineland. But he demanded overall command, bases in the Lower Saxon Circle and the port of Wismar, the support of an allied fleet, a guarantee of the neutrality of Danzig, agreed subsidies four months in advance and the exclusion of France from any agreement.[16]

The Protestant powers decided that they preferred a counter-offer from Christian IV: an attack by Denmark in north-west Germany at much less cost than that demanded by the Swedes. The latter could then operate in the Oder valley against Silesia, the northernmost of the Austrian Habsburg possessions. By 1625 the immediate threat of war between Sweden and Denmark had ended with an agreement which amounted to a humiliating climb-down by King Christian (see below, p. 64). His forces were not ready for conflict, and he was under strong pressure from his Council to reach a settlement. Gustavus had been less enthusiastic about a Danish war than his chancellor, and consequently, having rejected a proposal by Christian to co-operate in the enterprise to which he was now committed, reverted to the idea of landing in Polish Prussia at the mouth of the Vistula, and decided to renew the war in Livonia in preparation for this.[17]

The negotiations between the other Protestant powers and Sweden and the fears that these aroused of a Swedish army operating on the Weser drove Christian into the arms of Frederick's supporters. He was in a strong financial position, which gave him a certain independence of his suspicious councillors, whose influence was further weakened by the economic crisis faced by large landowners in Denmark in the early 1620s. The financial reforms carried out in the later sixteenth century had considerably increased the income from the crown's fiefs and ensured the Danish treasury of an annual budget surplus. The Sound Dues brought in annually some 200,000 daler, while the ransom paid by the Swedes for Älvsborg after 1613 plus his mother's considerable fortune, which she placed at his disposal, and interest on loans made by the crown to the nobility and offered on the international money market meant that in 1625 Christian had some 1½ million daler at his disposal. This was enough to support at least one year's campaign without resorting to additional taxation.[18]

In January 1625 he offered to intervene in Germany with 5,000 troops in the expectation of a further 7,000 from England but no advance payment, and finally forced his Council's hand by threatening to act independently of it as duke of Holstein. As such he had himself in April elected (though by a very narrow margin) captain or military leader of the Lower Saxon Circle, and two months later led an army of some 17,000 men over the river Elbe and advanced to the Weser.[19]

He did so, however, before he had received any firm guarantees of assistance from any other power, and he soon found himself faced with a foe far more formidable than the army of the Catholic League. The Emperor was finally forming his own army under the command of the Bohemian noble Albrecht von Wallenstein (Waldstein/Valdštejn), who was now marching to join Tilly. Christian drew back, and threatened the Protestant powers to make peace if they did not provide help. They finally agreed to do so at a conference at The Hague at the end of the year, and in August 1626 the Danish king again advanced in the belief that all Wallenstein's forces were engaged in eastern Germany by Frederick of Bohemia's general, Ernst von Mansfeld. In fact Wallenstein was facing Mansfeld in the east, but he had considerably reinforced Tilly's army, which decisively defeated Christian's forces at the battle of Lutter am Barenberg in August.[20]

After this the Danish king retired towards his kingdom while, deserted by his Council, he attempted to secure reasonable terms on which to withdraw from the war. Wallenstein, having driven Mansfeld further eastward, finally joined Tilly and in autumn 1627 proceeded to occupy Jutland as far as the Limfjord against weak resistance from the peasant militia, and the whole of the Baltic coastline between Holstein and the Polish border. Only the port of Stralsund defied him. Its overlord, Duke Bogislav of Pomerania, had submitted to the Emperor and agreed to admit an Imperial garrison. But Stralsund's citizens had been on bad terms with the duke for some time and now defied his orders and called on Denmark and Sweden for help. Denmark immediately sent troops, and Swedish engineers arrived to strengthen the fortifications.[21]

The neighbouring duchy of Mecklenburg, whose ruling brothers had sided with Christian and fled after his defeat, was sequestrated by the Emperor and granted to Wallenstein as a reward for his services. He was also ominously granted the title of 'Admiral of the Baltic and Ocean Seas'. To give substance to this, he began to build at Wismar a fleet with which to invade the Danish islands. In May 1627 the Elector of Brandenburg also submitted to the Emperor and formally allowed Wallenstein's troops to use his territories, a large part of which were already occupied.[22]

Such developments King Gustavus could hardly ignore. A victorious Imperial army, having disposed of Denmark, might well join with the Poles against Sweden. Wallenstein's nascent fleet could join the small Polish fleet (which the Spaniards had promised to afforce) in carrying Polish troops across the Baltic. Denmark had therefore to be kept in the struggle, at least until Sigismund had been decisively defeated in Poland. Only as a last resort, however, did either Gustavus or his chancellor wish to be drawn into the German conflict, the outcome of which was so uncertain and with the issues of which Sweden was only indirectly concerned. The Swedish king had offered to join the Anglo–Dutch–Danish alliance of The Hague, but in the hope of using it to extract aid against Poland rather than out of any enthusiasm for the anti-Habsburg cause in the Empire, and he drew back again when he discovered that he would not be able to do so.[23]

When the series of truces with Poland finally ran out in 1625, the Swedes had rapidly occupied most of the rest of Livonia north of the Dvina, retook Mitau and captured Dorpat in the east, although Polish resistance proved to be tougher than had been expected, and an expedition to Kurland to take Windau (Ventspils) and Libau (Liepāja) had to be abandoned. By now Gustavus appears to have determined to keep his conquests rather than to use them as counters in negotiations.[24]

After a crushing defeat of the Polish army at Wallhof south of the Dvina in January 1626, at which the new Swedish infantry tactics of rapid redeployment first showed to advantage, Gustavus was in a position to implement his plan to transfer the field of operations to royal Prussia. Such a move had been discussed already in 1624. But it was strongly opposed by both Brandenburg and the United Provinces. The action was now justified to the other Protestant powers as bringing the Swedish king closer to the borders of the Empire and placing him in a position to aid them more directly.[25]

In fact the final decision was taken only a month before it was implemented, and Gustavus's main motives were to force Sigismund to sue for peace by depriving Poland of the main outlet for its grain exports down the Vistula, to prevent the Poles from using the Prussian ports, with Spanish help, as bases for a direct assault on Sweden and to relieve Livonia of the burdens of war from which it had suffered so long. It was hoped that in Prussia, rich and untouched by conflict for a century, the war could be more easily made to pay for itself by exploiting local resources; Sweden's were under considerable strain, and social unrest in the country was growing.[26]

Denmark's defeat drew the two Scandinavian monarchies closer together in face of the common danger. But mutual distrust remained, and it was Denmark who had to make concessions in negotiations. The two kings had already met in Halmstad in February 1619 after the tension connected with the final payment of the Älvsborg ransom had relaxed and the fortress had returned to Swedish hands, and in the following year Christian had offered to enter into alliance negotiations. This the Swedes had then rejected. By 1624 the Danish king, alarmed by events in Germany and under pressure from his councillors, was, as has been seen, willing to give way to the Swedes on most disputed points, including the right to levy dues on Swedish ships.[27]

And after Wallenstein's occupation of the Baltic coastline in 1627, negotiations were begun for an alliance leading to joint operations against the Emperor and Sigismund. These came to naught, but in April 1628 agreement was reached on mutual naval assistance: Sweden was to help blockade Stralsund, while the Danes were to cut off supplies to Danzig. With Stralsund Sweden concluded a twenty-year alliance in June and the following month Wallenstein raised the siege after launching an unsuccessful assault. And he was never able to use his fleet. The thirteen ships gathered in Wismar were blockaded there by a Swedish squadron, and fell into Swedish hands when the city surrendered to them in 1632.[28]

Gustavus, however, failed to keep his neighbour in the war. A final Danish effort on land was defeated in September at Wolgast, which had been temporarily occupied, and a meeting between the two Scandinavian rulers at Ulvsbäck parsonage on the border between the two kingdoms in February 1629, after peace negotiations between the Danish king and the Emperor had already opened in Lübeck, ended stormily. Gustavus suspected that Christian had agreed to the meeting only in order to put pressure on the Emperor. He proposed a joint operation from Stralsund or Glückstadt, but this was to be under his command and to consist largely of Swedish troops.[29]

To this Christian could not agree, and in May he accepted the Emperor's generous terms: he was simply to abandon his claims to the German bishoprics and engage himself to play no further part in the war. Such magnanimity was outdoubtedly motivated by Imperial fears of Swedish intervention, which even Oxenstierna had by this time become convinced would be necessary. The assistance given to Sigismund by the Emperor and the threat of an Imperial navy sailing the Baltic highlighted the necessity of extricating Swedish troops from Poland even at the cost of failing to secure a decisive settlement there.[30]

Gustavus had found Prussia ill defended when he landed at Pillau at the head of an army of 14,000 in June 1626 and he rapidly established a strong position on the lower reaches of the Vistula. Only Danzig defended itself with any spirit after the Swedes had mismanaged negotiations for its neutrality. In its harbour King. Sigismund gathered a small navy of ten ships, which fought a fierce battle with and defeated the weakened Swedish force which was blockading the mouth of the Vistula in November 1627, sinking two Swedish vessels. In 1629, however, nine of the Polish ships evaded the Swedish blockade and sailed to Wismar to form the core of Wallenstein's naval force, and the Swedish navy was able to continue its blockade. This did, as Gustavus had anticipated, cause the Polish nobility considerable distress in their pockets, but it also complicated Sweden's relations with the Dutch.[31]

After the initial shock, Polish resistance to the Swedes stiffened; there was greater support for Sigismund's cause among the *szlachta* now that the fighting was on Polish soil. And the Polish commander was able to win back some of the ground which had been lost in the first onslaught. But encounters with the Polish cavalry at Dirschau on the Vistula while repelling a Polish counter-attack in August 1627 showed for the first time the Swedish cavalry to be its equal and by 1628 Gustavus was threatening Toruń (Thorn). In negotiations, worried as he was by developments in Germany, he offered to abandon Livonia in exchange for control of tolls on the Vistula. Resistance stiffened further as he penetrated deeper into Poland proper, and in June 1629 King Sigismund, his army having been reinforced by 12,000 troops sent to him by Wallenstein, inflicted a defeat on the Swedes at Stuhm which halted their advance up the Vistula towards Warsaw.[32]

Both the English and the Dutch were much concerned with the disruption to their trade in the Baltic which was being caused by the Prussian campaign as well as by the prospect of further disruption should Wallenstein be able to establish a Habsburg naval base on the southern coast of the sea. The Dutch mediated in fruitless Swedo–Polish negotiations in 1627 and 1628. But it was the French, anxious to use the Swedish army against the Emperor, who secured a six-year truce between Poland and Sweden at Altmark (Stary Targ) near Stuhm in September 1629. Although by this the Swedes had to evacuate most of the territory which they had occupied in Prussia, they gained recognition of their right for the duration of the truce to what had become since the beginning of the Prussian campaign an invaluable source of additional revenue: tolls of 3½ per cent from the ports along the coast of Prussia. Of the ports of Elbing, Braunsberg (Braniewo) and Pillau (Baltiysk) they were to have direct control. The duke of Kurland surrendered the dues from Windau and Libau by an agreement in 1630. Danzig made a separate agreement under English mediation in February of the following year; its tolls were to be shared, but the major part went to the Swedes. These 'Prussian tolls' amounted to some 600,000 daler annually or no less than a third of the total military expenditure of the Swedish crown, though much of the income was in fact devoted to general administration.[33] At last the Swedish army could be made ready for Germany.

The Secret Committee of the Riksdag had given the king their backing for intervention in Germany when he should see fit as early as January 1628, and the decision in principle to intervene was taken at a meeting of the Swedish royal Council on 8 January 1629, after all the political, economic and religious arguments had been well rehearsed. Even so, all hope of a peaceful settlement was not immediately abandoned; Christian IV pressed hard for one in order to prevent Swedish involvement, and secured the Emperor's agreement to a conference in Danzig to discuss Swedish proposals. This, however, did not open until Swedish troops had already landed in Pomerania, and it soon broke up.[34]

Gustavus's aims in 1630 seem, in any case, to have been limited: little more than to assist the German princes to drive the Emperor away from the Baltic, to restore the political situation in at least northern Germany to what it had been *ante bellum* and to erect some sort of system which would ensure that it would not again be disturbed, a system which would involve the establishment of Swedish bases on the southern coast of the Baltic, such as Stralsund and Wismar, from which Swedish troops could swiftly intervene as and when Swedish security appeared to be threatened. While there is no reason to doubt the sincerity of his religious convictions, and much was made of the threat to the Protestant settlement in Swedish propaganda, no mention was made of this threat in the Declaration which Gustavus issued in June 1630, and it was undoubtedly Sweden's security which was his prime concern. And with the main threat to that security coming from a fanatically Catholic Emperor, who had recently declared the restoration of everything which his co-religionists had lost in northern Germany since the middle of the sixteenth century, and from a Catholic king of Poland who was engaged to restore Sweden to Rome, there was no discrepancy between the repulse of the forces of the Counter Reformation and more secular objectives.[35]

Economic considerations also played a secondary role. Control of German trade routes into the Baltic which might result from victory in the conflict would undoubtedly provide a most welcome source of income for a poor country and would also bring nearer that *dominium maris Baltici* to which Gustavus was referring to increasingly in his correspondence with Oxenstierna. They did not, however, constitute the primary reason for taking the risks which he undoubtedly took (and realized that he took) in 1630.[36]

Like Christian IV, Gustavus entered the Thirty Years War without any guarantee of foreign aid and against a triumphant foe; neither England nor the Netherlands was willing to commit itself to aid, and the latter had even allowed its former alliance with Sweden to lapse. After Denmark's defeat, none of the German Protestant princes dared defy the Emperor. The Swedes' sole ally was the city of Stralsund, where their troops already formed part of the garrison. And Gustavus could never be sure that Christian IV would not use Sweden's engagement to attack him in the rear. For this eventuality he made plans before he sailed.[37]

But, unlike the Dane, the Swedish king went to war with the full approval of his Council, which he had obtained at the beginning of 1629 after a lengthy debate, and of the representatives of his subjects gathered in the Diet. An efficient propaganda machine, much assisted by the king's considerable oratorical gifts and a subservient clergy, stressed the threat of the return of popery and beat hard the patriotic drum.[38] Gustavus also had behind him an efficient administrative machine, which ensured the smooth running of the country in his absence and commanded an army trained in the latest military techniques.

The administrative machine was largely the brainchild of Oxenstierna, who had begun to establish a series of 'colleges' or committees, each chaired by one of the great officers of state and containing a number of members of the royal Council. The chancellor himself dominated the Chancery, a combined Home and Foreign Office, in which the administration of foreign affairs was clearly demarcated for the first time. A reorganized treasury ensured the more effective husbanding of financial resources, most of which fell within its purview and which could for the first time be seen as a whole. The process was completed two years after Gustavus's death by the so-called Form of Government of 1634, when a College of War and College of Admiralty were formally instituted. While the king continued to be accompanied wherever he travelled by a number of members of the royal Council, the remainder were expected to supervise the machinery of government in Stockholm, which became under Gustavus a capital city for the first time. For the first time also the composition, procedures and duties of the Diet were regularized by the Riksdag Ordinance of 1617 and the body was granted a permanent place in the constitution. It played, however, no part in the making of foreign policy.[39]

The recruitment of the Swedish army was made much more efficient under Gustavus. All adult male peasants were assigned to a 'file' (rota) of either ten (for freehold peasants) or twenty (for tenants of the nobility), each of which was expected to provide a foot soldier supported on a farm, whose tax or rent was reduced accordingly. Each regiment of eight companies was firmly attached to one of the ancient provinces of the country. Gustavus had no more success than his father in getting his nobility to perform their feudal service; his native cavalry was provided by wealthier farmers (among whom Finns were prominent) in exchange for tax exemptions. But it was a cavalry which was now trained to charge with the sword rather than, as was still the custom in western Europe, to advance at the trot and discharge their pistols at the enemy before retiring behind the protective screen of infantry. Against the Polish lancer such tactics had proved disastrous. Infantry equipped with muskets was provided with the protection of pikemen and body armour and trained to manoeuvre in such a way as to use its firepower to the maximum. Light field artillery, especially the three-pound 'regiment-piece' introduced in 1629, which could be easily moved from one part of the battlefield to another and intermixed with other arms, proved most effective. And Swedish troops were now armed largely with Swedish weapons, manufactured to uniform designs. The financing of the constantly expanding military machine from Sweden's limited resources was, however, always a problem.[40]

Gustavus finally left Stockholm in June 1630 with a fleet of twenty-seven ships and an army of 13,000 men on thirteen transport ships. These landed at Peenemünde on the northern end of the island of Usedom, which was rapidly occupied. Stettin was taken, but for the remainder of the year the Swedes remained penned into a small area at the mouth of the Oder river. Any hopes which Gustavus might have entertained that German allies would hurry to join him were soon dashed. Most German princes were as apprehensive of the Swedes as of the Emperor or were cowed by the thought of the possible consequences of joining Gustavus against Ferdinand should the latter be victorious. The example of Mecklenburg loomed large before them. Duke Bogislaw of Pomerania, under direct military pressure, agreed soon after the landing to place his troops under Swedish command and allow his foreign policy to be directed by the king. He was followed in August by the Imperial city of Magdeburg. But not even Gustavus's own brother-in-law, the Elector of Brandenburg, who had been much disturbed by the presence of Swedish troops in Prussia and whose claims to the succession in Pomerania when Duke Bogislaw died were threatened by the Swedish presence in the duchy and who required Imperial support for his investiture, would lift a finger to help.[41]

Any wish the Calvinist Elector may have had to aid his fellow Calvinist Fredrick of Bohemia had been thwarted by his pacific (and Lutheran) Estates and by his pro-Imperial and Catholic chief minister Schwartzenberg. He had before the beginning of the

Swedish campaign in Prussia refused King Gustavus's request for the use of the port of Memel (Klaipeda), only to see Pillau, also on his territory, used as a base for the Swedish expedition. This, and the threatening proximity of overwhelming Imperial forces, had even led him to consent to send 1,200 troops to join his Polish overlord in resisting his brother-in-law's forces, although the troops had proceeded to desert to the enemy. Now he agreed with the Lutheran Elector of Saxony to attend a meeting of Protestant German princes in Leipzig in February 1631 with the object of forming a home-grown alliance to defend German liberties against Swede and Habsburg alike.[42]

That Gustavus was able to establish his bridgehead at all was due largely to the absence of a large part of the Imperial army in northern Italy at the time of his landing. He was even more fortunate in that shortly after it the German Electors compelled the Emperor to dismiss Wallenstein, whose power they feared, as the price of electing Ferdinand's son as his successor on the Imperial throne.[43]

In January 1631, Cardinal Richelieu, now firmly in charge of France's foreign policy, agreed by the treaty of Bärwalde to pay the Swedes an annual subsidy of a million livres (400,000 dalers) for five years while they maintained an army in the Empire. But while the Polish tolls were enjoyed this represented a relatively small part of the Swedish war budget and was in fact not paid until 1632.[44]

Gustavus finally broke out of his bridgehead the following April, when he advanced into Brandenburg to attack the Imperial garrison which Elector George William had allowed to occupy the fortresses of Küstrin and Frankfurt am Oder. Even then it was only the horrific sack of Magdeburg by Tilly's troops in May, which decided the Elector to join his brother-in law. In June he agreed to place his army under Swedish direction.[45]

Gustavus's overwhelming victory over the Catholic League at Breitenfeld in Saxony in September transformed the situation. It began a triumphal march southward which drew the war further and further away from the Baltic and took Gustavus to within striking distance of Vienna. With military success, his dreams of a future settlement grew more ambitious; the whole of Pomerania was to be added to the territories envisaged as necessary for Sweden's future security, and the treaties he now made with German princes envisaged a permanent Swedish overlordship of a new Evangelical Union. Relations with Brandenburg were, however, still soured by rival claims to Pomerania and by Elector George William's hope to co-operate with Saxony in forming a third party to reduce Swedish influence in Germany, and many princes remained suspicious of Swedish ambitions.[46]

Only when his capital city was threatened did Ferdinand recall Wallenstein, who succeeded in luring the Swedes back into Saxony by threatening their lines of communication. The two armies met on the field of Lützen in November 1632. Technically the result was a Swedish victory, but Gustavus himself fell in the melee.[47]

He had, by the standards of the day, served his country well. While war had imposed heavy burdens on Sweden in manpower and resources, his leadership had united the country as never before and established its power firmly in the south-eastern Baltic. Out of the crisis which faced him at the beginning of his reign, the realm had emerged stronger. While other factors partly accounted for the weakening of Poland and Denmark since his accession, he and Oxenstierna had successfully exploited their embarrassments.

He left behind him a 6-year-old daughter, for whom a regency Council was appointed until she should be of an age to assume control. The Council was dominated by Oxenstierna, who remained in Germany to direct the war effort. The chancellor had never shared the king's more ambitious schemes in Germany; Sweden's main interests for him lay in the Baltic, where he was more aware of and interested in the commercial possibilities than his master. He determined that the burden of this should fall on the Germans in defence of whose liberties the war was ostensibly being fought. As native Swedish troops were withdrawn towards the Baltic coast to defend communications with their homeland, the chancellor organized the Heilbronn League, a union of smaller German Protestant states under his personal direction. For the remaining sixteen years of the war, while a succession of Swedish marshals commanded the principal anti-Habsburg forces in Germany, these forces were composed mainly of German troops.[48]

It was such an army which was defeated at the battle of Nördlingen in Bavaria in 1634, a defeat which cost Sweden control of southern Germany and forced France to enter the war as a principal against the Habsburgs. It also led to the rapid defection of most of Sweden's German allies, including the Elector of

Saxony and George William of Brandenburg, who had refused to join the Heilbronn League until given a guarantee of the succession to Pomerania and who now joined the Emperor. By the end of 1637 the Swedes held little more than Pomerania and Brandenburg, whose Elector had fled to Königsberg.[49]

The burden of the war had long led many members of the Swedish Council to call for Sweden's withdrawal from the conflict on the best terms which could be obtained which were at the same time in accordance with the country's security. In 1635 even Oxenstierna put out peace feelers to the Emperor and held talks with the Elector of Saxony. The outbreak of war between Poland and Russia in 1632 had at least ensured a continuation of the truce with Sigismund for the time being.[50]

Since the peace of Stolbova and the armistice of Deulino with the Poles the following year, Muscovite policy, dictated largely by the young tsar's all-powerful father, Filaret, to a subservient Council of boyars, had been cautious. Its main aim had been to prevent any permanent settlement of the conflict between Sweden and Poland which might tempt Sigismund to turn all his forces eastwards. This appeared to succeed at least until Altmark. Appeals from the Swedes to join Muscovy against Poland and share in its partition led to negotiations in 1626 but were finally rejected, and attempts by Gustavus to obtain the use of Muscovite troops in 1629 came to naught. The period of peace was used to rebuild the army, the organization of which had been seriously disrupted during the 'Time of Troubles': by 1630 it numbered some 90,000 men, including six infantry and a cavalry regiment (totalling some 12,000 soldiers) who had been trained on western European lines by mercenaries like the Scot Alexander Leslie, who was allowed in 1630 to leave Swedish for Muscovite service. The same period saw the foundation of a Muscovite armaments industry.[51]

The death of King Sigismund III in September 1632 promised a period of confusion in Poland–Lithuania until his successor was elected, and Filaret, urged on by Swedish diplomacy, decided that the time had come to attempt to recover the key city of Smolensk, lost by the terms of Deulino.[52] But the Polish army proved more than a match for the Muscovite forces, and with the resumption of Tatar attacks in the south, many boyars deserted to defend their estates while the mercenary elements melted away. In October 1633 the remaining troops were surrounded and in February

1634 forced to retire under an armistice. After this disaster, however, resistance to the Poles stiffened, and the latter offered to discuss peace. Negotiations finally brought this about on the eve of the expiration of the truce of Altmark in 1635. By the terms of the peace the terms of Deulino were confirmed and Władisław IV, who had succeeded his father on the Polish throne, finally gave up all his claims to the crown of Muscovy.[53]

Władisław wished to follow up the peace with an alliance with the Russians against Sweden, the claim to whose crown he had inherited and which, as with his father, largely dictated his foreign policy. He began to gather troops in Prussia and to build a fleet; the English royal agent in Poland, Francis Gordon, was used to seek help with the latter in Denmark and to hire ships and sailors in England. But he found little suppport among his subjects for a large-scale war, and Brandenburg and the Dutch wanted it even less. Much to the relief of the Swedes after their setback at the battle of Nördlingen, he agreed to renew the truce for twenty-six years after negotiations under Brandenburg, English, Dutch and French mediation at Stuhmsdorf (Sztumska Wieś). But for this the Swedes had to pay a high price: they had to abandon their right to levy tolls in the Prussian ports. It was a sad blow to Oxenstierna's commercial plans, which became less ambitious, and made the gaining of Pomerania (which he had before Nördlingen offered to exchange with Brandenburg for Prussia) more urgent.[54]

The financial weakness which resulted from this surrender certainly played a part in the military setbacks in Germany which the Swedes suffered during the following three years. Oxenstierna was able to put new heart into the Council after he returned to Stockholm in 1636 and to reach agreement with them on Swedish war aims, which included control of Western Pomerania, whose duke had died without issue in 1633, with the islands of Rügen, Usedom and Wollin and of the ports of Wismar and Warnemünde. But only after a new subsidy treaty had been made with France and been ratified in March 1638 were the armies under Swedish command able to advance southward again into central Germany.[55]

Denmark's intervention in the war had exhausted its treasury; the disturbance of trade in the Baltic reduced the income from the Sound Dues, and the king's credit was weakened. And the general economic situation in the country was worsening as a result of a decline in grain prices and a deterioration in the cattle trade. The Council was consequently able to wrest from the king control of military expenditure, which was in 1637 placed under the control of a commissariat.[56]

In matters of foreign policy, however, it found itself pushed aside by King Christian, who came to rely more and more on independent German advisers. These encouraged his efforts to exploit the fears and jealousies directed towards Sweden after its military successes in order to limit its gains in Germany, to defend what remained of Denmark's position in the Baltic, and, if possible, to extend Danish influence in northern Germany. Unfortunately in doing so he alienated most of his potential allies; the Dutch in particular, although concerned by the growth of Sweden's power in the area, were antagonized by Christian's doubling of the Sound Dues in an effort to restore his financial independence of the Council, and even in 1640 were driven to conclude with the Swedes an agreement on the defence of freedom of trade.[57]

Christian sent Malte Juels to Moscow in 1631 to try to establish links with the tsar against Sweden, but he found Sweden in favour there and came away empty-handed. Although King Władisław supported the idea of a Danish alliance directed against Sweden, his Council did not, and the Poles were incensed by attacks by Danish privateers on their shipping; in 1637 there had even been an attack on the Polish fleet trying to levy tolls on Danish merchant ships off Danzig. In 1642 Christian renewed approaches to the Polish king with plans for a war with Sweden into which the tsar was also to be drawn, but got cold feet, and Władisław turned towards the Turks.[58]

King Christian's main effort was, however, concentrated on the Emperor, to whom he offered Danish mediation in exchange for the right to raise a toll on the river Elbe and confirmation of his son's position in the bishoprics. The former he, in fact, secured in 1633 for four years and the latter in 1635.[59] In 1637 he even went so far as to offer the new Emperor Ferdinand an alliance against Sweden should that country not accept reasonable peace conditions. Ten years previously during his German campaign Gustavus Adolphus had himself considered a preventative war against Denmark. Rumours of such machinations made Denmark unacceptable as a mediator and finally helped to determine the Swedes, already incensed by the Danish refusal to allow war *matériel* through the Sound or to exempt ships from their newly acquired lands from Sound tolls, to end them by force of arms. The decision to attack their neighbour which was taken by the royal Council in Stockholm early in 1643 and approved by the Secret Committee of the Estates in October seems, however, to have been dictated by the weakness of Denmark's diplomatic position and the strength of Sweden's own. For Oxenstierna in particular the time seemed at last ripe to deprive Denmark of the command of the Sound which hindered Sweden's mercantile ambitions in the Baltic by winning the provinces of Scania, Halland and Blekinge.[60]

In December 1643 a Swedish army under the command of marshal Lennart Torstensson suddenly appeared on the southern border of Jutland, having marched from Bohemia, and in the course of two months this occupied the whole of the Danish mainland. In February 1644 another Swedish army under Gustav Karlsson Horn occupied all of Scania except the cities of Malmö and Kristianstad. There was even talk at this stage of crushing Denmark for good and all, an idea that was to re-emerge under Charles X in the next decade.[61]

The war was the first test of strength between the two great Baltic naval powers since the end of the Kalmar War thirty years previously. King Gustavus had taken a great interest in matching Christian IV's fleet and under the leadership from 1620 of Klas Larsson Fleming a more efficient administration had been introduced into the Swedish fleet, culminating in 1634 in the establishment of an Admiralty College. The problem of manning had been partly overcome by making areas on the coast responsible for supplying a fixed number of recruits. And more and bigger ships were built, although their design was not always ideal as evidenced by the fate of the *Vasa* in Stockholm harbour in 1628. Only one naval battle of any significance was fought in the Baltic in Gustavus's reign, but the Swedish navy was indispensable for blockade work, convoying troops and keeping open lines of communication. But the Danish navy had grown equally rapidly and by this time had also become a formidable and highly professional force. As early as 1618 Christian IV had founded at Copenhagen what was to be the great new naval base of Christianshavn, but growth had been particularly rapid after 1637 when Corfits Ulfeldt, the king's son-in-law, had taken charge.[62]

In May 1644 this fleet turned back off the island of Sylt in the

North Sea ships assembled in the Netherlands for Sweden by the industrialist Louis de Geer, and two months later it secured a famous victory over the Swedes under Klas Fleming at the ten-hour battle of Kolberger Heide, during which King Christian himself was wounded and lost the sight of one eye. As a result of this success the Danes managed to blockade the Swedes for three weeks in Kiel Bay, where Horn was slain. His ships, however, managed to escape and join a fresh fleet assembled by de Geer in the Netherlands, which reached Kalmar in August.[63]

With its help, they secured a crushing victory over a smaller Danish fleet in October off the island of Femern; the Danes lost no fewer than twelve ships of the line sunk or captured out of a total of seventeen, and a further three were beached. Two of their admirals were killed and two taken prisoner. Their command of the sea was lost. A Swedish landing on the Danish islands had been delayed long enough to force Torstensson, no longer able to support his troops and threatened by an Imperial army in Holstein, to withdraw from Jutland into Germany. But at the end of the year he sent a force of 4,000 men under Helmut Wrangel to reoccupy much of the peninsula. And the following year the Swedish fleet seized Gotland and Bornholm, and in June a Dutch fleet joined it at Køge.[64]

In the course of the peace negotiations between Denmark and Sweden which had begun at Brömsebro in February 1645, the French negotiator was for the Swedes ominously friendly towards the Danes, and the Dutch mediators were won over by Christian's giving way under pressure from his Council to most of their demands with regard to the Sound Dues, a reflection of the desire by both states to maintain a balance of power in the Baltic and limit Swedish ambitions there. The Dutch had also been taken aback by Sweden's failure to consult them before the war was launched, which they claimed to be a breach of the alliance of 1640. As a consequence, the Swedes had to abandon some of their demands: at the final settlement in August 1645 they failed to obtain all three Danish provinces to the east of the Sound, of which they had dreamed, and continued to dream. But Halland they would be allowed to occupy for thirty years, and the outright acquisition of the islands of Ösel and Gotland removed the last vestiges of Danish encirclement as well as in the case of the latter providing a possible naval base at Slite. They further gained the Norwegian provinces of Jämtland and Härjedalen. And Danish hopes of participation in the German peace negotiations, which had finally commenced in Osnabrück and Münster in Westphalia and at which Sweden found itself in a strong position, had to be abandoned.[65]

Indeed when peace finally returned to Germany by the treaty of Westphalia in October 1648 it was Denmark who was made to feel threatened by the settlement. By the acquisition of the bishoprics of Verden and Bremen (but not the Imperial city of Bremen) on the western side of the Jutish peninsula, of the port of Wismar (where a hostile fleet might be gathered) and, further along the Baltic coast to the east, of the western half of Pomerania, Sweden won not only control of the mouths of the rivers Elbe and Oder but also bases from which to launch at any time attacks on Denmark from the south.[66]

Christian IV had died at the beginning of the year, a sad and embittered man. A reign which had begun so promisingly with Denmark as the recognized leading Baltic power had been punctuated by a series of humiliations in foreign policy and loss of territory which ended all hopes of maintaining the *dominium* to which proud claim had been made. The king himself must undoubtedly bear some of the blame for this. He had entered the Thirty Years War without adequate preparation, and his intrigues in the 1630s to limit the growth of Swedish power had provided the Swedes with a fine excuse to impose fresh military defeat. At the same time he enjoyed a much broader view of his realm's position in northern Europe than did his councillors, fearful as they were of the results of a successful foreign policy on their own position and unwilling to provide the monarch with the resources to pursue one.[67]

Brandenburg had made peace with Sweden in 1641. The new Elector's effective rule was confined to East Prussia, to defend which he had only some 6,000 troops at his disposal. After the death of Schwartzenberg in March of that year, he sent envoys to Stockholm, who reached agreement on a ceasefire in July. Frederick William nevertheless maintained vigorously his claims to Pomerania, and it was not until February 1647 that, with French help, agreement had been reached on a partition of the disputed lands.[68]

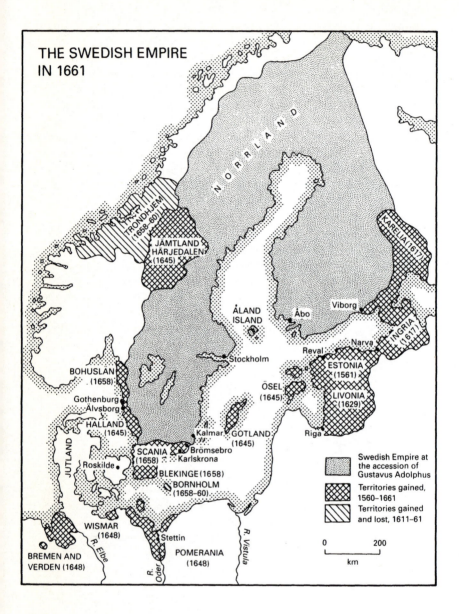

THE SWEDISH EMPIRE
IN 1661

N O R R L A N D

TRONDHJEM
(1658–60)

JÄMTLAND
HÄRJEDALEN
(1645)

KARELIA (1617)

ÅLAND
ISLAND

Åbo

Viborg

INGRIA (1617)

Narva

Reval

BOHUSLAN
(1658)

Stockholm

ESTONIA
(1561)

Gothenburg
Älvsborg

ÖSEL
(1645)

LIVONIA
(1629)

HALLAND
(1645)

Kalmar

GOTLAND
(1645)

Riga

JUTLAND

SCANIA
(1658)

Brömsebro
Karlskrona

Roskilde

BLEKINGE (1658)

BORNHOLM
(1658–60)

WISMAR
(1648)

Stettin

BREMEN AND
VERDEN (1648)

R. Elbe

R. Oder

POMERANIA
(1648)

R. Vistula

Swedish Empire at
the accession of
Gustavus Adolphus

Territories gained,
1560–1661

Territories gained
and lost, 1611–61

0   200

km

6

THE FIRST GREAT
NORTHERN WAR (1648–67)

While the territories ruled by the Swedish crown had still to reach their greatest extent, the peace of Westphalia established Sweden as the leading power in the Baltic. This had come about as the result of a combination of factors: the need to counter the ambitions of successive Danish rulers to reimpose the control they had exercised during the period of the Kalmar Union and more recently of the Vasa kings of Poland to gain their inheritance; the distraction of other great powers in the religious struggles of western and central Europe and the interest of the Maritime Powers in limiting Denmark's naval domination of the Baltic; the leadership of men like Gustavus Adolphus and Axel Oxenstierna; and the economic resources which compensated to a certain extent for the general poverty of the country. While certainly success bred ambition, it is difficult to see in the growth of Swedish power the evolution of a deliberate imperial plan for Baltic domination for longer than brief periods. It was, as with the foreign policy of most nations, a matter of using changing opportunities to pursue what were seen at the time as the best interests of the country. Oxenstierna in particular for a time did seem to have glimpsed the possibility of securing control of all the main export outlets in the Baltic, but all this belongs to a rather late stage in the development of the 'empire'. It re-emerges under Charles X and Charles XII, but permanent control of the Prussian ports and in particular Danzig, which is the only way such a monopoly could have been effective, always eluded the Swedes.[1]

It was by no means a uniform, integrated 'empire' which was ruled from Stockholm after 1648. The Swedish king's German possessions in Bremen and Verden, Wismar and Pomerania were

Imperial fiefs, for the administration of which he was answerable to the Emperor in Vienna and in which he did little to interfere with existing institutions. The Baltic lands were royal lands by treaty or conquest. Here he had a freer hand, but generally the rights of the local nobility were respected until the end of the seventeenth century, and only in Ingria were Swedish institutions introduced almost immediately. None of these territories sent representatives to the Swedish Diet.[2]

Westphalia did nothing to assuage Denmark's longing to regain its position, and it provided Sweden with a potential new challenger in the shape of Brandenburg–Prussia, whose Hohenzollern rulers would not rest until they had gained the western part of Pomerania. Swedish dominance also incurred the hostility of the Dutch with their formidable fleet, to which Sweden's own merchantmen were now a growing threat, while dependence on France limited the scope of Swedish action in foreign affairs and tempted it to seek alternative alliances. Furthermore the strain of the war and its aftermath caused formidable internal problems.[3] And for only seven years were the guns in the area silent.

In the year of Westphalia the Cossacks in south-eastern Poland rose in revolt against the king and at the beginning of 1654, after suffering defeat at the hands of their overlord, placed themselves under the protection of the tsar. In the war between Poland and Russia[4] which resulted, Russian armies advanced rapidly towards the Vistula as the Polish–Lithuanian Commonwealth seemed on the verge of utter collapse. The king of Sweden, Charles X, saw an opportunity to solve the Polish problem while blocking the Russian advance towards the Baltic and securing Swedish control of the mouth of the Vistula. His involvement in Poland tempted Denmark to strike at its traditional enemy, but at the peace Charles compelled the latter to withdraw from the southern Scandinavian peninsula, leaving the eastern shore of the Sound firmly in Swedish hands. This was a situation which was highly satisfactory to the maritime powers of England and the United Provinces of the Netherlands.

The peace treaties involving Sweden, Denmark, Russia and Poland signed in 1660 and 1661 confirmed the territorial extent of the Swedish 'Empire' at what was to prove its extreme limits (see map, p. 78) and ended the seventy-year-long struggle between Sweden and Poland over the latter's claim to the Swedish throne. They also marked a further stage in the emergence of

Brandenburg–Prussia as a Baltic power with the confirmation of its sovereignty over East Prussia. Peace between Poland and Russia in 1667 confirmed the supercession of the former by the latter as the leading power in eastern Europe and was followed by a period of co-operation between the two former antagonists against the Turks. Poland was indeed henceforth not an active factor in the struggle for Baltic dominance.

For Denmark, as for all the Baltic powers who participated in it, the Thirty Years War constituted an enormous economic and financial strain. Jutland had been twice occupied by enemy troops in the space of twenty years, and although recovery appears to have been comparatively swift, the drain on Denmark's resources was considerable. As has been seen, efforts by the Danish crown to recoup its financial losses by increasing revenue from the Sound Dues only made it enemies among the trading nations of northern Europe, and a budget with a regular surplus in the early years of the century was now converted into one where expenditure regularly far outran revenue.[5] In the circumstances Danish foreign policy had to be essentially defensive, aimed at isolating Sweden diplomatically to prevent further extension of its power in the Baltic.

But Sweden also faced serious problems. War had not 'fed itself' as had been hoped, French subsidies came to an end and the burden of taxation which had had to be imposed on the Swedish people was only increased by the large-scale grants of land and tax revenues to members of the nobility made in an effort to pay off the crown's debts and obligations. The financial situation itself might, however, tempt the state to indulge in further foreign adventures; in his instructions to the newly formed Chamber of Commerce in 1651, Axel Oxenstierna, who, though now a sick man and often absent from meetings of the royal Council, remained the single most important figure in Sweden's policy-making until his death in 1654 and who believed that the crown's income should be derived from customs dues rather than from landed property, stressed the desirability of gaining control of the Baltic staples; some half of all ships sailing through the Sound were still trading with Polish ports and some third of all Baltic trade flowed through Danzig. If the circumstances proved favourable, this might be achieved either by a blow against Denmark with the object of gaining control of the Sound and the Norwegian coast or by a revival of the struggle with Poland to gain those Prussian ports which had proved so lucrative before the expiry of the Altmark truce, the renewal of which was due to expire in 1661.[6] In fact both alternatives were to be tried before that date.

Brandenburg–Prussia had to sustain Swedish troops on its soil until outstanding problems in Pomerania had been settled. The frontiers between the two areas of Pomerania were finally agreed in November 1651 after the Elector had climbed down and agreed to surrender territory on the right bank of the Oder to the Swedes. But they continued to claim that the terms of Westphalia entitled them to continue to enjoy the tolls from both the ports of ducal Prussia and from those of the whole of Pomerania (i.e. including the eastern half, which had been granted to Brandenburg), as well as from Mecklenburg. Not until the Elector Frederick William agreed in May 1653 to grant Sweden half of these were the ports finally evacuated and not until after the accession of Charles X the following year was Sweden formally invested by the Emperor with its share of Pomerania. Sweden's quarrel with Mecklenburg lasted until the end of the eighteenth century.[7]

This all increased the Elector's determination to build up his army, which consisted of no more than 1,800 men at this stage, in preparation for the day when the opportunity presented itself to revenge himself on Sweden, which had, in his eyes, deprived him of half of what was rightfully his. In 1653 he obtained from the Brandenburg Diet, in exchange for a confirmation and extension of noble privileges and an undertaking not to conclude an alliance with a foreign power without its consent, a six-year subsidy with which to create a respectable military force.[8]

In all these countries peace also brought with it struggles within the ruling elites, struggles into which in Sweden the lower classes were also drawn. Such divisions might also impede initiatives in foreign policy. In Denmark the nobles were able to impose on the new king, Frederik III, as a condition of electing him to succeed his father in 1648, a charter which appeared to make him the mere tool of his Council to a greater extent than any of his predecessors. The principal aim for himself and his entourage, which included a number of German advisers he had brought with him from his bishopric of Bremen and his ambitious German wife, was to free the crown from such shackles. And within a few years indeed, by exploiting divisions within the Council and by building up a royal party within the organs of the state, he could boast considerable success.[9]

In Sweden, Queen Christina was even before the conclusion of peace in Westphalia already smarting under the tutelage of Oxenstierna and was creating her own party on the royal Council which was gaining ground at the cost of the chancellor's supporters. The non-noble Estates were also calling for a recall of royal grants of lands and taxes in order to ease their financial burden. This presaged a serious social crisis which came to a head in the Riksdag of 1650 and which the young queen exploited to force the Council to agree to accept her cousin Charles Gustavus (Karl Gustav) of Zweibrücken (son of Gustavus Adolphus's half-sister) as her heir as she had decided never to marry.[10]

In Brandenburg, as has been seen, the ruler made concessions to his nobility and endeavoured to separate it from the urban bourgeoisie by allowing the towns to raise their contributions to the treasury in the form of an excise tax, which was not dependent on the consent of the Diet.[11] He was never again to call a general meeting of his Estates. They were indeed not to meet again for two hundred years. In all the ex-belligerent countries bordering on the Baltic the bases were being laid during these years for the introduction of royal absolutism later in the century.

Of the non-belligerents, Poland had largely escaped the ravages of war after 1629, but neither King Władisław IV nor his brother and successor John Casimir (Jan Kazimierz) were able to reform the rickety constitutional system, and indeed monarchical power declined even further in mid-century to the benefit of the *szlachta*. Their local dietines had even acquired the right to raise their own troops, while the king had at his disposal only a small mercenary army. Of internal weakness, both the Cossacks and the Lithuanian nobility were ready to take advantage and threaten the survival of the Union.[12]

In Russia some efforts were made to modernize the army, and by 1640 the economy had begun to recover from the depression from which it had been suffering since the war with Poland, but the administration remained primitive as *prikaz* was piled on *prikaz*.[13] The attention of both Polish and Russian statesmen was in any case drawn temporarily away from the Baltic after 1648, though it was ironically the cause of this diversion which was to lead to a revival of the struggle for power there in the mid-1650s.

After the final resolution of the problems created by the Westphalian settlement in Germany during the remainder of Queen

Christina's reign, Sweden, with France as her sole reliable ally, endeavoured to avoid becoming embroiled in Europe's quarrels, especially the repercussions of the Anglo–Dutch War. At the same time it kept a wary eye on developments and, with the quarrel with Poland still unresolved, tried to ensure that it was ready for war if it should come; there was a constant fear of support for Poland from the United Provinces and Brandenburg which might make Sweden's position precarious. A *rapprochement* was sought with Denmark in an attempt to break that country's links with the United Provinces, and in fact both countries did draw closer together for fear of becoming embroiled in the Anglo–Dutch War, but no firm agreement could be attained.[14]

But in July 1654 Christina finally abdicated in favour of her cousin, who ascended the throne of Sweden as Charles X. She left her realm on a leisurely journey to Rome, in the course of which she was received into the Roman Catholic church. Charles had commanded the Swedish forces in Germany at the end of the Thirty Years War and was by profession a soldier. He was at the same time an astute politician who was able to manoeuvre a recalcitrant nobility into agreeing, under threat of the withdrawal of their taxation privileges, to the partial resumption of royal lands which had been alienated to them. The problem of maintaining the military establishment needed to protect Sweden's scattered 'empire' remained, and while the new king did not seek war for its own sake, and the hostile attitude of both Denmark and the Dutch and the uncertain policy of Brandenburg–Prussia made a foreign adventure risky, a successful war might not only help to sustain his troops and give employment and riches to a restless aristocracy but also strengthen his position at home.[15] In any case the situation developing in Poland could not be ignored.

The steady advance westward of a well-equipped Russian army opened up the threat of a Russian breakthrough to the Baltic on a broad front and the upsetting of all that Sweden had achieved in the early part of the reign of Gustavus Adolphus; Charles was particularly concerned that the navy of some forty-four warships formed by the ambitious Duke Jakob of Kurland might fall into the tsar's hands, and in the summer of 1654 ordered the defences of Livonia to be put in a state of readiness. In the autumn Smolensk and Vilna fell to the Muscovites, and Livonia was directly threatened. Charles, who acted as his own foreign minister after the death of Axel Oxenstierna's son Erik in the autumn of

1656, was faced with two alternatives: either to ally with the Poles in order to present a united front against the Russians in return for the abandonment of Polish claims to the Swedish throne and territorial concessions on the Baltic coast, or to intervene against both powers in succession and establish a Swedish presence on the southern coast of the Baltic such as would put an end once and for all to any threat to Swedish dominance, besides bringing decided economic benefits.[16]

Negotiations between Poland and Sweden in Lübeck under the aegis of France and Kurland in 1651 and in 1652–3 had come to naught; in spite of the Cossack threat in the south, King John Casimir had refused to make any concessions and continued to demand Livonia. The Poles now refused an alliance proffered to them, and urged on by the Lithuanian ex-chancellor Hieronymus Radziejowski, who had fled to Sweden in 1652, Charles decided to renounce the Stuhmsdorf truce. A decision to mobilize the Swedish army and navy was taken by the royal Council at the end of 1654. Though even at this stage no final decision was made as to who the enemy was to be or any detailed objectives drawn up, since for a country with Sweden's limited resources no large army could be maintained for any length of time without being used, intervention was now almost inevitable. And while some councillors spoke for peace, the majority supported an assault on Poland should it not make sweeping concessions, while leaving the final decision to the king.[17]

Sweden's demands were presented to the Poles in February 1655. The Poles offered only to negotiate for an alliance against the Muscovites. But Charles had already taken the decision to attack. In July 1655, in fact, a Swedish army of 14,000 men under marshal Arvid Wittenberg crossed into Poland from Pomerania, while an army from Livonia invaded Lithuania. Thus assaulted from all directions, Polish resistance collapsed. Only Danzig, defended by a Dutch garrison, held out. In August King Charles himself landed on Usedom with a further 15,000 men and joined Wittenberg.[18] In September Warsaw and in October Cracow fell to the Swedes, and John Casimir fled the country. At the same time the Calvinist Radziwiłł brothers in Lithuania concluded an agreement with King Charles which envisaged a Lithuanian union with Sweden. They acted, however, largely on their own behalf without the authority of their fellow nobles, and before the Swedes could reap any advantage, most of Lithuania was occupied by Russian troops and the grand duchy declared incorporated into the tsar's dominions.[19]

But at the end of the year a 'confederation' was formed by the crown hetman (royal commander-in-chief) in Poland, and Casimir returned to lead a national uprising against the invaders. Frederick William of Brandenburg had refused Russia's call for help against the Poles in exchange for Lithuania and also Charles's offer of sovereignty over Prussia and Ermland in exchange for 6,000 troops at the beginning of his campaign. He now turned to the tsar with an offer of mediation and concluded an alliance with the Estates of royal (West) Prussia. This latter action brought down on him the wrath of the Swedes, who secured the submission of all the Prussian towns except Danzig and forced the Elector to retire into Ermland. Finally, in January 1656, he had to agree by the treaty of Königsberg to accept ducal (i.e. East) Prussia and Ermland as fiefs of the Swedish crown. Sweden was to enjoy half the revenue from the Prussian tolls and the use of the ports of Pillau and Memel, and the Elector was to abandon his small navy of four warships. If the war continued he was to assist Charles with 1,500 men.[20]

In Russia there were fears of the formation of a Swedo–Polish confederation which would exclude it entirely from contact with western Europe. The dominant influence on the country's policy, Afanasi Lavrentevich Ordin-Nashchokin, sought to exorcize this danger by securing a peaceful settlement of the problem of the Ukraine with Poland so that Muscovite forces, possibly in alliance with Poland, could be concentrated against Sweden, which he was to describe as 'a well-known old enemy (who) slyly provoked quarrels and awaits the time to attack'.[21] He won over Tsar Alexis to the idea and, after making an alliance with Brandenburg, in April 1656 secured a truce with John Casimir on condition that the tsar would succeed him to the Polish throne, made an offensive alliance with Denmark and in May declared war on Sweden. Russian troops proceeded to occupy parts of Livonia and Ingria, and small fleets of Russian boats appeared on lake Ladoga and the river Dvina. A temporary base was even established on the Baltic at Nyen, and at the end of August Riga was besieged. The ultimate aims of the Russians were reflected in the demands made by Ordin-Nashchokin for the coastline between Narva and Viborg and for the duchy of Kurland, which he envisaged as providing a base for his nascent fleet.[22]

Charles X was now forced to retreat and he abandoned Warsaw in June. Under such pressure he agreed to surrender to Frederick William Sweden's gains in Poland, amounting to four Polish palatinates bordering on the electorate, in exchange for military aid amounting to the whole Brandenburg army for a year and 4,000 troops thereafter (treaty of Marienburg). Nearly half the army of 18,000 which was victorious over the Poles at the three-day battle of Warsaw the following month was made up of electoral troops, who proved that they had learned well the Swedish tactics they had been trained to employ.[23]

In the autumn the Swedes were forced to retire into Prussia but lost control of the land bridge to Pomerania; the Elector did not wish to penetrate further south and as has been seen, Russian forces were threatening Livonia. Polish troops entered Danzig, and Tatars raided as far as Hither Pomerania. Under the Emperor's mediation, Poland and Russia concluded a new armistice at Hadziacz in October, which enabled them to concentrate their forces against Sweden and Brandenburg. And the Emperor himself agreed to send military assistance to the Poles. All this led Charles to make even further concessions to Brandenburg: he finally offered to the latter full sovereignty in East Prussia together with the revenue from all its tolls in exchange for further military aid. Against the advice of a majority of his Council, who urged him to settle with Poland, but with the support of his pro-Swedish chief minister George Friedrich von Waldeck, the Elector accepted the offer by the treaty of Labiau in November. Thus strengthened, Charles was able at the beginning of the campaigning season in 1657 to advance once more into central Poland.[24]

But King Frederik III of Denmark chose this moment himself to declare war. To strengthen its naval position against the Swedes, much weakened by the war of 1643-5, Denmark had after the peace of Brömsebro turned to the Dutch, who had become increasingly alarmed by the growth of Swedish power and the threat to their economic position in the Baltic. As early as February 1647 the two powers had concluded a trade treaty, and in September 1649 they had agreed to a defensive alliance for thirty-six years on condition that Denmark accept a single annual payment of 140,000 daler instead of the tolls imposed on individual Dutch ships sailing through the Sound (the so-called Redemption treaty). The alliance was renewed in 1653, but the Redemption treaty was cancelled in face of English and

Swedish pressure.[25] Before his attack on Poland, Charles X had sought in vain to gain Denmark's support in excluding Dutch warships from the Baltic, and in July 1656 a Dutch fleet of forty-two ships was allowed to pass through the Sound in response to the Swedish blockade of Danzig, which Charles now raised. In September it was withdrawn from Danzig, together with the Danish ships which had joined it there after the Swedes had made trade concessions and after throwing troops into the city. The Dutch turned down further requests for aid and the offer of a new alliance from King Frederik.[26]

In February 1657 Frederik's Estates, meeting at Roskilde, did, however, agree to grant aid to meet a supposed threat from Sweden, and the Council, though with some reluctance, granted the king a free hand to take what measures he deemed necessary. In May the Emperor promised Denmark assistance, but then died, and diplomatically Denmark was weak; an alliance with Poland and Frederik's father-in-law, the duke of Holstein–Gottorp, promised little benefit.[27] In July a Danish fleet in its turn sailed for Danzig with the aim of preventing Swedish troops from embarking there for an assault on the Danish islands. But King Charles, having withdrawn most of his troops from the interior of Poland, chose to march west by land with a force of 9,000 men and to attack Jutland from the south. In October he captured the key fortress of Frederiksodde (present-day Fredericia), which commanded the narrowest crossing of the Little Belt to the island of Fyn. But the Swedish fleet had failed to secure sufficient command of the sea to allow a direct assault on the island; an engagement off Falsterbo at the south-western tip of Scania in September was indecisive and forced the Swedes to remain bottled up in Wismar until December.[28] In compensation the weather came to the Swedish king's aid.

An exceptionally harsh winter at the beginning of 1658 caused the narrow seaways between the Danish islands to freeze over to a depth which even permitted the passage over them of cavalry, and at the end of January Charles began a march which brought his army via the islands of Fyn, Langeland, Lolland and Falster to Vordingborg on Zealand in the second week of February, with the loss of very few lives. The Danes were unprepared for this manoeuvre, and at Roskilde concluded a humiliating peace. They surrendered the provinces of Scania, Halland and Blekinge in perpetuity, together with the island of Bornholm, the Norwegian province of Bohuslän north of Gothenburg and the whole of central Norway, thus giving Sweden a considerable Atlantic coastline. At one stage in the negotiations Charles had demanded considerably more: the islands of Møn and Læsø, as well as Iceland and the Faeroe Islands. Once peace had been concluded, however, he offered the Danes a close alliance while contemplating an assault on Brandenburg–Prussia, whose Elector had changed sides in the absence of the Swedish army.[29]

With the help of the Emperor, who needed Brandenburg's support in the College of Electors, Frederick William, who had already made his peace with the Muscovites, had obtained from John Casimir by the treaty of Wehlau in September 1657 full sovereignty over East Prussia, the town of Elbing and a number of districts adjacent to Pomerania as Polish fiefs in exchange for the surrender of Ermland and assistance against the Swedes with 6,000 troops.[30]

Control of the Prussian ports had, as has been seen, been one of Charles X's main objectives at the beginning of the war. Now, if Denmark could be brought to join him in closing the Sound against the Dutch, who would certainly not support an extension of Swedish power, a fresh attempt might be made in a campaign against Brandenburg. A partition of Poland by agreement with Brandenburg and Austria was also considered. But as the situation in the eastern Baltic became less favourable for Sweden (Austria, Poland and Brandenburg concluded an alliance and relations with Russia deteriorated) and it became clear that the Maritime Powers would not look kindly on a Prussian campaign, Charles turned to an alternative which was never wholly absent from his thoughts: a fresh attack on Denmark with the objective of outright conquest. This would give Sweden not only the ability to exclude all foreign navies from the Baltic but also control of the Sound Dues, providing an annual income roughly equivalent to that which might be expected from the Prussian ports.[31]

The Danes did finally give way to all Sweden's demands in the negotiations about the implementation of the peace treaty, and Sweden's relations with Russia improved. Charles consequently swung back to the Prussian project. But he did not trust the Danes to close the Sound to the Dutch should he become involved again in Prussia, and in July his Council agreed to the reopening of hostilities against Denmark to destroy Danish power once and for all. In August a Swedish army was brought from Kiel to

Korsør on Zealand and commenced a march on Copenhagen. The fleet was dispatched to the Sound. But instead of launching an immediate assault on the Danish capital, Charles chose to invest the city.[32]

In this second Danish war the odds were, however, more heavily stacked against Sweden than in the first. Frederick William of Brandenburg had followed his alliance with Poland with one with the Emperor, and when the Swedish attack came he led an army of 30,000 Brandenburgers, Austrians and Poles into Holstein. More valuable for the Danes was the arrival in October of a large Dutch fleet of thirty-five warships with no fewer than seventy provision ships in tow at the northern entrance to the Sound. Charles forbade Admiral Wrangel to attack, and the Dutch were consequently able to sail into the Sound, where they fought a five-hour battle with a superior Swedish fleet before breaking through to the shelter of Copenhagen. Seven Danish ships arrived on the scene too late to take part in the encounter.[33] Meanwhile the Dutch merchant ships slipped into the harbour of Copenhagen with much needed supplies for the city, which was being stoutly defended under the leadership of the king himself. The Swedish fleet, having lost four of its ships, was eventually compelled to retreat to Landskrona on the opposite coast, where it was bottled up by the Dano–Dutch fleet until the end of November.[34]

Charles launched a vain assault on the Danish capital in February 1659. He did succeed in occupying the islands of Langeland, Lolland and Falster, but at the end of April the main Swedish fleet was again forced to withdraw to Landskrona while a British fleet of forty-four ships under Admiral Edward Montagu joined a Dutch fleet in the Sound in May. In the same month a Brandenburg and Imperial army captured Frederiksodde, and at the end of October troops brought from Kiel were landed on Fyn and compelled the Swedes on the island to surrender after a battle at Nyborg. The Dutch fleet then sailed home. In spite of such setbacks and the occupation of Swedish Pomerania to the gates of Stralsund and Stettin by Brandenburg, Charles refused all offers of peace negotiations.[35]

The deadlock was broken only by his sudden death in Gothenburg at the beginning of 1660 while he was planning a campaign against Norway. He left behind him a 4-year-old son, and the regents for the boy opened peace negotiations with Denmark in Copenhagen the following March. The Dutch rejected Danish calls for an attack on Gothenburg, but forced the Swedes to raise a blockade of Copenhagen. The peace treaty finally concluded in May was, however, a sore disappointment for the Danes. France, England and the United Provinces had already agreed by the 'Hague Concert' in May 1659 that the terms of Roskilde should form the basis of a new settlement, and by a further agreement in July that the Swedes should lose central Norway, which had already expelled them. The only other modifications in the final settlement involved the return to Denmark of Bornholm, from which the occupiers had also been expelled but which Sweden demanded stubbornly until the Dutch began to arrest their ships.[36]

In the east peace was made between Sweden and Poland, Brandenburg and the Emperor under French mediation at Oliva near Danzig in the same month as that in Copenhagen. Frederick William had hoped to secure the remainder of Pomerania, but France, now freed from her war with Spain, wished to retain a Swedish presence in Germany and was able to isolate the Elector. He had to restore Elbing to Poland and rest content with a confirmation of his sovereignty over East Prussia. He was nevertheless the great gainer from the struggle. He had at his disposal an army of some 22,000 men, which he had already used during the war to extract taxes which had not been approved by his Estates, and the removal of the right of the nobles in East Prussia to appeal against him to the king of Poland enabled him to assert his power over the Estates there and exploit the rivalry between Königsberg and the other cities to crush their opposition.[37]

Under Russian pressure, the peace party in Poland, led by Queen Louise-Marie, had gained the upper hand. By the final settlement, the Swedes had to evacuate Kurland, which they had occupied in the previous September and to free Duke Jakob, whom they had taken prisoner. But King John Casimir surrendered all his claims to Livonia and above all to the Swedish crown (though he was allowed to retain the title of king of Sweden for his lifetime). So came to an end the dynastic struggle which had begun forty years previously when King Sigismund III had left Sweden for the last time and which had done little to forward his realm's interests. Poland was exhausted, and yet had to face a continuing conflict with Russia.[38]

In 1658 the *Sejm* rejected the mutual succession pact and in September concluded an agreement with the Zaporozhian Cossacks which would have created a triple Commonwealth and made war between Poland and Muscovy inevitable. In June 1659 a great army of Poles, Cossacks and Tatars inflicted a serious defeat on the tsar's army. But the Cossacks then changed sides and this enabled Alexis to regain the territory which he had lost. By 1667 both sides, faced by a common threat from the Tatars, were inclined to seek peace, and in January of that year they concluded a thirteen-and-a-half-year armistice at Andrussovo. John Casimir, faced at home with a noble confederation led by Jerzy Lubomirski, which had defeated the royal army in July 1666 as well as the Turkish threat, had to surrender all the territorial gains which had been made under Sigismund III. The return to Russia of Smolensk in particular was a triumph for Ordin-Nashchokin. The year following the peace, the Polish king abdicated, to die four years later in France.[39]

Oliva had released Swedish forces for operations against Muscovy, with whom, after the tsar had failed to take Riga, a three-year armistice had been concluded after tough negotiations at the end of 1658. Ordin-Nashchokin still hoped for Ingria and even offered money and troops for use against Poland in further negotiations in Kardis (Käärde) early in 1660. Faced, however, with the continuing war with Poland, he finally gave way and peace was concluded between the two powers on 21 June 1661. The terms were basically those of a return to the status quo, but it was not until July 1666 that final agreement was reached on the interpretation of all the clauses, and even after this relations between the two powers were soured by disagreement over trade restrictions and refugees.[40]

7

THE LATER SEVENTEENTH
CENTURY (1667–1700)

After 1660 the Baltic region enjoyed forty years of almost uninter-
rupted peace. The focus of European military and diplomatic
activity during this period centred to a much greater extent
than in the previous century on western Europe, where the
consequences of French ambitions involved all that country's
neighbours in almost continuous warfare, and on south-eastern
Europe, where the renewed struggle between Habsburg and Turk
also involved Russia and Poland. The Baltic returned to the somewhat peripheral position it had occupied before 1620.

During the long reign of Charles XI of Sweden (1660–97)
the problems of reconciling the country's limited economic and
manpower resources with the responsibilities of governing and
defending the newly acquired territories, as after 1648, precluded
foreign adventures. Sweden was a satiated power. The *dominium
maris Baltici*, of which some of her statesmen had dreamed, had
eluded her and no further attempt was to be made to gain it.[1]
When war came to the country again in 1674 it came very much
against the will of those in charge of its foreign policy and
reinforced the pacific and defensive predilections which had
marked the 1660s.

In Denmark the programme of internal reform which followed
the introduction of absolute monarchy in 1661 (which included a
form of collegial administration less regular in organization than
that introduced in Sweden by Oxenstierna) and the financial
weaknesses which these did little to solve also dictated caution.
When the opportunity seemed to present itself in 1675 to restore
something of Denmark's former power and influence, it soon
became apparent that it was not militarily strong enough to support its claims against Sweden. On the other hand, Denmark's

foreign policy was potentially revisionist and its rulers were on the look-out for alliance combinations which would lead to a reduction of Sweden's influence in the area.

Poland was not yet the passive victim of its neighbour's greed that it was to become in the eighteenth century, and it had not yet abandoned Baltic ambitions; it retained links with the East Prussian estates during their struggle with the Elector of Brandenburg[2] and under King John III Sobieski in the 1680s and under Augustus of Saxony at the end of century there was considerable interest in developing the country's Baltic trade. But its economy had suffered grievously during the constant warfare on its territories during the First Great Northern War – a period referred to in Polish history as 'The Deluge' (*Potop*). It lost something like a quarter of its total population during these years. The decline in the demand for its grain on European markets in the course of the early seventeenth century was a further blow. The privileges enjoyed by its magnates prevented the growth of its towns, and its rulers consequently had great difficulty in maintaining an efficient military machine in the face of a suspicious and complacent nobility, unwilling to grant the necessary additional taxes and from 1652 able to reject any piece of royal legislation by the single vote of one of their number in the *Sejm* (*liberum veto*). This forced them onto the defensive against Russia in the east, and after 1680 their attention was drawn southward by first the advance and then the retreat of the Ottoman Turks.[3]

Russia, while increasing its military potential under Peter the Great's immediate predecessors and making sporadic attempts to improve the terms of the peace of Kardis, remained backward compared with other European powers and unable to conduct a vigorous foreign policy; the *otchina* policy of reclaiming lands supposedly once part of Kievan Russia which had been pursued by Ivan III and Ivan IV had been abandoned. Russia also turned away from the Baltic towards the Black Sea. The long internal crisis which followed the death of Tsar Alexis in 1676 was followed by a long struggle against the Turks.[4]

Finally, the Electors of Brandenburg–Prussia, having secured sovereignty over East Prussia, were too often drawn into the struggles between France and its opponents in western Europe to pay more than occasional attention to the Baltic. Their policies tended to be dictated by circumstances rather than by any fixed principles.

The Baltic was, in spite of all this, not isolated during the period. It retained strong diplomatic and commercial links with powers outside its bounds and played a not inconsiderable part in their policies. The Maritime Powers of Britain and the United Provinces, in spite of their rivalries, both supported the balance of power in the Baltic which had been achieved in mid-century and intervened on a number of occasions to ease tensions which might both upset it and interfere with trade. France, on the other hand, could benefit from a conflict in the Baltic which would disrupt its enemies' economies and distract the attention of the north German princes from the Rhine. Louis XIV was willing to satisfy the need of both Denmark and Sweden for subsidies in exchange for their putting pressure on the Empire and could offer naval support to counterbalance that of the Dutch; in 1674 Sweden was drawn into war by succumbing to French blandishments, while in the early 1680s it was France which largely determined whether a crisis in the Baltic should escalate into open warfare.[5]

And the old causes of conflict were far from dead; favourable circumstances might well revive the struggle for power at any time. Denmark sought in the short term to rid itself of the threat coming from the duke of Holstein–Gottorp, whose lands straddled the southern part of the Jutish peninsula and whose alliance with Sweden in June 1661 made him little better than a Swedish satellite, and in the longer term to restore its position on the Sound by regaining its ancient provinces to the east of it and to destroy Sweden's Baltic hegemony. Some Danish statesmen even dreamed of expansion along the southern shore of the Baltic as in the days of the medieval Valdemars. Brandenburg continued to resent deeply Sweden's control of the mouth of the river Oder in western Pomerania and the loss of revenues represented by the customs agreement of 1653 with Sweden. Its rulers looked to extend the coastline of East Prussia further eastward.[6]

In Russia Ordin-Nashchokin fell from power in 1671. His successor Artamon Matveev was more interested in the Turkish threat, but ambitions to establish a Baltic coastline lived on; Russo–Swedish relations became more amicable as Matveev sought Swedish aid against the Turks and Sweden sought to escape from the isolation with which it was faced after the death of Charles X. But Russian mercantile policy was now decidedly anti-Swedish.[7] Even in Poland–Lithuania ancient claims to Livonia only awaited revival by an ambitious king who might use them to increase his popularity and power at home. And in the last decade of the century circumstances fed such ambitions and led to the formation of an anti-Swedish coalition which plunged the Baltic into over twenty years of war.

In spite of the arrival of Brandenburg–Prussia on the Baltic scene and the growing power of Russia, the principal rivals for dominance there remained Denmark and Sweden. But for some time after 1660 the game was played out only on the diplomatic level. Both powers sought to strengthen their position by seeking alliances with states outside the area and at the same time to isolate the other. Their choices were limited by developments in western Europe and in particular by the alignment of powers in response to the ambitions of Louis XIV of France in the Low Countries and on the Rhine in west Germany. In such alignments the opposition to France of the United Provinces and the Emperor was a fairly constant element. For a brief period after the end of the Dutch War in 1679 disillusionment with their former allies drew the two Scandinavian powers together, but the ancient suspicions remained and antagonisms soon re-emerged; only in defence of their trade was there genuine co-operation.

But the behaviour of other countries was less predictable; Anglo–Dutch rivalry and the domestic ambitions of Charles II and his brother James II made England an uncertain factor until the 'Glorious Revolution' in 1688. In Denmark, Hannibal Sehested, the dominant statesman during the early years of absolute government, turned away from his country's traditional allies and sought friendship with both Britain and France, the latter in particular for the subsidies which he needed in order to restore the financial stability of the Danish crown. He had some initial success. A commercial treaty with Britain in 1661 was followed by a similar treaty and defensive alliance with France two years later.[8]

Both, however, proved somewhat disappointing in their results: the French subsidies did not materialize, and the British alliance dragged Denmark into the Second Anglo–Dutch War. After Sehested's death in 1665, Denmark reverted to its earlier links with the United Provinces. After England had in 1665 concluded a treaty with Sweden which guaranteed the territories of the duke of Holstein–Gottorp, Denmark swung decidedly to the side of the Dutch.[9] This was in fact one of the patterns for alliances in the Baltic in the seventeenth and eighteenth centuries:

alliance with one Scandinavian monarchy drove the other into the opposing camp.

Swedish policy lacked firm direction in the 1660s. The constitutional settlement reached after the death of Charles X left the Estates with considerably more power over the Council than hitherto, and its Secret Committee (from which representatives of the peasant Estate were excluded) could make its voice heard in matters of foreign policy, especially when the Council was divided. Magnus Gabriel de la Gardie, the chancellor throughout the regency, was closely associated with Sweden's traditional French connection. But he lacked the authority which Oxenstierna had enjoyed during the previous regency, and was strongly opposed within the Council, which believed increasingly that Sweden should look to the Emperor and his anti-French allies for its security.[10]

As has already been noted, Sweden concluded an alliance with Britain in 1665. This threatened to draw it into war over Louis XIV's claims on behalf of his wife in the Spanish Netherlands after the death of King Philip IV of Spain (the War of Devolution), but war was something which no party in Sweden desired, and in 1666 the country declared its neutrality and even managed to get itself accepted as mediator at the peace negotiations at Breda which ended the conflict.[11] As so often, however, this peace contained the seeds of future conflict, and war broke out again in 1672 with France's direct attack on the United Provinces. And in this Sweden was not so fortunate.

It found itself isolated after the end of the War of Devolution, and de la Gardie could argue that an alliance with France would provide the country with the subsidies needed to maintain a military potential essential for the defence of its status without drawing it into open conflict with its neighbours and would keep France from turning to Denmark. After the treaty of Dover between Charles II and Louis XIV in 1670 and the Anglo–Danish alliance of the same year, a British alliance was no longer an alternative, and it was the United Provinces which appeared to be isolated. Consequently in 1672 the Council agreed to return to a pro-French policy and to conclude an agreement with Louis by which 16,000 troops would be stationed in Pomerania from 1673 in order to discourage the German princes from giving aid and succour to the Dutch. In return, France would grant subsidies of 400,000 daler, increased to 600,000 should war break out. It also guaranteed the possessions of the duke of Holstein–Gottorp against an attack from Denmark. Britain offered assistance should Sweden be drawn into war because of the French alliance.[12]

In accordance with this agreement, there was a large build-up of Swedish troops in 1672–3 to put pressure on Brandenburg, whose Elector had joined the Dutch. Frederick William had used his new excise tax as well as his other income to build up an army which in wartime could be raised to 45,000 men. A large proportion of these he took with him to the Rhine at the beginning of 1673 to face the French and their allies. In June, however, he was persuaded to withdraw from the war by the offer of French subsidies and at the end of the year he renewed the alliance he had made with Sweden in 1666. It seemed that Sweden might be able to keep out of the conflict after all.[13]

In the spring of 1674 France offered to increase subsidies to Sweden if it would raise its garrison in Pomerania to 22,000. But it then made it clear that the bulk of the money would be paid only in the event of an attack on Brandenburg, which had re-entered the war against France. De la Gardie, unable to sustain the troops in any other way, had to agree, while he endeavoured to delay action as long as possible. Finally, at Christmastide 1674 the Swedish commander in Pomerania, Karl Gustav Wrangel, unable to maintain his troops where they were, marched into the Uckermark of Brandenburg with an army of 20,000.[14]

In May 1675 he was standing at the gates of Berlin. The Elector marched rapidly back from the Rhine to defend his capital and the Swedes retired. Brandenburg forces pursued them to Fehrbellin where, in spite of a superiority of two to one, the Swedes were defeated. Strategically the battle was of minor importance, but it was a moral blow to Sweden's military prestige, and diplomatically Fehrbellin had serious consequences for the defeated: both the Dutch and the Emperor declared war.[15]

In Denmark, count Griffenfeld, the chief minister of the new King Christian V, had struggled to maintain the peace between the Scandinavian monarchies in face of the more bellicose attitude of his master. The country had no firm alliances, and he considered the rapprochement between Sweden and France which resulted in the alliance of 1672 as particularly threatening. In May 1673 he concluded a defensive alliance with the Dutch, and Jens Juel was sent to Stockholm to seek Swedish collaboration in working for a peace settlement in the hope of weakening Sweden's French ties and also in order to frighten the Dutch into ratifying the alliance. There was talk of a marriage between the Danish king's sister Ulrike Eleanora and the young Charles XI of Sweden.[16]

But in spite of Griffenfeld's efforts, Denmark after Fehrbellin decided to fulfil its treaty obligations to Brandenburg and entered the struggle against France and Sweden. By the terms of a new agreement with Frederick William, King Christian laid claim not only to the old Danish provinces on the other side of the Sound but also to Wismar and to the island of Rügen at the mouth of the Oder. The Elector was to take Greifswald and Stralsund as his share of the booty. In September 1675 he declared war on Sweden. The duke of Holstein–Gottorp was seized and his fortresses occupied by Danish troops. The Danish fleet under Admiral Niels Juel rapidly achieved supremacy in the Baltic.[17]

Christian V took considerable interest in his navy, and by the outbreak of war it consisted of nineteen warships and twelve smaller vessels. By contrast the Swedish fleet though larger (twenty-four large and fifteen smaller ships) suffered from neglect during the regency and lacked competent leaders.[18]

Juel succeeded in occupying Gotland at the beginning of May, and a month later a combined Dano–Dutch fleet under admiral Cornelis van Tromp defeated in a series of encounters the Swedish fleet which was sailing to retake the island and relieve the beleaguered Swedish troops in Germany. The Swedes lost three of their largest ships, including the *Krona*, the largest warship in the Baltic. Even a small Brandenburg fleet of frigates, hired through a Dutch merchant after the Swedish attack, operated off the southern Baltic coast from Pillau in East Prussia. Swedish communications with its German possessions were cut, and in Pomerania the commander soon found himself holding on desperately to only Stettin, Greifswald and Rügen. And Stettin had to be surrendered to its Brandenburg besiegers at the end of the year.[19]

Meanwhile Danish troops, exploiting their navy's command of the seas, crossed the Sound into southern Sweden, where they received considerable support from pro-Danish partisans known as *snapphanare*. Only the city of Malmö held out against them. The tide, however, turned against them with the arrival on the scene of an army led by King Charles himself. This won a decisive victory at Lund in December. The Danes withdrew across the Sound leaving only Landskrona and Kristianstad to defy the Swedes. They returned in 1677, but failed to take Malmö and suffered a further defeat at Landskrona in July. Once more they withdrew to Zealand. At sea, however, the honours continued to rest with the Danes and their Dutch allies; the Swedes, although superior in number of ships, suffered a further defeat at the hands of Juel when they attacked him in Køge Bugt before he had been joined by the Dutch; in the action they lost a further eight large ships. In 1678 the Swedish fleet did not go to sea at all, and during the autumn of that year the last Swedish *pointes d'appui* in Pomerania were lost. As peace in Europe approached, Sweden's position appeared extremely weak.[20]

After France had come to terms with the Dutch at Nijmegen in August 1678, Sweden tried to put pressure on Brandenburg by attacking East Prussia from Livonia. But this action ended in fresh humiliation. Not only was the invasion repulsed but Horn's army was able to regain Riga only after losing four-fifths of its original strength. It was, however, in France's interests to maintain a Swedish presence in Germany, and the Emperor was opposed to Denmark's claims to bases on the Baltic coast; he had guaranteed Sweden's possessions in his peace treaty with King Louis. At the peace of St Germain between France and Brandenburg in June, the Elector had to rest content with the small piece of Hither Pomerania on the right bank of the river Peene which he had had to surrender in the final frontier agreement of 1653 and with full control over Pomeranian tolls. And the Swedes now hoped for French assistance against the Danes. But in August Louis made peace with Denmark, and Sweden followed at Lund in September.[21]

The peace terms constituted ostensibly a return to the status quo. Secret clauses, however, envisaged close collaboration between the two monarchies. They were largely the work of John Gyllenstierna, Charles XI's chief adviser, who had opposed de la Gardie's pro-French policy and had helped to engineer the chancellor's fall from power in 1678. For ten years each party was to inform the other of any agreements which might be made with third parties, and no such agreement was to be directed against the other. Both Denmark and Sweden had indeed much to gain from co-operation aimed at excluding foreign influences from the Baltic and preventing future conflicts. France's high-handed attitude at the peace negotiations and Louis's breach of the terms of his alliance with Sweden by making peace with the Dutch without securing commercial concessions from them which would benefit Sweden caused considerable resentment in Stockholm. The Danes felt equally let down by their Dutch ally, who had proved lax in the payment of promised subsidies and should not have made a separate peace. Agreement with Sweden might also give King Christian a freer hand against the duke of Holstein–Gottorp. An alliance concluded in September 1679 confirmed the promises made at the peace, and the new policy was symbolized by the marriage in April of Charles XI and Princess Ulrike Eleanora.[22]

Unfortunately the new spirit was of brief duration. Gyllenstierna had no intention that any union should be one between equal partners, and it soon became apparent to the Danes that Swedish interests were to be paramount. Even had Gyllenstierna lived, old rivalries and resentments would soon have resurfaced. The Swedish king regarded Denmark as his realm's principal opponent, and under the cautious Frederik Ahlefeldt, who led its foreign policy until 1686, Denmark again began to seek alliances which would give it protection against its neighbour.[23]

After the death of Gyllenstierna in 1680, the direction of Swedish foreign policy fell to Bengt Oxenstierna, grandson of one of the great Axel's uncles. He never, however, enjoyed exclusive access to the king's ear and often had to defend his policy with some vigour in the Council. Oxenstierna abandoned his predecessor's attempts to establish close links with Denmark, but he shared Gyllenstierna's aversion to an alliance with France, whose policy on the Rhine and in the Low Countries appeared to be the main threat to peace in Europe. This meant inevitably an approach to the Emperor and, in order to compensate for French support at sea, to the Dutch, from whose support the Danes had profited so greatly in the war.[24]

In September 1681 Oxenstierna boldly drove through the Swedish Council approval of a treaty with the United Provinces to guarantee the settlements made at Westphalia and Nijmegen, which were now threatened by France. This compact was joined by the Emperor at the beginning of the following year and by Spain in the summer.[25]

All of this strengthened the hand of the more aggressive elements of the Danish Council. They favoured an alliance with France, who offered large subsidies as a further inducement, and in March 1682 the two countries reached agreement. With the renewal of the French alliance with Brandenburg–Prussia, whose Elector was even more anxious to eliminate the Swedish presence on his borders after his experiences in the recent war, Sweden understandably felt itself under threat and made preparations for its defence; the Diet agreed to grant additional taxes, substantial forces were drawn up in the south of the country and an expanded fleet was mobilized at the end of 1682.[26]

The establishment of absolute monarchy in Sweden in the course of the 1680s reduced still further the influence of the Council (significantly now named the 'Royal Council' rather than the 'Council of the Realm'), though it continued to meet regularly and in it Oxenstierna had to defend his policies against a pro-French faction which tried to win the ear of the king. The self-effacing monarch, conscious of Sweden's military weakness after the end of the war and fearful of repeating the experiences of the 1670s, wished above all to avoid involving his country in the current European struggles in order to be able to pose as a mediator between the belligerents. Such a role also promised to win for Sweden material gains as well as prestige at little cost. Any entangling alliances should be avoided, even though this would threaten Sweden with isolation in the face of its jealous neighbours.[27]

In the absence of foreign subsidies, the military force needed to defend Sweden's neutrality, especially against Denmark, had to be paid for out of the realm's own rather limited resources. These were husbanded in the 1680s and 1690s by the resumption of alienated royal lands and taxes in the so-called *reduktion* and by the encouragement of overseas trade, which as a neutral Sweden was able to exploit; the Swedish merchant marine based on Stockholm grew to some 750 ships, of which about a tenth were of large size. It also benefited from the shift of emphasis in Baltic trade from grain through Danzig, which had dominated the scene in the earlier part of the century, to naval stores through the Swedish-controlled port of Riga after 1660.[28]

On the basis of this new wealth a native army with a wartime strength of 63,000 men was planned without the need for additional taxation. The allotment system, by which groups of farms were made responsible for providing and supporting an infantryman and the richer farmers for providing the cavalry, while officers and non-commissioned officers were provided with royal farms (see above, p. 68), was improved and regularized, so that each province could mobilize a foot regiment of 1,200 men and a cavalry regiment of 800 to 1,000 horse.[29]

The navy was also refurbished and, building on the experience of what for it had been the disastrous war of 1675–9, a new naval base was created in 1682 at Karlskrona, an easily defended anchorage much closer than Stockholm to the likely fields of action in the southern Baltic and enabling the fleet to put to sea earlier in the year. As early as 1658 Charles X had ordered a search for a new base. Landskrona had been the first choice, but it proved to be too easily blockaded. For most of the 1680s the fleet spent the winter in Kalmar. Not until the end of the decade were preparations in Karlskrona advanced enough for it to be taken into commission. Under the direction of Hans Hansson Wachtmeister, assisted by English shipwrights, the fleet grew from the thirteen ships of the line to which it had been reduced in 1679 to thirty-nine with eight frigates at the end of the century. In addition the rapidly expanding merchant fleet could be called on in wartime to provide additional help; in 1697, no fewer than 111 Swedish merchants ships were capable of carrying at least twenty-four cannon. Such ships were allowed reduction of a third in customs duties, though referred to as *helfri* (i.e. wholly free), while smaller ships were allowed reduction by a sixth and referred to as 'half free'. More coastal areas of the country were organized to provide crews, although their training continued to leave much to be desired.[30]

The improved financial situation meant that the Diet was rarely called; it no longer had any influence on foreign policy and learned in 1686 that it would be informed on foreign affairs only if it was required to grant supplies for its execution.[31]

In Denmark the Diet had ceased to meet after 1660, and the king called to his small advisory council whomsoever he chose. King Christian V, a man of no great intellect, feared the emergence of a new all-powerful minister like Griffenfeld, and liked to play off one faction against another to maintain his authority. Men like Ahlefeldt had to battle constantly against the influence of a court circle which tended to encourage the king's aggressive instincts and his desire for revenge against Sweden. In spite of Sehested's reforms and the sale of a considerable amount of royal land in Denmark and Norway, the crown's financial position was by the 1680s again precarious, and a choice of foreign partners was dictated to a considerable extent by expected financial rewards. Shortage of funds also limited military preparedness, but considerable attention was devoted to the Danish fleet, which had served the monarchy so well in the 1670s. A naval base was established at Kristiansø, north-east of Bornholm, in 1684 to keep an eye on the new Swedish base at Karlskrona, and under the direction of Nils Juel from 1679, fifteen new line of battle ships were built to bring the Danish fleet up to thirty-seven, or only slightly inferior to the Swedish by the end of the century, though these proved difficult to man, and recourse had to be made to press gangs.[32]

In 1683 the Baltic threatened again to burst into flames. Ever since Denmark had concluded its alliance with France in 1682, it had been discussing with Brandenburg–Prussia plans for an attack on Sweden, for which it was hoped that French support could be obtained. Denmark was to occupy the lands of the duke of Gottorp and Bremen and Verden, while the Elector was to occupy Western Pomerania. The Danish fleet, aided by French subsidies, would prevent the Swedes from reinforcing their possessions to the south of the Baltic. It was even hoped that Russia might be persuaded to join in. The Danes actually put pressure on the duke of Gottorp, who fled to Hamburg in September 1682 and appealed for support to Sweden and the Emperor. The Swedes called on the Dutch for naval assistance, which, however, they were unable to supply immediately because of the poor state of their fleet. In spite of military threats from the dukes of Brunswick, Denmark and Brandenburg felt confident enough to proceed with preparations for an attack on Sweden.[33]

King Charles refused to provoke a conflict by ordering the reinforcement of his much depleted garrisons in Germany. Offensive alliances were nevertheless concluded in the spring between Denmark, France and Brandenburg–Prussia. The Baltic allies endeavoured to win the dukes of Brunswick for their enterprise, and in April concluded a 'concert' detailing the gains they intended to make from the enemy. A French naval squadron prepared to sail to the Sound to counter the Dutch one finally being put together in response to the call from the Swedes. A Dutch fleet did in fact sail in August, but after cruising in the North Sea did not reach Gothenburg until the end of October and set sail for home almost immediately. And in June thirteen French ships of the line joined the Danish fleet outside

Copenhagen. Troops were taken on board, and all seemed set for a Danish attack on Sweden.[34]

But Louis XIV, who had encouraged his allies in the North only to bind them more closely to him, did not want a Baltic conflict at a time when he was seeking a peaceful settlement of his claims on the Rhine and in the Netherlands. He consequently sought to restrain the ambitions of Brandenburg and Denmark and rejected the 'concert'. As a result Brandenburg refused to ratify the alliance and became lukewarm towards the whole enterprise. Without French support, the project had to be shelved for the time being. The French squadron sailed home in October.[35]

As a result of the tame outcome of the crisis for which it had been largely responsible, France's influence in northern Europe declined. Brandenburg began to turn to the Dutch, and at the end of 1683 even offered an alliance to Sweden in exchange for Stettin. Denmark was equally disenchanted.[36] At the truce of Ratisbon Louis XIV obtained temporary confirmation of the territorial gains he had made in the Spanish Netherlands and on the Rhine by his 'Reunion' policy without an armed conflict, while the Emperor Leopold, the German princes and the Poles drove the Turks back from the gates of Vienna.

Relations between Denmark and Sweden worsened as the result of the actions taken by Christian V against Sweden's close ally, Duke Christian Albert (Albrecht) of Holstein–Gottorp. In 1684 Danish troops occupied his territories in Slesvig, which were declared confiscated to the Danish crown. For the moment Sweden lacked the resources to take counter measures, but its position was strengthened by a reversal of policy by the Elector of Brandenburg.[37]

Louis XIV's persecution of his Protestant subjects, which culminated in 1685 in the revocation of the Edict of Nantes and the cancellation of all their rights and privileges, led Frederick William finally to abandon his alliance with France. In February 1686 he concluded a secret alliance with Sweden by which each party guaranteed the other's possessions and the integrity of the Empire and the Elector agreed to defend the rights of the duke of Holstein–Gottorp against Denmark.[38]

Negotiations to settle the Gottorp dispute opened at Altona outside Hamburg in 1687. In the course of them Brandenburg put forward suggestions of an exchange of territories involving the acquisition by the duke of the counties of Oldenburg and

Delmenhorst in north-west Germany. But at this stage Denmark was not willing to countenance such proposals, and Sweden wished that 'Denmark be always kept occupied with the Holstein dispute'. Sweden in 1689 made an alliance with the dukes of Brunswick Lüneberg to the south of Holstein. This effectively isolated the Danes at a time when a fresh war was breaking out on the Rhine following the French devastation of the Palatinate (see below). The Swedish navy was mobilized at Ystad and troops gathered in the south for an attack on Denmark. In face of this, the hostile attitude of William III, now king of England as well as *stadholder* of the United Provinces of the Netherlands, and also the lack of support they received from France, the Danes gave way, and in June 1689 agreed to restore the duke's lands.[39] Many problems, however, remained unresolved, to prove a serious cause of tension in the Baltic throughout the succeeding decade, and to be an important element in the twenty-year war which engulfed it at the beginning of the new century.[40]

Louis XIV's devastation of the Palatinate in 1688 was an attempt to frighten the German princes into agreeing to make the truce of Ratisbon a permanent modification of the settlements of Westphalia and Nijmegen and led to nine years of conflict. At the same time the 'Glorious Revolution' united the Maritime Powers under a leader determined to join with the Emperor in opposing all France's pretensions and to mobilize the strength of all other powers in a crusade to drive Louis XIV back to the frontiers defined by the Nijmegen settlement. While Denmark did hire a small number of troops to William III for use in his campaigns in Ireland and Flanders, it did so for purely financial reasons and had no wish to be drawn further into the struggle. Sweden, although obliged by its treaties with the Emperor to send a contingent of troops to the Rhine, did so with reluctance and was determined on a policy of neutrality. The belligerents' interference with Danish and Swedish merchant shipping led the two powers to agree in 1691 on joint convoys outside the Baltic, an agreement renewed in 1693. But, in spite of efforts by Oxenstierna's pro-French critics in the Swedish council led by Sten Bielke, governor of Pomerania, this did not lead to any closer relationship in other fields; Holstein–Gottorp and the Scanian provinces lost to Denmark in 1660 formed seemingly insuperable barriers to cordial relations between the two Scandinavian monarchies.[41]

The succession of Duke Frederick of Holstein–Gottorp in 1695 again brought the threat of conflict between Denmark and Sweden. Sweden agreed to provide him with a small number of troops and he himself began to build forts on his territories in defiance of Denmark. Both sides looked round for allies, while the Maritime Powers sought to prevent the outbreak of armed conflict in the Baltic; Sweden renewed its alliance with Brandenburg in July 1696. The latter supported Sweden in taking the side of Duke Adolf Frederick of Mecklenburg–Strelitz, nephew of the Swedish queen, against Duke Frederick William of Mecklenburg–Schwerin in a dispute over the succession to the lands of Sweden's old ally the duke of Mecklenburg–Güstrow. When the Emperor decided in favour of the latter, troops under Swedish command occupied Güstrow and opposed Duke Frederick William's entry at the beginning of 1697. Negotiations over the Gottorp dispute finally opened at Pinneberg near Hamburg in August 1696. But in the middle of 1697 the Danes, emboldened by an alliance with the Maritime Powers in the previous December and by the death of Charles XI, suddenly attacked the duke's forts and razed them to the ground. The duke fled to Tønning. But Dutch threats caused the Danes again to withdraw.[42]

The Nine Years War ended in 1697 with the peace of Ryswick. Sweden had acted as official mediator but won meagre material advantages from the honour and indeed had little influence on the settlement.[43] Charles XI died in the knowledge that at least one of his ambitions had been achieved. But the 15-year-old son he left behind him to ascend the throne as Charles XII was faced with daunting problems at home and abroad. Disastrous harvest failures in 1696–7 may have carried off half the population of Finland as well as large numbers in the western half of his dominions. There was unrest among the nobility, particularly in Livonia where they had been hard hit by the *reduktion* and their privileges seriously undermined by the absolute monarchy in the 1690s. Abroad Sweden's neutrality had left it diplomatically isolated and confronted by an evolving coalition among neighbours eager to exploit Charles's difficulties to cut Sweden down to size. Denmark had at last found allies for a war of revanche in the shape of the new king of Poland and the young tsar of all the Russias.[44]

As has been seen, after the fall of Ordin-Nashchokin in 1671 tensions between Sweden and Russia had relaxed somewhat.

Frederick William of Brandenburg and King Christian V of Denmark tried to involve Russia against Sweden in the Pomeranian War of 1674–9, but it was not until after this war was over that there was again a serious crisis in Russo–Swedish relations. Russia demanded part of Ingria as compensation for slights it claimed to have suffered. But the Turks were again on the march, and in October 1683, when they stood before the walls of Vienna, Tsar Alexis agreed to confirm the terms of the Peace of Kardis.[45] The repulse of the Turks and their swift retreat down the Danube tempted the Russians even more to concentrate their forces on their southern border in order to be ready to exploit the situation. At this time their thoughts were focused on the Black Sea rather than the Baltic. As always, resources were inadequate to deal satisfactorily with a war on two fronts at the same time.

The Russian army was by the 1680s, however, much more formidable than it had been fifty years before. Out of a total force of 130,000 men at least two-thirds had been trained on western European lines by western European officers. Though the engineering and commissariat departments still left much to be desired in the face of western or northern European forces and training was largely confined to a brief period every year after the harvest had been gathered in, the abolition of the *mestnichestvo* system of promotion by family seniority in 1682 did much to improve the efficiency of the higher command.[46]

In 1686 Russia confirmed in an 'eternal peace' the terms of Andrussovo with Poland, whom it joined in the Holy League against the Turks. Matveev's successor Vasili Golitsyn, the author of this 'southern' policy, fell from power three years later after a number of military setbacks. But the young Tsar Peter I, who acquired sole power in 1689, followed in Golitsyn's tracks. His 'window on the west' was at this stage of his reign to be the Black Sea rather than the Baltic. He rejected Denmark's first approaches for an anti-Swedish alliance early in 1697, and his first trip to western Europe in 1697–8 was partly aimed at persuading the powers there to join him in a Turkish crusade at a time when their military might had been freed by the peace of Ryswick.[47]

Only when such hopes were dashed did he begin to listen seriously to renewed Danish proposals, now backed by Saxony, to join in an assault on Sweden, a Sweden led by a young and inexperienced monarch, diplomatically isolated and plagued by discontent throughout its social structure. An exaggerated impression of the latter was given by the leader of the Livonian discontents Johann Reinhold Patkul, who had fled after being condemned to death for treason by the Swedish Council in 1693 and eagerly supported Danish efforts in both Moscow and Warsaw after 1697.[48] In October 1699 he presented the tsar, who had already concluded a defensive alliance with Denmark in August, with a plan, agreed with King Augustus, for an attack backed by both France and the Emperor; in the event of victory Russia would gain Ingria and Karelia and with them the direct access to western technology which his predecessors had long been seeking and which he had himself recently witnessed at first hand.[49]

In Poland the Turkish advance had provided King Sobieski with an opportunity to regain some of the prestige which his realm had lost in the 1660s. It was largely his victory over the Turks which indeed had led to his election to the throne in 1674, and his main interests were always directed southwards. But the outbreak of war between Sweden and Brandenburg tempted him to turn against the latter in the hope of regaining East Prussia. By a treaty with France in July 1675 he promised to attack the Elector as soon as peace had been made with the Turks. To free his hands he concluded a preliminary peace with the Turks in October 1676, and a year later he signed in Danzig an alliance with Sweden, who agreed to aid his reconquest of Prussia. This new orientation was, however, difficult for many Poles to accept, and the Lithuanians under the leadership of the Radziwiłł and Sapieha families were more interested in regaining Livonia at Sweden's expense in alliance with the tsar. In any case Sweden's defeat at the hands of Frederick William's army, the failure to make a permanent settlement with the Porte and the success of the Russians in doing so effectively put paid to such a plan. After making tentative approaches to Brandenburg, Sobieski turned finally once more against the Turks in alliance with Russia in an enterprise which might have brought personal glory but which further drained Poland's resources. He did much to improve the quality of the Polish army and increased it to 54,000 men, some three times the size it had been under his predecessor. But he did little to change the administrative or financial system of his realm, and the economy was further shattered by the years of campaigning which followed the relief of Vienna in 1683.[50]

After Sobieski's death in April 1696, an exhausted Poland was politically paralysed by an interregnum of over a year before the election to the throne of Elector Augustus of Saxony. Augustus, an ambitious but somewhat impractical intriguer, dreamed of creating in Poland a strong hereditary monarchy by means of conducting a successful foreign policy. After the failure of the Turkish war and the conclusion of peace in the south in 1699, this meant above all the reacquisition of Livonia at the expense of Sweden and the development of Polish sea power. The idea of a Russo–Dano–Saxon alliance against Sweden attracted him greatly, and in March 1698 an alliance between himself and Denmark constituted the first element in a pact which was completed in November 1699 by the adhesion of Peter of Russia. By these treaties Sweden's possessions in the Baltic were to be partitioned: Livonia was to go to Poland and Ingria to the tsar. The latter agreed to attack in Livonia as soon as an armistice had been concluded with the Turks.[51]

Brandenburg was also invited to the feast. It had long been its rulers' ambition to gain the mouth of the Oder and Memel and the coast between East Prussia and Kurland, which might be made the price for an alliance. But the new Elector Frederick III's Rhineland possessions were threatened by the Dutch and he had set his heart on acquiring the royal title, which he hoped to obtain by assisting the Emperor to defend Austrian claims to the crown of Spain against France in the war which was looming in the west. His relations with Augustus had been strained by his seizure in October 1698 of the port of Elbing. This had been pledged to Brandenburg by the treaty of Bydgoszcz (Bromberg) in 1657 for the sum of 300,000 daler, which had not been paid. Under pressure from Tsar Peter, he finally agreed in December 1699 to accept the Polish crown jewels in place of the port as a pledge for the promised sum. In February 1700 he further promised to allow Augustus's troops free passage through his territories. But it was not the time to tie himself down in a Baltic struggle.[52]

8

CHARLES XII, PETER THE GREAT AND THE END OF SWEDISH DOMINANCE (1700–21)

The twenty-year war which now engulfed the Baltic saw the emergence of Russia as the leading power in the area and the loss by Sweden of most of the gains which it had made in the southern and eastern Baltic since the middle of the sixteenth century. From the conflict Denmark gained little in power or prestige, and the territory which it did win in the Duchies was to cause the main problems in its foreign policy over the next forty years. The war, during most of its progress, was paralleled by that over the Spanish succession, which until 1713 and the peace of Utrecht absorbed most of the energies of the other great European powers: France, Britain, the United Provinces and the Empire. By the time these could again devote their full attention to the Baltic the fate of Sweden was already sealed. Their general policies henceforward were to try to prevent the delicate balance in the area being completely upset by Russia, a largely unknown quantity in western Europe, which at one stage had stood menacingly on the river Elbe.

At the beginning of the war Sweden had at its disposal an army of some 67,000 men, made up of 25,000 foot and 11,500 horse raised by the peasant *rotar* and *indelning* system and 22,000 foot and 8,500 horse contracted with the crown. These latter were mainly stationed outside Sweden–Finland proper. Denmark had about 23,000 troops in Denmark itself and 10,500 in Norway, mostly volunteers and including a large number raised in the German states. Cavalry was supported on royal lands specifically set aside for the purpose. A national militia was re-established in 1701. This was intended for home defence but could be used to

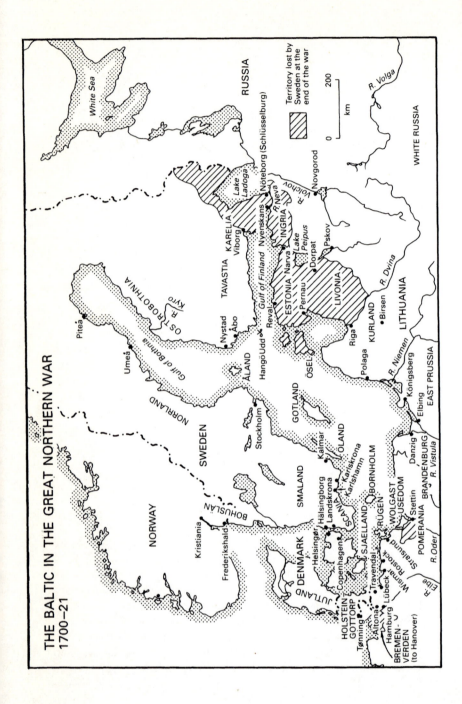

THE BALTIC IN THE GREAT NORTHERN WAR
1700–21

Territory lost by Sweden at the end of the war

0   200
km

White Sea

RUSSIA

R. Volga

Lake Ladoga

Nöteborg (Schlüsselburg)
Nyenskans
R. Neva
Novgorod
R. Volchov
Lake Peipus
Pskov

TAVASTIA
KARELIA
Viborg
Gulf of Finland
Hangö Udd
Revat
Narva
Dorpat
INGRIA
ESTONIA
Pernau
LIVONIA

OSTROBOTHNIA
R. Kyro
Nystad
Åbo
ÅLAND

Piteå
Umeå
Gulf of Bothnia
NORRLAND
Stockholm

WHITE RUSSIA

Riga
KURLAND
Birsen
R. Dvina
LITHUANIA
R. Niemen
Polaga
Königsberg
EAST PRUSSIA
Elbing

SWEDEN

GOTLAND
ÖSEL

SMALAND
Kalmar
ÖLAND
Karlskrona
Karlshamn
BORNHOLM

NORWAY
Kristiania
Frederikshald
BOHUSLÄN

Hälsingborg
Helsingør
Landskrona
SCANIA
Copenhagen
SJAELLAND
RÜGEN
USEDOM
WOLGAST
Stettin
POMERANIA
BRANDENBURG
R. Oder
R. Vistula
Danzig

DENMARK
JUTLAND
Travendal
Lübeck
Wismar
Rostock
Stralsund

HOLSTEIN-
GOTTORP
Tönning
Altona
Hamburg
BREMEN-
VERDEN
(to Hanover)
Elbe

fill gaps in the regular army. Denmark's naval programme in the 1680s and 1690s had, as already seen, brought its battle fleet up to thirty-seven ships of the line, slightly fewer than Sweden's and with appreciably fewer guns, but with all the other advantages over its neighbour already noted.[1]

The conflict opened in February 1700 with a Saxon invasion of Livonia and assault on Riga. In March 1700 the Danes occupied Holstein and prepared to attack the duke of Gottorp's fortress of Tønning.[2]

Before the Maritime Powers were drawn into the war against France in 1702 they were able to fulfil their obligations to Sweden and the duke of Holstein–Gottorp under the treaty of The Hague of February 1700, which confirmed the Altona agreement in exchange for a Swedish guarantee of the treaty of Ryswick. In June an Anglo–Dutch fleet of twenty-three ships arrived in the Sound, where it was joined by the main Swedish fleet under Admiral Hans Wachtmeister after a daring run through a shallow channel. Together they drove the Danish fleet, which was outnumbered by two to one, into the harbour of Copenhagen, and under their protection 4,000 Swedish troops were transported from Landskrona to the island of Ven, whence they were ferried in smaller boats to the coast of Zealand at Humlebæk, south of Elsinore. An army of 10,000 was soon stationed within the bridgehead thus formed ready to march on Copenhagen. Before it did so, however, came news that Denmark, under pressure from Britain, the United Provinces and the dukes of Brunswick, and faced by an army of 20,000 men under the Elector of Hanover in Holstein, had agreed to negotiate. By the treaty of Travendal King Frederik agreed to restore the duke's lands and to withdraw from the coalition with Saxony. Since the Dutch and British admirals refused to do more in the circumstances than to escort the Swedish army back across the Sound, the Swedes had reluctantly to give way.[3]

But while the Maritime Powers' guarantee of the duke's possessions and the treaty of Travendal provided some protection in the west, there was no certainty until King Frederik's army, and to an even greater extent his navy, had been decisively defeated that he would not, as his grandfather Frederik III had, take advantage of Sweden's involvement with his former allies in the east to renew his drive for revenge. This meant that considerable forces had to be maintained in southern Sweden which could have more usefully been employed elsewhere during the coming years. It also meant that Sweden's communications with its trans-Baltic possessions were under constant threat.

In October King Charles, having under pressure from the Maritime Powers abandoned the idea of striking at Saxony direct from Pomerania, led a large army over to Pernau in Livonia with the object of relieving Riga, still under siege by the Saxons. Contrary to Patkul's prediction, the Livonian nobility largely remained loyal to the Swedish crown, and while Dünamünde fell to the Saxons, an assault on Riga itself was beaten off in February and the besiegers defeated in battle in May. On learning of Travendal, Augustus requested an armistice through France and Brandenburg. Charles refused to agree until Livonia had been evacuated. Augustus did indeed withdraw the bulk of his forces over the Dvina into Kurland and again sued for peace.[4]

Peter of Russia was, however, made of sterner stuff. In September, the month after Travendal, having received news that his negotiators had succeeded in making a thirty-year peace with the Turks, he laid siege to Narva with an army of 23,000 men. Thither the Swedes, having learned of Augustus's withdrawal, now turned. The tsar had built up his army rapidly in preparation for the war in the north, but it remained far inferior to that of Charles XII in equipment, training and leadership, and a Swedish force less than a third its size swiftly defeated the besieging Russian contingent and freed the city in November. The haul in both prisoners and war *matériel* was enormous.[5]

Charles and his advisers were then faced with the choice of pursuing the defeated but still unbowed Russian foe and forcing him to conclude a decisive settlement or of first clearing their right flank by striking south against the Saxons, who at Birsen (Birzai) in February 1701 concluded a new and favourable alliance with the tsar, thereby gaining the help of a considerable body of Russian troops. A winter campaign in Muscovy was in fact planned by the Swedes, but they encountered serious logistical problems and finally abandoned the idea in favour of a two-pronged summer campaign across the river Dvina into Kurland, and against Pskov in the east. But after the Dvina had been crossed and Kurland occupied in August without bringing the main Saxon army to battle, the second part of the programme was temporarily abandoned in favour of deeper involvement in Polish affairs. In Lithuania the Swedes could count on support from the rebel faction led by the Sapieha family which in November 1701 had been defeated in a civil war but which was now much encouraged by Charles's success. It was planned with its help to topple Augustus from the Polish throne and replace him with a more amenable Swedish nominee from among the Polish–Lithuanian nobility, among whom there was much distrust of Augustus's ambitions. The primate cardinal Michal Radziejowski sought Swedish support to counter these, though he had no wish to commit himself further than was necessary, and James (Jakub) Sobieski, the Swedes' choice for the new Polish king, entered into negotiations.[6]

Augustus himself failed to get any support from the *Sejm*, which wished Poland to remain neutral in the struggle, and again offered to negotiate. But a deeply mistrustful King Charles rejected his approaches and, against the advice of many of his councillors, who did not wish to antagonize the Poles, headed his army into Lithuania and on into Poland. In May 1702 he entered Warsaw.[7]

In July 1702 he won a great victory over Augustus's troops at Kliszów, and in the spring of 1703 a lesser Swedish victory at Pułtusk, the first one in which the king himself enjoyed independent command, opened the way for the seizure of the key fortress of Thorn on the Vistula. This and a new less favourable treaty between Augustus and Peter, in which Polish claims on Livonia were not mentioned, encouraged Augustus's Polish opponents at the beginning of the following year to declare him deposed at an assembly of nobles in Warsaw. The next July, James Sobieski having been seized by supporters of Augustus, the noble Stanislas Leszczyński was elected king on the understanding that he would abdicate in favour of Sobieski once the latter were freed. But the action drove many leading Poles into the camp of Augustus's supporters. These formed the Confederation of Sandomierz (Sandomir). In May they had finally declared war on Sweden on behalf of the Commonwealth, and in August they concluded the alliance of Narva with the tsar. By this Peter promised them Livonia, an army of 12,000 and limited subsidies. In October 1705 Stanislas was crowned, and in November he in turn signed a treaty with the Swedes which revealed the extent of Swedish ambitions in Poland at this stage: the port of Polaga, north of Memel, which Augustus had planned to develop as an outlet for Saxon manufactured goods, was to be closed, and all Poland's exports were to pass through Riga, while Swedish merchants were granted extensive privileges in the country.[8]

No territory was transferred, but like his grandfather, Charles certainly had his eyes firmly fixed on the Prussian ports and Kurland, with Poland possibly receiving compensation for these at Russia's expense; an attack on Danzig in 1704 had been postponed only under pressure from the Maritime Powers. The treaty in fact brought the Swedes little benefit; Stanislas could provide no military aid, being kept too busy in opposing the Confederation of Sandomierz and a continuing threat from Augustus. In August 1706, however, after virtually annihilating the Saxon army at Fraustadt (Wschjowa) in February and driving Peter's forces from eastern Poland, the Swedish king marched into a largely undefended Saxony. The allies' victories over Louis XIV at Blenheim and Ramillies had removed their former objections to such a move. At his headquarters at Altranstädt King Augustus was compelled to surrender the Polish crown and abandon his alliance with the tsar.[9] Only Russia was now left for Charles to deal with.

But Peter had not been idle since the defeat at Narva. He had expanded his army with the formation of forty-seven infantry and nine new cavalry regiments, had formed his first artillery regiments, and had improved training and organization. As early as October 1702 he had managed to take Nöteborg, which he renamed significantly Schlüsselburg (literally 'key fortress'). Nyenskans fell to him in May of the following year. This gave him a firm base at the eastern end of the Gulf of Finland, and he began to lay plans for his new capital on the newly occupied territory at the mouth of the Neva. By the end of 1703 all that remained to the Swedes in Livonia were Riga, Dorpat, Reval, Narva and a few minor fortresses. In July 1704 Dorpat was lost, and a month later Narva. The German nobility of the region largely welcomed the Russian occupation as likely to guarantee their ancient privileges, which Peter was careful to promise them. They also hoped for the reversal of the *reduktion* of their estates. While Charles and Augustus negotiated in Altranstädt, Russian troops poured into Poland.[10]

Of greater significance for the future, these years saw the foundation of the Russian fleet, based on the fortress being constructed at the mouth of the river Neva. Its first ships were launched in August 1703, and by the end of 1704 it could boast six frigates and some oared galleys. These latter marked the revival of an instrument of naval warfare in the Baltic which the Swedes were long to neglect at their peril. Under Gustav Vasa they had possessed a large fleet of these shallow-draft vessels which could support the land forces among the many islands along the coasts of Sweden and Finland into whose waters ships of the line could not penetrate. They had built a new galley fleet during the struggles with Muscovy in the 1590s. But while Sweden's main antagonist was Denmark and its navy's main tasks were to keep open lines of communication and encounter the foe's battle fleet in open waters, galleys had again been abandoned. By 1710 the Russians had over a hundred of them, while the Swedes still had no more than five.[11]

When King Charles finally turned an army of some 40,000 men against his remaining antagonist in the autumn of 1707, Peter again evacuated not only Poland but also Livonia; only the area around the emerging St Petersburg would he not give up; indeed he had claimed that he would fight on for ten years rather than do so. Otherwise he professed a willingness to make peace with Sweden under the mediation of the western powers, an offer which Charles rejected.[12]

The Swedes failed to reach Moscow in 1708. They managed to divide Peter's forces and inflict a severe defeat on the main Russian army at Holovzin (Holowszyn) in July. But they had hardly crossed the border between Russia and Lithuania in September before the first of a series of disasters struck them. Reinforcements of some 12,000 men from Livonia under Adam Lewenhaupt were intercepted by Peter's forces and largely destroyed just after crossing the river Dnieper. Charles consequently decided to march south to winter in the Ukraine, which had been largely untouched by Peter's scorched earth policy and where he hoped to join up with Cossacks and Turks in a decisive march on Moscow from the south in 1709. But after an exceptionally harsh winter spent on the open southern plain, his forces, reduced to some 25,000 men, suffered further heavy losses in an unsuccessful assault on the fortified position which the main Russian army had taken up at Poltava and were compelled to retreat southward toward Turkish territory, preceded by the monarch. At Perevolochna, the Swedish commander Lewenhaupt surrendered the whole remaining army of 16,000 men to the much smaller Russian force which had been pursuing it.[13]

The news was the signal for both Denmark and Saxony to re-enter the struggle. Denmark made Sweden's supposed abuses of its privileges at the Sound a pretext to declare war in October, and in November an army of 15,000 was transported into Scania for an attack on the Swedish fleet in Karlskrona. In response the Swedes raised a force of 16,000 men under Magnus Stenbock. This drove the enemy back to Hälsingborg where, at the end of February 1710, the Danes were defeated and compelled to recross the water.[14]

Augustus of Saxony made a new treaty with the tsar at Thorn in October. In it he was promised Livonia, but he had to allow Peter to station his troops on Polish soil and in effect placed his kingdom under Russian control.[15] Meanwhile King Charles was a virtual prisoner of the Turks, whom he tried to persuade to renew their war with Russia. He rejected a convention drawn up by England and the United Provinces in March 1710 neutralizing the Empire as it would have prevented his using Pomerania as a base and also ordered the formation of a new army in Sweden which was to be brought over to Pomerania to recommence the campaign in Poland.[16]

In the Baltic the war was turning decisively against the Swedes. The territory from which Peter had withdrawn his troops in order to face King Charles's invasion in 1707 was reoccupied, and in the summer of 1710 both Viborg and Riga fell to him. Reval followed in September. In 1711 an army of 24,000 Russians, Saxons and Poles laid siege to Stralsund, while the Danes attacked Wismar. The Swedish Council did manage to form an army of 16,000 in accordance with the king's orders. This Stenbock managed to transport from Karlskrona and Karlshamn to Rügen under the protection of the Swedish fleet, which was withdrawn from the Sound for the purpose. The *indelning* and *rotar* systems had worked reasonably well up to the time of Poltava, though even in the early stages of the war additional troops had had to be raised by grouping the 'files' in fours and fives, with each new group expected to provide an additional infantryman. Now the shortage of manpower began to be a serious problem, and out-right conscription had to be resorted to, though at the end of his reign Charles XII was still able to raise large armies of able-bodied men from among his subjects, even if agricultural production suffered as a result.[17]

Stenbock's campaign fell victim to Sweden's weakness at sea.

Soon after he landed in Pomerania his supply ships were captured or destroyed by Danish frigates, which had been detached from the main fleet for this purpose, before the Swedish fleet could intervene. Weather conditions prevented the sending of new supplies and instead of striking eastward into Poland, Stenbock was forced to march westward along the coast. He defeated the Danes and Saxons at Gadebusch near Wismar at the end of 1712, and marched into Holstein in the hope of forcing the Danes to conclude a separate peace. There, however, he was shut up by superior forces in the fortress of Tønning, while the Danish fleet blocked the sea lanes. He was forced to surrender in May 1713.[18]

Stettin fell to a Russian army in September, and in a treaty signed the following month between a still officially neutral Brandenburg–Prussia and the tsar, the king was promised the city together with Wolgast, Usedom, Wollin and Pomerania to the Peene river in exchange for payment of 400,000 daler. Russia was to take Ingria, Karelia and Estonia. This partition treaty was joined in the summer of 1715 by Denmark, who again hoped for the island of Rügen and part of Western Pomerania, and by the Elector of Hanover, who lusted after the bishoprics of Bremen and Verden on the Elbe.[19]

The Elector Frederick of Prussia had joined the anti-French coalition at the end of 1701 and beginning of 1702; in exchange for Imperial recognition of his royal title in Prussia, he committed 5,000 out of his 30,000 troops to the campaign on the Rhine. Narva and the crossing of the Dvina by the Swedes caused some alarm in Berlin, where it was feared that Augustus might make peace at Brandenburg's expense and in particular that Kurland might be ceded to Sweden. The new king sought recognition of his title from the Poles as the price of his support, but they responded with demands for the abandonment of his claims on the sum promised as compensation for Elbing. With little hope of an agreement with Saxony–Poland and with the Swedes on the river Vistula threatening the Prussian coast and Danzig, at the end of July 1703 he signed a defensive alliance with Sweden, which, in exchange for recognition of his new title, allowed the latter to use his territories for the passage of troops. But while some of his advisers urged him to adopt an active policy in the conflict and seek territorial gain by armed intervention, more cautious counsel represented by his principal foreign policy adviser Heinrich Rüdiger von Ilgen prevailed; both the military and diplomatic situation was too fluid to risk committing the country to one side or the other. Policy must aim at limiting the gains of both Sweden and Russia while attempting to use the situation to strengthen Brandenburg's position in the area; in negotiations with both Sweden and Poland, Brandenburg's bids for royal Prussia, Ermland and the succession to the duchy of Kurland in a partial partition of Poland–Lithuania indicate the direction of the new king's ambitions at this time: a continuous coastline from the Oder to the Dvina leaving Danzig untouched to humour the susceptibilities of the Maritime Powers. But the fortunes of war were still too uncertain to lead him to commit himself and Charles compelled Brandenburg troops to withdraw from Elbing and occupied Ermland, from which he could threaten East Prussia. In August 1704 Danzig obtained from King Frederick a promise of limited protection.[20]

After Altranstädt Charles had given some support to Frederick's claims to Elbing and promised to allow him to occupy it once Swedish troops had withdrawn. In August 1707 Sweden and Brandenburg had concluded an 'eternal' treaty of friendship and mutual assistance by which the latter recognized Stanislas's claims to the Polish throne. King Frederick had resisted Russian and Saxon blandishments until after Poltava, and even then he hesitated before committing himself; to Sweden's enemies his somewhat extravagant demands for territorial compensation did not match Brandenburg's likely contribution to the struggle. At the beginning of 1712 Ilgen even negotiated with Sweden and Augustus for an alliance to force on the tsar, harrassed by the Turks, a peace settlement out of which Brandenburg would gain Elbing, a land-bridge through West Prussia and the succession to Kurland, and Stanislas Leszczyński would win the reversion of the Polish throne. But the plan was decisively rejected by Charles XII, who not only counted on the success of Stenbock's campaign and of his own negotiations with the Turks but could not bring himself to fight side by side with Augustus.[21]

With the accession in February 1713 of Frederick William I, who was much less fearful of Russian expansion than his father had been, and the growing success of the anti-Swedish coalition after the failure of Stenbock's mission, the influence of Ilgen on Brandenburg–Prussian policy waned. With the conclusion of his treaty with the tsar the following year, the king finally committed his realm to the ranks of Sweden's enemies in exchange for the promise of gains at the expense of Sweden rather than of Poland.[22]

By the time Charles XII finally returned to the Baltic theatre at Stralsund in November 1714, after a dramatic ride from the Turkish frontier in the Balkans across the Empire, nearly all his trans-Baltic possessions had been lost. Russia had the whole of Estonia and Livonia in its grasp. The Swedish defensive line in south-eastern Finland had been turned in May 1713 by a landing at Sandviken, which forced the Swedish commander Karl Gustav Armfelt to retreat northward into Tavastia (Tavastland/Häme). In February 1714 he suffered a serious defeat on the Kyro river in southern Ostrobothnia. In Pomerania only Rügen and Stralsund held out.[23]

Even at sea the Russians had established their supremacy. Shortage of funds and manpower had hindered the Swedes from developing a galley fleet to meet Peter's. A Swedish squadron had in August 1714 been severely defeated off the south-western tip of Finland (Hangö Udd/Hankoniemi) by the Russian galley fleet with the tsar himself on board, and in September Russian galleys had raided and burnt the town of Umeå on the northern coast of Sweden itself. Even the Swedish high seas fleet was weak. It numbered only twenty-four ships of the line, less than two-thirds of its strength at the outbreak of war, and many of these were in poor shape and scattered in different ports.[24]

Wolgast on the Peene and the island of Usedom were temporarily regained from Prussian troops who had occupied them, and Charles opened negotiations with Frederick William of Brandenburg to try to entice him into the Swedish camp. But these talks broke down when the Swedish king refused either to recognize Frederick William's claim to Stettin or to compensate him for the 400,000 daler he had paid for it. In April 1715, using the Swedes' activities on Usedom as an excuse, Brandenburg finally declared war on Sweden. The ring of Charles's enemies was completed by the alliance concluded between Russia and Hanover in October. The Elector of Hanover had since 1714 also been king of Great Britain and Ireland, but Britain was not involved as such in the commitments entered into by George I as ruler of Hanover.[25]

The two Maritime Powers were nevertheless, as in the past, much concerned by the effects on their commerce of war in the Baltic, especially after Charles XII had in February 1715 ordered his privateers to stop all trade with his enemies. A British squadron under admiral Sir John Norris sailed into the Baltic in May 1715 with orders to join with Dutch units to protect British and Dutch merchant ships there. This had the effect of confining Sweden's main fleet to Karlskrona, and the squadron's anti-Swedish bias was demonstrated by Norris's detaching eight of his ships to join the Danish fleet assisting in the siege of Stralsund, which, with King Charles still in residence, began in July. With the help of the British vessels, the island of Rügen protecting Stralsund was captured by a Danish, Prussian and Saxon army in November. Stralsund fell shortly after, King Charles escaping from it only at the last moment. With the fall of Wismar in April 1716, Sweden's last foothold on the southern Baltic coast and its last possession in the Empire had gone.[26]

Indeed Sweden itself was soon under direct threat. In accordance with a plan worked out between Denmark and Russia at Altona in June 1716, an army of 30,000 Russians was in September transported on Prussian ships from Warnemünde in Mecklenburg to Zealand, where it joined a Danish army of 24,000. The Danish navy of twenty-four ships of the line was joined by the main Russian fleet and galley force together with British and Dutch squadrons, sixty-seven ships of the line and frigates all told. The combined force was intended for an invasion of Scania. But Tsar Peter suddenly announced the postponement of the whole enterprise until the following year, when King Frederik could no longer guarantee the troops' transportation. It is usually claimed that Peter had found the Swedish defences too formidable. But he may also have been influenced by Swedish offers to negotiate which had been instigated by Charles in the hope of exploiting the now obvious divisions developing within the coalition ranged against him. The Russian troops were marched back to Mecklenburg.[27]

For Mecklenburg Peter had developed ambitious plans: it was to be an advanced Russian base on the Baltic. At one stage he seems indeed to have envisaged transplanting the duke to the duchy of Kurland and incorporating his German lands into his own realm. Duke Charles Leopold, who had succeeded to the title in 1713, sought Russian support in the struggle he was waging with his nobles over the powers of taxation wielded by his Estates, a struggle in which they had gained the support of the Emperor. In April 1716 an alliance was concluded which involved the engagement of the duke to the tsar's niece, Catherine

Ivanovna, with Wismar as her dowry as well as Peter's assistance against the Mecklenburg Estates. After the marriage, Mecklenburg became little better than a Russian satellite. There were plans for a canal to link the duchy with the North Sea via the river Elbe on which to carry Russian commerce to Hamburg, thus avoiding the Sound with its irritating dues. But Russia's presence so far westward alarmed Russia's allies, especially the Elector of Hanover, whose territories marched with those of Mecklenburg, and in order to please France, from whom Peter hoped for both subsidies and mediation for peace, he ordered the withdrawal of his troops from the duchy in July 1717, with the exception of 3,000 who entered the duke's service. This was followed in January 1719 by the occupation of the duchy by 12,000 troops from Hanover and Wolfenbüttel executing the Emperor's sequestration order against the duke, who fled.[28]

The situation in Sweden at the time of King Charles's return was desperate. The crown's income was much reduced by the loss of territory, and expenditure far outpaced income; great difficulty was being experienced even in servicing the loans on which the government more and more relied. Baltic trade had been little affected by the war until 1709, but it was now seriously disrupted, and the Swedish merchant marine was largely confined to local commerce. Harvest failures and outbreaks of plague, which carried off over 100,000 Swedes in 1710-11, undermined morale and exacerbated the discontent already caused by the burden of taxes and conscription. A meeting of the Diet in 1713, called on the initiative of the Council and soon repudiated by the absent king, had revealed a vocal opposition to the continuation of the war. Charles, however, was determined to fight on until an honourable peace could be won whatever sacrifices this might entail.[29]

He proceeded to order forced levies of food and iron at fixed prices and replaced the existing governmental apparatus with one centred on five ministries or 'expeditions'. He also made all overseas trade a state monopoly and put through a number of financial measures which temporarily improved the crown's liquidity, including a state loan serviced by graded taxes and the issue of copper tokens and paper notes. Such measures have long been associated with Georg Heinrich von Görtz, chief adviser to the administrator of Holstein–Gottorp who had joined the Swedish camp after the Danes had occupied the Gottorp territories and

soon after the king had arrived at Stralsund. But many of the
reforms had been envisaged before Görtz appeared on the scene.[30]
Görtz engaged in a flurry of diplomatic activity with both King
Frederick William and the tsar. To the latter he proposed the
marriage of Charles Frederick of Gottorp to Peter's daughter,
Anna, in exchange for Peter's support of the duke's claim to the
Swedish throne after the death of the childless Charles XII. In
June 1716, after Charles's invasion of Norway to force Denmark
out of the war had been frustrated by King Frederik's superiority
at sea, Görtz was sent off to the United Provinces to attempt to
secure a loan and to France to try to persuade the duc d'Orléans,
regent for Louis XV, to pay the arrears of subsidies promised to
Sweden under an agreement made in April 1715. There was also
some hope of getting France to mediate between Sweden and the
tsar on a settlement in the eastern Baltic. In none of these tasks
was Görtz particularly successful. His contacts with the Jacobites
in exile, who offered money for the use of Swedish ships and
troops in an invasion of England, led to his arrest in Arnhem by
the Dutch in February 1717 and of Gyllenborg, the Swedish
envoy in London.[31]

While Charles was gathering an army of 65,000 men and a
large naval force for a second invasion of Norway which was
probably to be followed by an attack on Denmark, Görtz and
Gyllenborg (once more at liberty) in May 1718 opened negotiations with the tsar's representative Heinrich Ostermann on
Lövö in the Åland Islands. Peter, as suspicious of his allies as
they were of him, had agreed to this at a meeting with Görtz at
Loo in the United Provinces in August 1717. Swedish feelers also
went out to the western powers; negotiations were going on with
a Hanoverian representative at the king's headquarters at Lund in
Scania with the object of obtaining King George's assistance
against Russia in exchange for territorial concessions.[32]

The main Norwegian campaign opened in October 1718 when
Charles advanced into the country at the head of a well-equipped
and organized army of 40,000 men against only slight opposition.
At the end of the following month he fell in the trenches before
the Norwegian fort of Frederikshald which blocked the Swedish
advance on Kristiania.[33]

To him the best hope of a favourable peace had long seemed
to lie in that policy of dividing the opposition which had been
commenced after the king's return. This was continued after his

death by the ministers for his sister Ulrika Eleanora and her husband Frederick of Hesse who succeeded him, though the accent was now on securing peace with the western powers even without the guarantees of compensation on which Charles would have insisted. With the western powers peace did come in the course of 1719 and 1720 at the cost of most of Sweden's German possessions. Hanover acquired Bremen and Verden in November 1719, and in January of the following year Brandenburg–Prussia won Wollin, Usedom and Western Pomerania south of the river Peene with Stettin. British mediation secured an armistice between Sweden and Denmark in October 1719, and peace between the two was signed in June of the following year. King Frederik, under pressure from Britain, surrendered his claim to Stralsund and Rügen, which had been promised to him, in exchange for a guarantee by the Maritime Powers of his possession of the Slesvig lands of the duke of Gottorp, who had turned to the tsar for assistance (see below, p. 133). He also gained Sweden's surrender of the freedom from the Sound Dues which it had enjoyed since 1645 and a payment of 600,000 daler.[34]

Such sacrifices were made in the hope of gaining the support of the western powers in the continuing struggle against the tsar, who broke off the negotiations on the Åland Islands in September 1719. In August, Britain, anxious to keep Russia from the Baltic and control of its naval supplies, had agreed to renew the alliance of 1700, and a British squadron under Norris appeared in the Baltic that year and the following two. This did lead to the withdrawal of the Russian high seas fleet to Reval and Kronstadt, but it could not prevent the Russian galley fleet, based on the Åland Islands, from penetrating the Stockholm archipelago, where it landed 6,000 troops. Though this attack was repulsed, the coastline to the north and south of the capital was raided in the summer of 1720.[35]

The whole northern coastline of Sweden was again ravaged in 1721 and Umeå burnt anew. The British minister Stanhope failed to win either the king of Prussia, who demanded the whole of Pomerania, or the Emperor for a crusade to limit Russian gains, and internal crises in both Britain (the South Sea Bubble and the renewed threat of Jacobitism) and in France (the failure of John Law's scheme) led them to advise the Swedes to make the best settlement they could with the tsar.[36]

At one stage in the Åland negotiations the Russian

representatives, aware of Swedish negotiations with the western allies and of the opposition to Görtz in Sweden itself, had gone so far as to offer to retain only Viborg, Narva and Ingria and to persuade the duke of Mecklenburg to surrender his duchy in exchange for territory in Russia. But Charles had in return demanded help against Denmark, which Peter had refused.[37] Now the Swedes' military situation was much more desperate and they had to agree to much harsher terms. By the peace of Nystad (Uusikaupunki) in November 1721 they surrendered the whole of Livonia, Estonia and Ingria, and the southern part of Keksholm with Viborg. The only concession they won was permission to import (except in famine years) 50,000 roubles' worth of Livonian grain free of customs dues. Russian indirect control of Kurland had been ensured in 1710 by the marriage of the young duke to Peter's niece Anna.[38]

Charles XII may well have secured peace with less loss of territory at several stages during the war: in the first year Augustus of Saxony would have withdrawn; before the Poltava campaign Tsar Peter offered to return all Swedish territory except the mouth of the Neva; the acceptance of the Brandenburg–Prussian offer of an anti-Russian alliance in 1713 might well have persuaded the tsar, embarrassed by the Turks, to agree to reasonable terms and, as has been seen, during the Åland negotiations he seemed willing to retain only a foothold on the Baltic. But a peace secured without a convincing military defeat of Sweden's enemies would have been a precarious one, which Sweden could not have sustained for more than a limited period. The beginning of the eighteenth century, with the Maritime Powers engaged in the War of the Spanish Succession, Russia under the dynamic leadership of Peter I and Sweden isolated diplomatically after a long period of peace, was particularly unfavourable for her, but even had the Russian enterprise not been dogged with misfortune and other powers been more willing and able to come to Sweden's assistance after the death of Charles XII, the eventual collapse of Sweden's 'empire' was inevitable.[39]

The position which it had secured in the earlier part of the century, after decades of seemingly fruitless struggle in Livonia, was due to temporarily favourable conditions. Russia was exhausted by Ivan IV and the 'Time of Troubles', and on recovery concentrated its energies on struggles with Poland and the Turks. Denmark's embroilment in the Thirty Years War weakened it militarily and economically. Brandenburg–Prussia had yet to build up an army which was to be the largest in Europe per head of population. For all the reforms of Gustavus Adolphus, Sweden's national army was small and manpower resources limited. Although the effects of the Great Northern War on the population and economy of Sweden have often been exaggerated, the country was put under considerable strain in maintaining the defence of the overseas possessions even in time of peace, and the financing of a war of any duration created enormous problems. As Sven Lundkvist has expressed the situation so cogently:

> Sweden's position as a great power was the result of the favourable accident of having weak neighbours, and of *ad hoc* solutions with resources too small for the great objects in view. When one of these conditions vanished, and the other was partly destroyed as the result of the weakening or removal of the basis on which it rested, the day of Sweden as a great power was over for good.[40]

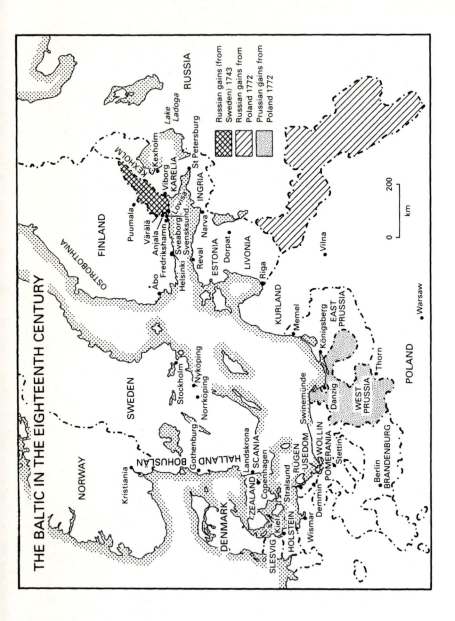

THE BALTIC IN THE EIGHTEENTH CENTURY

Russian gains (from Sweden) 1743

Russian gains from Poland 1772

Prussian gains from Poland 1772

0   200
km

RUSSIA

Lake Ladoga

Kexholm

KEXHOLM

Viborg
St Petersburg

KARELIA

INGRIA

Puumala

Väräiä

Anjala

Fredrikshamn

Loviisa

Sveaborg

Svensksund

Narva

Reval

ESTONIA

Dorpat

LIVONIA

Helsinki

Åbo

FINLAND

OSTROBOTHNIA

Riga

KURLAND

Memel

Königsberg

EAST PRUSSIA

Vilna

Danzig

WEST PRUSSIA

Thorn

Stettin

POMERANIA

Swinemünde

WOLLIN

USEDOM

RÜGEN

Demmin

Stralsund

Wismar

Berlin

BRANDENBURG

POLAND

Warsaw

Stockholm

Nyköping

Norrköping

SWEDEN

Gothenburg

HALLAND

BOHUSLÄN

SCANIA

Landskrona

ZEALAND

Copenhagen

DENMARK

HOLSTEIN

Kiel

SLESVIG

NORWAY

Kristiania

9

A NEW BALANCE (1721–51)

The settlement which brought to an end the Great Northern War in 1720/1 led to the replacement of Sweden by Russia as the leading power in the Baltic. Denmark's acquisition of the duke of Holstein–Gottorp's lands in Slesvig under the guarantees of Britain and France was the kingdom's only real gain, and it was one which was to complicate Denmark's relations with both Russia and Sweden for nearly fifty years and was to bring it to the brink of war with both. Not until 1788, however, was the country actually drawn into armed conflict with another state. Brandenburg–Prussia's winning of the control of the mouth of the river Oder with the port of Stettin was of some economic significance, but without a navy Prussia's role in Baltic politics was bound to be limited; its rulers' ambitions to secure West Prussia and so close the gap between Brandenburg and East Prussia at Poland's expense competed with those further south, which brought the Hohenzollerns into conflict with the Austrian Habsburgs. Poland was to be for much of the period little more than a Russian satellite and in general was the passive victim of its neighbours' ambitions. Before the new century was out it disappeared from the scene altogether as an independent state.

Consequently the power struggle in the Baltic in the eighteenth century was basically one between Sweden and Russia. In the course of it, Sweden made two unsuccessful attempts to exploit Russia's preoccupations elsewhere to regain something at least of what had been lost by Nystad, and Russian rulers attempted to secure sufficient influence over Sweden's internal political life to ensure that the country would not be able to distract them from larger ambitions; as in the case of Poland, Russia preferred indirect to direct control of Sweden and the acquisition of its territory,

although the exposed position of St Petersburg to Swedish operations from Finland (the frontier of which lay only a day's march
from the Russian capital) made the idea of the transformation of
the latter into a nominally independent client state an attractive
one.[1] But while Sweden's relations with Russia were always of
prime importance for her, Russia's interest in the Baltic was, as
in the seventeenth century, much more sporadic. Sweden's continued possession of a small area of German territory in Pomerania and of the city of Wismar added little to its prestige and was
indeed a distraction, which, as in 1674, involved it in war with
Brandenburg–Prussia and led to military and diplomatic humiliation which increased internal political instability.

After the death of Peter the Great in 1725 the concept of a
dominium maris Baltici passed into history. Peter I's successors
never strove for it, and Russia never enjoyed the degree of domination which Sweden had in the early seventeenth century.[2]
During the reign of Tsarina Anna in the 1730s, Russian policy
was essentially defensive and conservative. Under Elizabeth in
the 1740s and 1750s, her chancellor Bestuzhev-Ryumin adopted
a more aggressive line, directed particularly against Prussia. But
his attitude to the latter, while it had irrational elements, was
dictated largely by his fears of Frederick the Great's designs in
Poland and the south-eastern Baltic and that king's place in a
French-led alliance of states aimed at destroying Russia's position
in eastern Europe.[3]

One of the leading objectives of Baltic diplomacy in the eighteenth century was the 'Tranquility of the North', something at
which indeed the Maritime Powers had always aimed in the
seventeenth century and something which Sweden also sought
after 1660 in order to protect its existing 'empire'. The main
protagonist of the idea was now, however, Denmark, fearful as
it was of the possible effects of Sweden's revanchist aims and of
Russian power on Baltic stability. It sought to protect such stability by cultivating friendly relations with all its neighbours as
well as by securing the support of one of the great powers outside
the area who had similar aims.[4]

Only in Sweden was the machinery of foreign policy making
changed drastically after the end of the Great Northern War. By
a written constitution approved by the Diet in 1719/20, the ruler
was deprived of any real control over foreign affairs. While this

constitution remained in force (i.e. until 1772) the ultimate authority for all state matters rested with the four Estates of the Diet and particularly with its Secret Committee (*sekreta utskott*) of over a hundred members and the smaller 'deputation' (*mindre sekreta deputation*) of sixteen which it appointed. To this body (from which peasant representatives were generally excluded) the Council (now again named 'Council of the Realm'), on which the king had only two votes and a casting vote, was answerable for its conduct between the triennial sessions of the Diet. Even over the composition of the Council the monarch had little control; when a vacancy in it occurred, he was presented by the Estates with three names, of which he chose one. Within the Council it was the chancellor (its only *ex officio* member) who was largely responsible for relations with foreign powers. His personality could be a significant factor in foreign policy, but in the circumstances no eighteenth-century Swedish chancellor was able to wield the power once possessed by Axel Oxenstierna; ultimately he had to answer for every move he made to the Secret Committee whose members appointed him but who were not as well informed as he of the international situation. In all it was a system which did not allow for swift decision-making and was more open to foreign intrigue than the more unified autocratic system of Sweden's neighbours, especially when in the 1730s organized political parties with contrasting views of foreign policy began to emerge.[5]

The first chancellor of the new regime, Arvid Horn, could nevertheless for some two decades stamp Swedish foreign policy with his interpretation of the country's best interests. While he looked forward to a time when circumstances might allow Sweden to regain something of its former power and influence and was indeed already in 1720 authorized by the Diet to exploit any favourable opportunity to do so without further reference to it, he realized that the most immediate requirement was for peace and the avoidance of conflict with neighbours to enable the country, diplomatically isolated as it was, to recover from the traumatic twenty years through which it had just passed. And peace was again threatened within a few years of the signing of Nystad.[6]

While the fundamental principles of government in Russia remained unchanged, Peter towards the end of his reign did much to modernize the creaking administration. In 1711 he established a Senate of nine to advise him, in place of the old boyar council, which had come to have little influence on policy, and from 1718 replaced the old *prikazy* with eleven colleges on the Swedish model. After his death foreign policy was largely the responsibility of the chancellor, although the monarch could often exercise a decisive influence when opinions within the Senate were divided. The *zemsky sobor* had in the later seventeenth century passed from a purely advisory committee into oblivion; it met for the last time in 1682 after the death of Tsar Fedor and then consisted wholly of nobles.[7]

In Denmark, King Frederik IV (1699–1730) and his son and successor Christian VI (1730–40) conducted their own foreign policy with the assistance of a small body of councillors, but with the accession of Frederik V in 1740, the reins of government in general were taken over by one or more ministers acting in the king's name.

In Brandenburg–Prussia, Frederick William I (1713–40) kept foreign affairs outside the competence of the General Directory which he set up at the beginning of his reign to supervise financial and economic affairs and relied heavily on his foreign minister in the making of policy. His successor Frederick II ('the Great') himself conducted his relations with other monarchs. Both kings were, however, directly concerned with the organization and growth of their kingdom's military potential, to which a large proportion of their income was devoted. While continuing to rely heavily on recruitment from other German states, Frederick William reorganized his army's home conscription on the basis of a 'cantonal' system by which each unit, as in Sweden, was given a defined area from which to draw its manpower. He doubled its size from the 40,000 of his father to the 80,000 inherited by his son.[8]

The accession of Charles XII's younger sister Ulrika Eleanora to the Swedish throne after her brother's death was not unchallenged. Her sister's son, Duke Karl Friedrich of Holstein–Gottorp, also put forward a claim. Not only did he dream of the Swedish throne but also of the recovery of his lands in Slesvig, the loss of which to the Danish crown he refused to recognize and which command of Sweden's resources might help him to win back. For his Swedish supporters Slesvig was an attractive substitute for Bremen and Verden, which Sweden had lost to Hanover.[9]

His fate was thus also of concern to the Danes, whose foreign policy for the next five decades was to be dominated by the need to obtain a permanent settlement in the Duchies. Denmark's economy took long to recover from the effects of the Great Northern War, and the crown's parlous financial situation precluded any vigorous action which might involve a further conflict.[10]

The duke's ambitions would, however, have been of little significance had they not been backed by the might of a great power. Tsar Peter's relations with Denmark had already become strained after King Frederik had made a separate peace with Sweden, had refused not only to address Russia's ruler as 'tsar' but also to marry his son to Peter's daughter Anna and had rejected an offer of a Russian guarantee of Denmark's possession of Slesvig in exchange for exemption for Russian ships from the Sound Dues. He consequently took up the duke's cause. Kiel in Holstein might, as a free port, well replace Wismar as a desirable base for Russian trade in the western Baltic and through to the North Sea.[11]

In 1723 Anna and the duke were engaged. The latter's supporters in Sweden emerged in strength in the Diet which met in that year. A Russian naval demonstration, in which both the tsar and the duke took part, and the mobilization of Russian troops in Livonia rather alarmed them and indeed from the Russian point of view proved counterproductive. But collaboration between Horn and the Holsteiners resulted in February 1724 in a twelve-year treaty of friendship with Russia, which aimed to secure the choice of the duke as heir to the Swedish throne and then to recover not only his Slesvig lands for himself but also Bremen and Verden for Sweden. The alliance did not commit the Swedes as far as Peter had hoped but in the marriage contract between Anna and the duke which was drawn up at the end of the year, he committed himself to supporting the latter's claims to the Swedish throne and Slesvig. The spectre was raised of war between Sweden and not only Denmark but Hanover (behind which stood Britain) as well.[12]

The path to the alliance had been smoothed by the discontent felt both by the Diet and the chancellor with King Fredrik, who had replaced his seemingly less compliant wife Ulrika Eleonora on the Swedish throne in 1720 but who tried to conduct his own foreign negotiations as well as to modify the constitution in his favour. But British-Hanoverian diplomacy now worked hard to achieve a reconciliation as part of its aim to prevent a new Baltic conflict, which would probably lead to a strengthening of Russia's position there, and to bind Sweden to the Hanoverian Alliance with France and Prussia.[13]

In fact Peter, who died the following year, failed to back up the duke's cause with any vigour once he had secured the Swedish alliance to balance that between Denmark and Britain. But his widow Catherine I championed the Holstein cause with much more enthusiasm.[14]

Schleswig–Holstein figures largely in a memorandum drawn up at the beginning of her reign by Andrei Ivanovich Ostermann, vice-president of the College of Foreign Affairs and the main architect of Russian foreign policy for a decade. It outlined Russia's relations with its neighbours and explained the principles which should guide Russia's attitudes to them. It placed great emphasis in general on the Baltic as a field for Russian activity, and in particular on Kurland, administered by the still unmarried niece of Peter the Great; Mecklenburg, whose exiled duke continued to receive Russia's diplomatic support, and on Slesvig, whose recovery (by Duke Charles) Russia was committed to by the marriage agreement of the previous year. In August 1726 Russia finally concluded an alliance with Austria, which was to prove one of the cornerstones of its foreign policy for much of the eighteenth century. In it Austria promised support for the duke of Gottorp. In the same month came an alliance with Prussia, by which Russia was granted the right of passage for its troops on their way to Denmark.[15]

In response to such threats both Scandinavian monarchies strengthened their ties with Britain and France, at this time temporarily working together in international affairs. Horn, who, fearful of the danger into which his Russian alliance seemed to be drawing his country, had been distancing himself from the Holstein party for some time, openly broke with it in the Diet of 1726–7, and in March 1727 he brought Sweden into the Hanoverian Alliance which was directed against Russia, Austria and Spain. In Denmark, King Frederik IV, probably the ablest king of his line, was unwilling to commit himself to this extent, but did conclude a separate four-year treaty with Britain and France. In this he promised to maintain an army of 24,000 men in exchange for French subsidies and a renewed guarantee for the Gottorp possessions in Slesvig. A British naval squadron was dispatched to the Baltic in 1726 and 1727 to discourage the Russian fleet from leaving harbour.[16]

The crisis came to an end with the death of Tsarina Catherine in May 1727. Under her successor, Peter the Great's 12-year-old grandson Peter II, the duke was forced to leave Russia to take up residence in Kiel, where he died in 1739. Russia and Austria had already in 1732 guaranteed Denmark's claim to his territories in Slesvig.[17] But a potential threat to Denmark remained: the fruit of the duke's marriage had a strong claim to both the Russian and the Swedish throne, and a new crisis might well develop should he come into possession of either of them.

After Tsar Peter's death, his ambitious maritime plans in the Baltic were shelved and his fleet, which had numbered thirty-four ships of the line and fifteen frigates by the end of his reign, was neglected for some fifty years. During the brief reign of Peter II (1727–30) indeed the navy was even threatened with extinction.[18] This was part of a general reaction which can be seen as a protest by the lesser Russian nobility against an ambitious foreign policy which had imposed heavy financial burdens on them and deprived them through conscription of a high proportion of their labour force for little return. Unlike the Swedish nobility of the seventeenth century, they could not hope for extensive new estates and lucrative offices as the result of Russian expansion.[19]

The installation of Peter I's niece Anna of Kurland[20] on the throne in 1730 ensured, however, that his work would not be wholly undone. This was certainly true in the sphere of foreign policy, which under her was largely the responsibility of Ostermann, a German like most of Anna's advisers. He, as has been seen, was already an important force in government under Peter I, who prized his diplomatic talents. Ostermann was a cautious man, who sought to strengthen Russia's position and defend it against potential threats from France, Sweden and Turkey by means of an alliance system led by Austria and Brandenburg–Prussia. The friendship of Denmark should, he believed, also be courted by offering a settlement of the Slesvig problem. Above all, French influence in Poland must be guarded against.[21]

The death of King Augustus of Poland in 1733 led to yet another struggle for control of his unhappy realm, a struggle which led to another European war (ironically fought mainly in Italy between France and Austria). Augustus's hopes of turning his kingdom into a strong monarchy able to hold its own against both Russia and Brandenburg–Prussia had come to naught. By an agreement reached with the *Sejm* in January 1717 under Russian pressure but also in the interests of the nobility, the royal Polish army had been limited to 24,100 men supported by a permanent tax, gathered locally where the units were stationed. Although intended to be only a temporary arrangement, it in fact lasted for half a century. And in practice even this puny force could not be raised; only about half this number ever took the field, and only a small proportion of these were trained and equipped on western European lines; discipline was lax and corruption rife. The magnates' own private armies were probably as large and were certainly better equipped, and the better able to call on the services of the petty nobility.[22]

The agreement of 1717 marked the beginning of a Russian domination of Poland which lasted until the extinction of the republic three-quarters of a century later. It was in the interests of its neighbours to keep Poland–Lithuania weak, and Russian rulers hoped to dominate it and even eventually incorporate it in their dominions without the need of conquest. And the best way to keep it weak, it was generally agreed, was, as in the case of Sweden, to ensure the maintenance of the existing constitution. Peter I had already agreed with Frederick William of Prussia on this in the alliance made between the two rulers in February 1720, and a Russian guarantee of the Swedish constitution figured in the seventh paragraph of the treaty of Nystad, where ironically it had been inserted at Sweden's request as a barrier against the duke of Holstein–Gottorp. It also figured in the Russo–Swedish treaty of 1724.[23]

After Augustus's death, elements of the broken Holstein party in Sweden joined with young militant elements of the nobility in supporting the claims to the Polish throne of Charles XII's protegé Stanislas Leszczyński. He was backed by France against Augustus's son, the new duke of Saxony, the candidate of the Russians, whose fleet blockaded Danzig in 1734. The young Swedes hoped to create a new Swedo–Polish alliance which would, as in the days of John III, drive Russia back from the Baltic. Horn, his position weakened by the breach between Britain and France in 1731, came under pressure to join the latter in Stanislas's cause and negotiations were entered into with France which envisaged Sweden's involvement in the struggle. But he resisted a final commitment. He succeeded in securing a fifteen-year defensive alliance with Denmark in October 1734 and even in August 1735 renewed the Russian alliance, two months after concluding a subsidy treaty with France in accordance with the instructions of the Secret Committee. The defeat of Stanislas's supporters in October 1734 by those of the new elector, King Augustus III since January, seemed to confirm Russia's dominance in Poland and to justify Horn's suspicion of France's effectiveness in eastern Europe, although France's refusal to ratify the subsidy treaty he had negotiated was to play a large part in his eventual downfall.[24]

New heart was put into the Swedish militants by the outbreak of war in 1735 between Russia and the Turks, who put up unexpectedly stiff resistance to the tsarina's troops. These militants, now organized as the so-called Hat party, seized control of the Diet in 1738 and forced Horn, whom they charged with the responsibility for the loss of the French subsidy treaty, to retire from the chancellorship.[25]

The new Hat regime looked to Sweden's old ally France, to Denmark and to the Turks for support and to a crisis in Russia as a signal to launch a war of revenge. The Danes, however, demanded the cession of the province of Bohuslän and recognition of Oldenburg claims to the Swedish throne as conditions for an alliance, while Russia's position was strengthened by the victorious ending of their war with the Turks. And though the French concluded a three-year subsidy treaty with the new regime, their response to the suggestion of a war in the Baltic was consequently cautious. The attack in 1740 by the new king of Prussia, Frederick II, on the new ruler of Austria, Maria Theresa, and the death of the tsarina Anna shortly before seemed, however, to provide just the crisis on which the Hats had pinned their hopes.[26]

A common interest in a weak Poland might have been expected to draw Prussia and Russia together, and, as has been seen, Ostermann wished to include Prussia in his defensive alliance system. But King Frederick William saw a new Saxon king in Warsaw as a potential threat and refused to co-operate with Russia in the War of the Polish Succession. He advised his son, however, to remain on friendly terms with St Petersburg; from war with Russia, Prussia had little to gain, and Frederick did open negotiations for a treaty of mutual guarantees soon after coming to the throne and concluded an alliance at the end of the year. But his attack on Austria dashed all Ostermann's hopes.[27]

With some reluctance, a Russia whose moral and material

resources had been seriously undermined by the hard struggle with the Turks came to the assistance of Austria after the Prussian attack in the hope of compelling Frederick to return to the status quo; suggestions by Saxony of a partition of the latter's realm, from which Russia would receive East Prussia, were rejected.[28]

France backed Frederick against its traditional Habsburg foe. Consequently it welcomed a chance to draw Russian forces away from central Europe, where they might help the Austrians to defeat Prussia, agreed in March 1741 to pay to Sweden further subsidies for three years to enable it to arm for an attack on Russia, and assisted Swedish intrigues in St Petersburg with Princess Elizabeth, Peter I's youngest daughter. The latter promised monetary compensation and even hinted at territorial concessions (*témoinages les plus réels de ma reconnaissance*) in exchange for Swedish military support in her bid to topple from the throne the boy tsar, Ivan VI, son of Tsarina Anna's sister, and ascend it herself. The Hats in fact dreamed that, with the help of Denmark, Prussia and the Turks, they would regain at least Karelia and Ingria, including the mouth of the Neva and St Petersburg, and at best a Russo–Finnish border which ran from lake Ladoga to the White Sea and Estonia and Livonia into the bargain.[29]

The Secret Committee of the Swedish Diet agreed to a declaration of war, which was delivered in August. Subsequent military operations proved how far the Swedish army's standards had declined since the days of Charles XII; preparations for an attack by land or sea were quite inadequate, the officer corps riven by political rancour and the commander-in-chief Carl Emil Lewenhaupt incompetent. By withdrawing forces from central Europe, Ostermann was easily able to stem a dilatory advance on St Petersburg.[30]

But when at the beginning of December 1741 the crack guards regiments in St Petersburg were ordered to the front, their officers called on Elizabeth to carry out the coup which she had been planning. This she did successfully with their support. Ostermann, widely blamed for the unpopular war and hated as a foreigner, was dismissed and condemned to exile in Siberia. The coup was immediately followed by a truce with Sweden and the withdrawal of its troops across the border.[31]

The Swedes, who had hoped so much of the new tsarina, became rapidly disillusioned. Elizabeth genuinely set out to reverse Ostermann's foreign policy by seeking a rapprochement with Sweden and France, whose culture she admired, and repeated her offer to pay the costs incurred by the former in the war. But of any territorial concessions which involved the gains hard won by her father she would not hear. In the course of subsequent negotiations, the Swedes reduced their demands to Viborg, but this was seen by the Russians as a vital part of the defences of St Petersburg. At the end of February they denounced the truce.[32]

At the same time a Russian manifesto was distributed in Finland which promised its inhabitants support in establishing their own government independent of Stockholm and at the same time threatening to lay waste the country should there be any resistance to invading troops. This appears to have been the result of reports of discontent in Finland received from Michael Petrovitch Bestuzhev-Ryumin, the Russian envoy in Stockholm. In 1740 he had established contact with elements opposed to the Hat administration, and pressed his government to seize Finland as the only way to secure Russia from a future Swedish threat. But it may equally have been inspired by Colonel Lagercrantz, the representative of the Holstein cause in St Petersburg.[33]

The manifesto in any case evinced no response, and in June the Russian army crossed the border. The Swedish officers opposing it, their spirits undermined by enforced idleness and political faction, were quite unprepared for a fresh campaign and retreated before it. In August Helsinki surrendered after a siege of only two weeks. The Swedish fleet, though stronger than the Russian, was put out of action by disease. Encouraged by this success, Elizabeth again called on the Finns to free themselves, although on this occasion there was no mention of Finnish independence, and with the withdrawal of all Swedish forces from the country, she claimed it as hers by right of conquest.[34]

The Hat government sought to save itself by raising the question of the succession to the Swedish throne. Queen Ulrika Eleanora had died childless in November 1741, and support grew for the young duke of Holstein–Gottorp, Karl Peter Ulrich, whom Elizabeth had called to her court after her coup and whose claims to Slesvig she championed. Such a choice of heir, it was believed, might win from Russia concessions at the peace negotiations. King Christian VI of Denmark, alarmed by the threat of a duke of Holstein–Gottorp with the resources of Sweden at his disposal, also put forward a claim to the succession on behalf of his son

Prince Frederik, backed by promises of aid from the Danish army and fleet in the reconquest of Finland. He was strongly supported by the Swedish peasantry. The tsarina further informed Sweden in December 1742 that she had chosen the duke to be her own heir, and a majority on the Russian Council supported the idea of retaining Finland or at least of the establishment of a Finnish puppet state, to form a barrier against a Francophile Sweden.[35]

This idea was favoured by Alexei Bestuzhev-Ryumin, brother of the Russian envoy in Sweden and Elizabeth's chief adviser on foreign affairs.[36] His views on Russia's alliance system were not dissimilar to those of his rival Ostermann, but he favoured a more aggressive approach and one which would justify the continuation of the war. For him Prussia was a threat in particular to Russia's hold on Poland and its ambitions must be opposed in collaboration with England and Austria.[37]

The tsarina herself, faced with the possibility of a Danish prince on the Swedish throne and an eventual Scandinavian union, rejected the idea in favour of returning most of the country to Sweden in return for Sweden's acceptance as prospective ruler of the duke's cousin and heir, Duke Adolf Frederick of Holstein–Gottorp–Eutin, bishop of Lübeck, to whose brother Elizabeth had once been engaged. The Hats were faced by a peasant revolt on behalf of the Dane and decided to accept the offer. On these terms therefore peace was finally concluded in Åbo (Turku) in June 1743. Finland was deprived of another slice of southern Karelia including the port of Fredrikshamn (Hamina), and its frontier was pushed still further from St Petersburg, to the Kymmene river.[38]

Since the previous crisis in 1727, Denmark had sought closer relations with Sweden with the object of lessening Russian dominance in the Baltic and its reliance on alliances with great European powers, which might have deleterious consequences. After the breach between France and Britain in the early 1730s, Denmark had received subsidies from Britain, then closely associated with Russia and Austria. But Britain was always reluctant to pay subsidies in peacetime and consequently an unreliable paymaster. King Christian VI, who came to the throne in 1730 and, like his father, took direct control of foreign affairs, hoped for a dynastic union between the two Scandinavian monarchies, and in 1731, with French encouragement, offered his neighbour an alliance. Negotiations on this broke down, however, on the question of Slesvig and in May 1732 Denmark concluded an alliance with Russia and the Emperor. Christian had more success three years later when the Hats captured the Secret Committee and agreed to a five-year defensive alliance. After the fall of Horn and against the increasing likelihood of war with Russia, Christian, as has been seen, did offer assistance in exchange for the return of Bohuslän.[39]

Denmark even followed Sweden into the French camp in.1740, and in 1742, after the expiry of the treaty it had made with England in 1739, it concluded a five-year alliance with that country promising neutrality in exchange for subsidies and French support in negotiations being conducted in Stockholm. The election of Adolf Fredrik as heir to the Swedish throne not only dashed King Christian's hopes of an eventual union of the two monarchies but also revived the immediate danger to the Slesvig settlement, which it had become the main aim of Danish foreign policy to defend. Adolf Fredrik might well use Russian support to back his own claims to the Gottorp inheritance in the event of the death of Duke Peter without heirs. The Danish king therefore refused to recognize Adolf Fredrik unless he should renounce his claims in Slesvig. When the latter refused to do so, the Danish army and navy were mobilized for an attack on Scania from Zealand and on Bohuslän from Norway. In response, the Russian high seas fleet put to sea to join the Swedish navy in protecting the Swedish coast, and 12,000 Russian troops were in October brought over to Sweden and stationed in the vicinity of Norrköping and Nyköping.[40]

A Baltic war seemed inevitable. But King Christian found himself isolated. Under strong British and French pressure but in face of Russian intrigues, both sides agreed in February 1744 to reduce their forces. The tension consequently eased, and the Russian troops were withdrawn from Sweden in July.[41]

In Adolf Fredrik the tsarina had imagined she had found a ready tool of Russian policy in Sweden, now even more necessary for Russia to gain because of its loss of Brandenburg–Prussia to France. In June 1745 she forced on the Swedes an alliance which promised the latter 400,000 roubles for four years in exchange for a Swedish engagement to back Duke Peter of Holstein–Gottorp's claims to Slesvig. But the new Swedish heir fell more and more under the influence of the Hat chancellor Karl Gustav Tessin, who worked hard for reconciliation with Denmark and who had even envisaged a Danish marriage for Adolf Fredrik. This had, however, been strongly opposed by Britain, and in July 1744 Adolf Fredrik had in fact married Princess Lovisa Ulrika, the sister of France's ally, Frederick II of Prussia, which opened for Sweden the possibility of closer ties with the latter to balance Russian influence. Lovisa dominated her pliant husband from the start and, in exchange for vague promises to modify the constitution to strengthen royal power, worked with Tessin to persuade Adolf Fredrik to abandon his claims to the Gottorp inheritance.[42]

Largely as a result of the clumsy attempts made by the new Russian envoy Johann Albrecht von Korff and his government to influence by bribery the elections, the pro-Russian Cap party failed to gain the power it hoped for in the Swedish Diet of 1746–7. More and more frustrated, Bestuzhev resorted to military threats: twenty-six galleys with 4,000 men on board were sent to Reval and at the urgings of the Caps, backed by Korff, at the beginning of 1747 100,000 troops were drawn up on the Russo–Finnish border, and a Russian squadron appeared in the waters off Helsinki in the summer.[43]

Korff threatened Adolf Fredrik himself. The king, however, countered with a bold declaration of his loyalty to the regime, whose authority was only strengthened by such measures; an alliance, which Russia had long tried to frustrate, was at last concluded with Prussia and the alliance with France renewed for ten years. The Cap party disintegrated. Russia failed to get either British or Danish support for action, and tension relaxed again in the spring of 1748, when 37,000 Russian troops left for the Rhine to fight in the last campaign of the War of the Austrian Succession.[44]

But when this came to an end with the peace of Aix-la-Chapelle in August, the danger of war in the Baltic returned. A Russian army again gathered on the border, and the Swedes countered with defensive measures. But now Bestuzhev, who had appeared in an unassailable position within the Russian administration, found that the failure of his aggressive plans was seriously threatening his standing within the circle of Elizabeth's advisers.[45]

His attempts to gain Denmark's support had proved unsuccessful in 1747. With the death of Christian VI in 1746, domestic and foreign policy had slipped from the royal grasp; the new king, Frederik V, faithfully supported his ministers but took little interest in what they were doing. In foreign policy this did not result in any appreciable change of direction; Count Johann Sigmund Schulin, who had been chief secretary in the foreign section of the Chancery since 1735, continued in office and came to direct Danish diplomatic activity with his main aim to ensure the security of Slesvig by peaceful means. War was to be resorted to only as a final option. In 1748 he again turned down Bestuzhev's proposals for an attack on Sweden to replace Adolf Fredrik as heir and deprive it of Finland; in spite of the carrot of the Scanian provinces held out to him, Schulin would not risk involvement. And Britain, having just emerged from an exhausting war in the west, warned Russia against any disturbance of the 'Peace of the North'.[46]

Even the tsarina, in spite of her hatred of Adolf Fredrik, failed to back her chancellor. He found himself faced with the threat of an attack from both France and Prussia. At the beginning of 1749, fearing that war might yet break out, he made a final bid for Danish support. This time Schulin, not wishing to risk a rift with Russia, himself proposed an alliance by which Denmark would gain Scania, Halland and Bohuslän in the event of a war aimed at changing the succession to the Swedish throne.[47]

Frederick of Prussia had encouraged his sister in the spring of 1748 to take advantage of the expected death of the king and the absence of Russian forces on the Rhine to restore the power of the Swedish monarchy. Now, however, alarmed by these threats of war, he warned Lovisa to avoid giving the tsarina any excuse to intervene in Sweden on the pretext of the seventh clause in the peace of Nystad, which, so the Russians claimed, forbade any changes in the constitution. He now persuaded Britain to join him in urging caution also in St Petersburg and in the spring mobilized his army.[48]

In fact, under the combined pressure of Tessin, his own wife and the French envoy, who offered subsidies, Adolf Fredrik finally agreed to surrender his rights of inheritance to the Gottorp lands in both Slesvig and Holstein in exchange for the duchies of Oldenburg and Delmenhorst near the Dutch border, which had been inherited by the Danish crown in 1667. A preliminary agreement based on this was concluded in Stockholm in August 1749 and ratified the following April. With it the Danes lost interest in a Russian alliance. The Dano–Swedish alliance of 1734 was indeed renewed for fifteen years in October, and France concluded a six-year subsidy treaty with Denmark. Even closer links between Denmark and Sweden seemed envisaged with the engagement in January 1751 of Crown Prince Gustavus to the Danish princess Sofia Magdalena. The accession to the Swedish throne of the prince's father Adolf Fredrik three months before had been accepted by the Russians without demur. The crisis was finally over. Bestuzhev decided to confine himself for the time being to a threat to send troops into Finland should a new king of Sweden attempt to change the constitution, and negotiations for an alliance with Denmark came to an end in November with the latter's rejection of Russian proposals.[49]

The problem of the Gottorp lands, however, remained a bone of contention between Denmark and Russia, where Duke Peter stubbornly refused to surrender any of his claims. As Sweden seemed to be slipping from her grasp Tsarina Elizabeth proved more willing to accommodate Denmark. In 1746 she had promised to try to persuade the duke to reach a settlement and to work for an amicable solution. But until this could be achieved, Elizabeth's death could be expected to cause a further crisis in the Baltic.[50]

10

MID-CENTURY CRISES
(1750–72)

The Baltic crisis which followed the peace of Åbo had ended in a sharp rebuff for Russia's attempts to turn Sweden into a satellite state; it was never again to come so close to achieving this goal. The crisis had also brought about a rapprochement between Denmark and Sweden under the aegis of France, symbolized by the abandonment of Adolf Fredrik's claims to the Gottorp inheritance, the betrothal of his son Gustav to the Danish princess Sofia Magdalena and an agreement in October 1751 concerning the delimitation of the frontier between Norway and Sweden. This was all fully in accord with the aims of Johan Hartvig Ernst Bernstorff, who was effectively in control of Denmark's foreign policy from 1750 to 1770.[1] Years of suspicion, however, stood in the way of long-lasting genuine friendship between the two powers.

At the same time Frederick of Prussia found himself dangerously isolated; by the end of 1750 his relations with Russia had been broken off and those between Sweden and Prussia, in spite of the dynastic ties between them, cooled until in August 1755 the Prussian envoy in Stockholm was withdrawn. This isolation played its part in the build-up to the Seven Years War, in which all the Baltic powers except Denmark were involved.[2]

The so-called 'Diplomatic Revolution' of 1756, on the eve of the war, involving as it did both Prussia and Russia, had itself widespread repercussions in the Baltic; when the Seven Years War broke out the following year with Frederick of Prussia's attack on Saxony, he found himself faced by his former ally France allied to its age-long enemy Austria and to Russia. Bestuzhev-Ryumin regarded Prussia as the most immediate threat to Russia's position on the Baltic ('its eternal and natural enemy') and entertained ambitious plans to partition Frederick's territories and extend Russian influence to the Elbe as had been done briefly in the days of Peter the Great. Sweden's French ties brought it into the war against Prussia in Pomerania, with humiliating consequences. The accession to the Russian throne in 1762 of the pro-Prussian duke of Holstein–Gottorp as Tsar Peter III brought peace between Russia, Prussia and Sweden, but led to a threat of war between Russia and Denmark, from which only Peter's murder saved the Baltic.[3]

The new Russian regime led by Peter's German widow Catherine II agreed to settle the Gottorp question by negotiation rather than force of arms. But in order to achieve this Bernstorff abandoned Denmark's long-standing ties with France and agreed to work with Russia to prevent any strengthening of Swedish power. In Sweden the triumph of the 'Younger Caps', opponents of the pro-French Hats, in the Diet of 1765 was seen as a triumph for Russian influence in the country a year after Tsarina Catherine's former lover, Stanislas Poniatowski, had been elected to the Polish throne. Russian influence again appeared to be dominant in the Baltic; it seemed that the anti-French and -Austrian 'Northern System' of alliances devised by Catherine II's foreign minister Nikita Panin was carrying all before it. His dream was, however, shattered by the reaction in Sweden which enabled the young King Gustavus III to carry through a bloodless coup d'etat in 1772 with French support. This not only destroyed Russian influence in Sweden but, as Catherine had feared, revived Swedish thoughts of revanche in the east. The following year the First Partition of Poland represented a further blow to Russian hopes of surrounding itself with satellite states.

In Denmark after 1750, J. H. E. Bernstorff continued Schulin's policy in its broad outlines: to secure a peaceful settlement with Russia of the Gottorp problem; to avoid entangling Denmark in wars in which her national interests were not directly involved; to prevent the emergence of a strong monarchical government in Sweden; to maintain friendship with France, who could hopefully keep Russian ambitions in check; and in general to maintain the 'Tranquility of the North', any breach of which would most likely strengthen Russian power still further and interfere with Baltic commerce on which the wealth of the kingdom so largely depended. Peace also appealed to Bernstorff as director of

Denmark's economic policy, which could benefit so much from the country's neutrality while other powers exhausted themselves.[4]

His anxiety to achieve the settlement of the Gottorp question intensified with the birth of a son to Duke Karl Peter of Gottorp in 1754. With French encouragement, he and the Swedish chancellors Anders Johan von Höpken and Carl Fredrik Scheffer worked amicably together to maintain tranquillity in the area, from which both could benefit, and in July 1756 the two powers concluded a new neutrality league.[5] When war threatened between the great powers the following year and news came of a British fleet sailing for the Baltic, Sweden proposed the closing of the Sound. Bernstorff, however, rejected the idea, and shortly afterwards Sweden became a belligerent. The Diplomatic Revolution and Anglo–French colonial rivalry had brought war to the Baltic once more.[6]

The Diplomatic Revolution can be traced to the conclusion of an agreement between Britain and Russia in 1755 by which, in exchange for subsidies, Russia would dissuade France's ally Prussia from an attack on Hanover in the event of the Anglo–French colonial struggle spreading to Europe by drawing up an army of 80,000 men in Livonia and adjacent regions. It seemed that Bestuzhev might at last have the war to destroy Prussian power of which he had dreamed so long. To counter this in January 1756 Frederick of Prussia concluded with Britain the so-called Convention of Westminster which committed the two parties to defend the peace in the Empire. France regarded the convention as a hostile act and gave way to proposals from its ancient enemy Austria for a defensive alliance. By means of this the latter, long disillusioned by its alliance with Britain, hoped to recover Silesia from Prussia, to which it had been lost in the previous conflict.[7]

The Convention of Westminster had seemed to remove the *raison d'être* of the Russian subsidy convention with Britain; again Bestuzhev appeared to have been deprived of an opportunity to destroy Prussian power. But in March 1756 at a meeting of a small 'conference' of ministers which Bestuzhev hoped to dominate more easily than the full Senate, he won over the tsarina to the idea of war with Prussia and outlined Russia's war aims: Frederick was to be deprived of East Prussia, which was to be exchanged with Poland for areas round Smolensk and Pskov, and of Pomerania which was to go to Sweden. Kurland was to become a Russian dependency.[8]

Bestuzhev also considered acquiring Memel as an advanced base for the Russian galley fleet. The dismemberment of Brandenburg–Prussia would not only end the potential threat that it would lead an anti-Russian coalition in the Baltic, but the acquisition of large slices of Lithuania would give Russia complete control of valuable hemp- and timber-growing areas and of the main trade routes between the Baltic and the Black Sea. The chancellor had managed to maintain the bulk of the Russian foot regiments in the area of the Baltic provinces, whence they could strike against either Sweden or Prussia, and by the autumn of 1756 they were ready for action against the latter. The mobilization of the cavalry, the most neglected arm of the service, however, took longer, while the artillery lacked horses.[9]

But in any case, fearing, with some justification, an Austrian-inspired assault on his dominions, Frederick II replied in August 1756 with what he regarded as a pre-emptive strike at Austria through Saxony. In fulfilment of its treaty obligations, Russia was at last able to march against Frederick through Poland. While Bestuzhev had long dreamed of striking such a blow, he had never imagined that it would be carried out as an ally of France.[10]

Sweden, summoned by Austria to fulfil her obligations as guarantor of the Westphalian peace settlement, finally assaulted Prussia from its Pomeranian base in September 1757. In the late 1740s, the Hats had adopted a much needed programme of strengthening Sweden's defences. The defences of Scania, based on Landskrona, were improved, and the great fortress of Svea-borg on the archipelago outside Helsinki was developed under the direction of Augustin Ehrensvärd from 1748. This was to serve as the base for an expanded galley fleet, which numbered as many as forty-two two-masted ships as early as 1749. Henceforward this was to be superior in all respects to its sole potential opponent – the Russian galley fleet. In 1756 it was decided to separate this from the main fleet and place it under army command. But for the high seas fleet, which it had been envisaged by a plan drawn up in 1734 to make as large as the largest fleet in the Baltic, little was done. This was partly because of lack of resources, partly because of disagreements about the type of ships needed and partly because it was assumed that the main threat came from the east rather than from the much larger Danish fleet in the south. Preparations for a German war were inadequate. The army of some 48,000 men was better trained and led than in the war with Russia, but in spite of the French subsidies, there was simply not enough money to pay for adequate equipment for the forces in Pomerania and on two occasions in the course of the subsequent campaign the commander had to pledge his own fortune to ensure supplies for his men.[11]

As in 1674, France looked to Sweden to draw Prussian forces away from the main battlefields further south and east. But to the more bellicose elements within governing Hat circles, led by the brothers Carl and Ulrik Scheffer, an attack on the seemingly isolated Prussian king offered an opportunity for territorial gains, in particular control once more of Stralsund and the mouth of the Oder, and possibly the rest of Pomerania, at apparently little risk; the new chancellor Höpken even hoped that a grateful France might surrender one of its West Indian islands. War with Prussia also offered a further chance to punish Frederick II's sister, Queen Lovisa Ulrika, for an attempt which she had made to overturn the existing constitution in 1756 but which had led only to a further diminution of the powers of the crown. Frederick had been generally blamed in Sweden for having encouraged the royalists' ambitions, although he had in fact done his best to restrain them. He was also suspected of having designs on Sweden's Pomeranian foothold.[12]

But the Swedish Council was divided. Its instruction from the Estates was unclear since this called for a policy of peace while using any possibility to expand the realm, and constitutionally an offensive war needed the Estates' approval. At first Sweden tried to confine itself to diplomatic action, but Austria and France insisted on binding agreements, which were concluded in September 1757. They promised to restore to Sweden the parts of Pomerania which had been lost since 1648. The Estates were never consulted and, as in the 1670s, war was never officially declared. The action was justified largely as one to restore the peace of the Empire which Frederick had disturbed by his attack on Saxony.[13]

The subsequent Pomeranian campaigns brought no greater glory to Swedish arms than had those of the 1670s, and only exacerbated the financial and economic crisis into which Hat policies had already plunged the country. In 1757 Swedish troops did succeed in occupying the mouth of the Oder, but the following year were driven back to Stralsund. Only after Frederick II's defeat at the battle of Künersdorf in 1759 and the wholesale withdrawal of Prussian forces from Pomerania to face the more serious threat in the east was the Swedish commander tempted to return to the offensive; a Prussian flotilla of four galiots and four small galleys on the Stettiner Haf was captured by Swedish galleys, and the islands of Usedom and Wollin at the mouth of the Oder were again occupied.[14] But in accordance with what was becoming an established pattern, the Prussians were back on the Peene in 1760. The Swedish war chest was now empty, and the opposition in the Diet to the war threatening. At the end of 1761 the Secret Committee urged the conclusion of peace on the best possible terms. Humiliatingly the government turned to the queen with a request to intercede with her brother. In April 1762 she wrote to Frederick, who agreed to open negotiations in Hamburg the same month.[15]

Russian armies in 1757 had marched into East Prussia, taking Memel on the way. They had defeated the Prussians at Gross Jägersdorf in August, but had then had to withdraw because of their faulty supply system. For this failure Bestuzhev had to pay the price; he was dismissed and banished to his estates. In the course of the war, however, the Russian army, though still with weaknesses, grew to be a formidable force. Danzig was occupied and Frederick withdrew into Brandenburg, where he fought a desperate action against Russian, Austrian and French armies in turn. He was defeated by the Russians at Künersdorf, and Berlin was occupied for a time. East Prussia was declared annexed and given a Russian governor.[16]

At the beginning of 1762 the whole situation in the Baltic changed dramatically. The fiercely anti-Prussian Tsarina Elizabeth died and was succeeded by the duke of Holstein–Gottorp as Peter III, an equally passionate admirer of all things Prussian. News of the tsarina's illness had already led to the withdrawal of Russian troops from East Prussia. Now all hostilities between Russia and Prussia came to an abrupt halt. Peter had refused all the efforts of Bernstorff and Elizabeth to reach a settlement of his claims to the Gottorp lands in Slesvig, and he now dreamed of using the resources of Russia to back up these claims and even to drive the Oldenburgs off the Danish throne. In anticipation of Elizabeth's death, Denmark had already begun mobilizing in 1761 and sought help from both Britain and Prussia.[17]

Sweden's anxiety for peace encouraged Peter to hope for its assistance in his enterprise. Under Höpken, Sweden had been drawing closer to Russia while relations with Denmark cooled, and in 1758 had rejected an invitation from Bernstorff to join the Russo–Danish agreement on Slesvig for fear of offending the tsarina. In June Höpken renewed the Russo–Swedish alliance for twelve years. Both Denmark and Sweden were alarmed in 1760 by a Russian demand for East Prussia as its price for entering the Franco–Danish–Austrian alliance, but this was dropped in face of protests from France and Britain, and in the autumn of 1761 the Swedish Council had come out strongly in favour of close collaboration with Russia.[18]

Peter particularly needed the Swedish fleet. Russia's fleet, in spite of efforts under Elizabeth to build it up, consisted in 1762 of no more than fifteen ships of the line and four frigates. Even with the Archangel squadron, which Peter immediately ordered to the Baltic from the White Sea, this was no match for the naval resources of Denmark–Norway. The Swedes, however, did not wish to be involved beyond granting the right of passage to Russian troops in Pomerania, in spite of a suggestion that it take Norway as a reward for participating in the war with Denmark and of support from Prussia for Russian diplomacy in Stockholm.[19]

In May 1762, Frederick of Prussia, having at first demanded Usedom, Wollin and Demmin, or at least the closing of the Oder at Swinemünde (Świnousście) as his price of peace with Sweden, agreed to conclude on the basis of the status quo 'out of love for his sister'. The next month he bound himself to Peter III by agreeing to use diplomatic means to secure the restoration of Slesvig to the house of Holstein–Gottorp and to provide 20,000 troops for a forceful solution should this fail. The tsar drew up an army of 40,000 in Pomerania, while 27,000 Danish troops advanced into Mecklenburg from the west. A clash seemed inevitable, when news came in July of Peter's overthrow in favour of his wife Catherine and his subsequent murder.[20]

Catherine ordered the withdrawal of Russian troops from north Germany and finally engaged with Bernstorff to reach a peaceful settlement of the Gottorp question by the time that her son Paul, the inheritor of the Gottorp claims, should come of age in ten years' time. She wished to settle the dispute so that she could devote her energies to the (for Russia) much more pressing problems of Poland and Turkey. In all this she was backed by Nikita Ivanovitch Panin, former Russian envoy in Stockholm and court chamberlain to Tsar Peter III, who was effectively in charge of

Russian foreign policy from the end of 1763. He was joined by Casper von Saldern, a Holsteiner who had entered the service of Peter III but who believed in a peaceful settlement of the Gottorp question as part of a general 'Pacification of the North'.[21]

Panin also wished for a pacification as part of his 'Northern System'. This involved close alliances with Denmark, Britain and Brandenburg–Prussia and support of pro-Russian factions in Sweden and Poland. Bernstorff on his side was willing to abandon Denmark's ties with France and to allow Catherine a free hand in Poland, where the death of Augustus III in October 1763 threatened to bring about a new crisis, if agreement over Slesvig could be reached. He had become disillusioned with France, who had been remiss in paying subsidies and who was suspected of encouraging royal ambitions in Sweden. At the same time, while he wished to keep Sweden weak, he feared that Russia aimed to turn it into a satellite kingdom, and Catherine for her part long treated Denmark with some suspicion, especially after Bernstorff had appointed Danish regents in Holstein in accordance with an agreement reached with Adolf Fredrik.[22]

A Dano–Russian eight-year defensive alliance was finally concluded in March 1765, but it was not until April 1767 that agreement was reached over the Gottorp lands by means of the *Mageskifte* or exchange of territories. This followed the lines of the agreement which Denmark had made earlier with the Swedish king: the Danish crown was guaranteed permanent possession of all the Gottorp lands in the Duchies in exchange for heavy monetary compensation and the counties of Oldenburg and Delmenhorst on the North Sea coast of Germany, which were to be ruled by a younger branch of the Gottorp family as soon as Paul should come of age. The treaty thus did not come into force until 1773. But with its conclusion one of the principal aims of Danish foreign policy for the previous fifty years, indeed since the middle of the previous century, had been achieved. From Russia's point of view the danger of a Danish alliance with France, which would increase Russia's isolation, had been averted. And from a wider perspective, the danger of a Russian naval base at Kiel was also removed.[23]

Part of the price which Denmark had to pay for its settlement with Russia over the Gottorp lands was agreement to assist the tsarina in maintaining the existing Swedish constitution against attempts by rulers to strengthen monarchical power, which was seen to be inevitably in the interest of France. It thus ran the risk of becoming involved in a large-scale war, from which it could expect little benefit.[24]

Frederick II of Prussia, more isolated than ever after the Seven Years War, also turned to Russia for support, and also had to pay a price. In April 1764 he concluded an eight-year defensive alliance with Catherine by which each party engaged to take joint action should the Swedish constitution seem to be threatened by its domestic critics. Prussia was also to support the Russian candidate on the throne of Poland, where Frederick regained some of the influence which had been lost with the ascendancy of Bestuzhev. Denmark confirmed its commitment to act similarly in its alliance concluded the following year. In fact Panin's policy in Sweden was to break the links between the Hats and the court and to bind the royal couple (in whom, however, he had little faith) to the Caps with promises to restore the constitution at least to its original form with the Council more dependent on the Estates than it had shown itself to be in 1756.[25]

But the annihilation of the Hats was not considered in Russian interests, and the triumph of the Caps in the Diet called at the beginning of 1765 to deal with the rapidly deteriorating financial situation was much greater than either Catherine or Frederick of Prussia had envisaged or considered desirable. And it did not lead to the Russian hegemony in Sweden which Panin had planned and which both Bernstorff and King Frederick feared. The Caps were disillusioned by Britain and Russia's failure to replace with any tangible benefits the French subsidies enjoyed by their predecessors and by Panin's aggressive policy in Poland. Their deflationary economic policy proved to be no more successful than the inflationary one of their predecessors, and the court, disappointed in its hopes of constitutional reform, swung back again to the Hats. These returned to power at the beginning of 1769 after the king had forced the calling of the Diet by threatening to vacate the throne and by a strike of the Hat-dominated civil service.[26]

In these circumstances, rumours soon spread that a new attempt would be made to increase royal power in Sweden. Russia consequently called on the Danes to mobilize, at the same time dangling before their eyes the lure of Swedish territory. In February Denmark responded. Indeed French threats drove Bernstorff even closer to Russia, to which he offered yet more binding agreements; he proposed a landing in Scania and the immediate implementation of the *Mageskifte*. In these, however, Catherine could see no profit, though she did agree to guarantee Holstein. The new Hat regime in Stockholm ordered military counter-measures, in face of which Denmark began to back down. Frederick of Prussia was not convinced of the danger which the Hat victory was supposed to represent and had no wish to be drawn into war. He attempted to calm the waters, but in October nevertheless renewed his agreement with the tsarina and promised to occupy the Swedish part of Pomerania should the Swedish court threaten the constitution in specific ways. Denmark, fearing isolation, made a new treaty with Russia at the end of the year; any change of the Swedish constitution was now to be a *casus belli*, and both sides were to seek territorial compensation in the event of intervention. A joint Dano–Russian squadron had already been sailing the waters of the southern Baltic.[27]

Meanwhile in Sweden party rancour reached new heights. The accession of Prince Gustav as Gustavus III in 1771 offered new hope to his subjects. In Potsdam, on his way back to his country from France, where he had been when he received the news of his father's death, his uncle, King Frederick, urged on him the desirability of reconciling the Hats and the Caps and of retaining Russia's friendship. But the Caps swept to power in the Diet called to mark the change of ruler, and used their position in such a way as to make all the king's attempts at reconciliation vain. He decided on more drastic action. On 19 August 1772 he carried through a bloodless coup d'etat which led to the introduc-tion of a fresh constitution. This restored to the crown something of the position it had enjoyed in the earlier seventeenth century. Panin's 'Northern System' lay in ruins.[28]

His ability to act in Sweden had been hampered by distractions in Poland, by the renewal of hostilities against the Turks and by developments in Denmark. Events in Poland after the election in September 1764 of Catherine's former lover Stanisław-August Poniatowski to the throne as Stanislas Augustus with the help of Russian bayonets had revived the 'alliance of the three eagles' (i.e. those in the arms of Austria, Prussia and Russia) which had been broken at the beginning of the War of the Austrian Succession. The Russian action had been taken in accordance with an agree-ment the previous April between the tsarina and Frederick of Prussia, who wished to exclude the new Elector of Saxony. A

Russian hegemony was imposed through Catherine's envoy, prince Nikolai Repnin, who used the cause of religious dissidents to defeat all attempts to introduce political and military reforms such as had been effectively quashed by Russian intervention earlier in the century but which now threatened to make Poland once more an effective force in eastern Europe and thus menacing to both Russia and Prussia. In reply, confederations of Polish nobles were formed to fight for such reforms. The tsarina countered with her own confederations and troops. When these violated Turkish territory the Turks declared war in October 1768.[29]

At the time of the Swedish crisis of 1769 the Russian fleet was preparing to sail to the Mediterranean and troops had been withdrawn from the Russian frontier with Finland to march to Poland or to face the Turks. In Denmark Bernstorff had been toppled from power in September 1770. The new dominating figure in Danish politics was the German court physician Johann Friedrich Struensee. Having been pushed forward by a group of young nobles who wished to use the royal powers to introduce reforms in the monarchy, he acquired dictatorial powers to conceal his illicit relationship with the young English queen. Struensee did not wish to break the Russian alliance, but he did aim to make Denmark less dependent on the tsarina and had no wish to be drawn into Swedish affairs. He called Adolph von der Osten from the Danish embassy in Naples to take charge of foreign affairs, of which Struensee himself had no experience. At the beginning of 1772 he was overthrown and executed after having alienated all the influential groups in Danish society by a stream of reforms. Catherine was much happier with his conservative successors led by the king's ex-tutor Ove Høegh-Guldberg. And in August she signed with Prussia and Austria the First Polish Partition treaty.[30]

The idea of a partition of Poland had, as has been seen, a history reaching back to the middle of the sixteenth century. It had more recently been discussed in the Russian College of War before the election of Stanislas Poniatowski; Count Zachar Chernyschev, the College's vice-president, had then proposed on strategic and economic grounds the annexation, when the throne should again fall vacant, of the area east of the Dvina and Dnieper rivers. But on this occasion Catherine and Panin preferred an undivided Poland as long as it could be under Russian tutelage.[31]

Which power was most responsible for beginning the process

which led to the the actual implementation of the plan is the subject of dispute. Certainly Frederick of Prussia had most to gain. He had no wish to be drawn into another war, and his engagements to Catherine II now threatened to involve him in a conflict with Austria, whose relations with Russia were becoming strained because of a clash of interests in the Balkans. A partition would also allow him to gain at a stroke West or royal Prussia, his only remaining territorial ambition but one which he had written of as acquiring 'like an artichoke, leaf by leaf'.[32]

From Catherine's point of view partition was a *pis aller* after attempts to control the whole country had proved to be too expensive. But it would give her large areas of territory which could be absorbed into the Russian Empire and might bind both Prussia and Austria more closely to her. An initial plan put forward by Prussia in 1768 came to naught, but gradually Panin, threatened by continuing resistance to Russian forces in Poland and by a nascent anti-Russian coalition between Austria and Turkey, had to give way before the urgings of his critics, and negotiations between Russia and Prussia opened in 1771. The final treaty, completed on 25 July/5 August 1772 after Austria's agreement at the beginning of the year, gave to Russia just those areas which Bestuzhev-Ryumin had envisaged exchanging with Poland for East Prussia, and to Prussia the long desired links between Brandenburg and East Prussia, though without control of the mouth of the Vistula; Danzig, which Frederick had originally demanded as part of his share, remained nominally under the Polish crown, though separated from the rest of the Commonwealth by Prussian territory. The *Sejm* had no choice but to submit to the butchery of the Republic, which it did formally in September 1773.[33]

11

THE AGE OF GUSTAVUS III
(1772–90)

Gustavus III's coup d'etat caused an immediate crisis in the Baltic, more serious than the one which had threatened its peace after the Hat victory in 1768. The guarantee of the Swedish constitution of 1720 to which Russia, Denmark and Prussia were committed was thereby activated. But both Russia and Prussia were deeply involved in Poland, where the First Partition treaty was to be implemented the following year, and Russia failed to bring an end to its war with the Turks. Denmark was in no position to act alone, and was easily persuaded to accept Gustavus III's assurances of his peaceful intentions towards it.

During the following two decades, the relations between the powers in the area were largely dictated by the supposed intentions of the Swedish monarch. Neither Denmark, Prussia nor Russia had any serious ambitions for territorial expansion in the Baltic; Frederick II was only vaguely tempted by the small area of Pomerania still under Swedish control, and even if Catherine II would have been glad to have seen an autonomous Finland under Russia's protection, her attention was drawn more and more to the Black Sea for the remainder of her reign. And for the first ten years of his reign Gustavus himself appeared to be content with the status quo; while his relations with Denmark were never cordial, he entered into personal negotiations with the Russian empress.

As opposition to his domestic policies grew, however, he turned more and more to foreign policy as a means not only of strengthening his position at home but also of fulfilling his dreams of reviving Sweden's past glories. Plans to strike at Denmark in 1784 in order to deprive it of Norway had to be abandoned after the tsarina had made her opposition clear and indeed led to a rapid cooling in Swedo–Russian relations. Catherine's involvement in a new war with the Turks seemed, as to Swedish rulers in the past, to offer him a chance to make gains in the eastern Baltic. His attack over the Finnish frontier in 1788 brought Denmark into a war for the first time in nearly seventy years, and while the situation enabled Gustavus to establish what amounted to an absolutist system of government in Sweden and brought the Swedish navy its final triumph, peace was made in 1790 on the basis of the status quo. Gustavus's only gain was the abandonment by Catherine of Russia's claim to interfere in Sweden's internal affairs. The last serious challenge to Russia's dominant position in the Baltic before the twentieth century had ended in failure.

The constitution which Gustavus introduced after his coup allowed the monarch much greater scope in foreign affairs than had its predecessor. He was able to make treaties and conduct a defensive war without reference to the Diet, which was now to be called only when he felt he needed to consult it. He also had a free hand in the selection of his councillors, whose advice he was, in any case, not obliged to follow. On the other hand he was not to launch an offensive war without the approval of the Diet, on which he continued to rely for the extraordinary taxes without which his operations would be hamstrung. Gustavus was intensely interested in foreign policy as a means to restore the prestige of his realm to that which it had enjoyed in the days of his hero Gustavus Adolphus. That his ambitions underestimated the resources he commanded and paid too little attention to the current diplomatic situation in Europe was to become apparent in the second decade of his reign after the retirement of Gustavus's first chancellor Ulrik Scheffer, an experienced and respected diplomat who exercised a moderating influence on the much younger monarch.[1]

His coup in 1772 was regarded with some justification as a triumph for French diplomacy and a blow at the Russo–Danish–Prussian alliance system in the Baltic, with which Britain was associated and which had aimed during the 1760s both to exclude French influence and to keep a potentially revanchist Sweden weak by guaranteeing a constitution which was believed to hinder the execution of an effective foreign policy. A new northern war now threatened. And it was one into which France, to defend its protégé, and Britain might be drawn on opposing sides. Denmark in particular feared a pre-emptive strike by the new Swedish regime, and not without justification, for Gustavus made threatening troop movements on the Norwegian border. But Lovisa Ulrika, who was in Berlin at the time of her son's coup, was able to persuade her brother, who saw no particular advantage in intervening against his nephew except to maintain his good relations with Russia, to make representations in St Petersburg on his behalf. The tsarina's forces were in any case tied down by the war with the Turks and her energies taken up by this and the consequences of the Polish partition treaties. Denmark consequently found itself somewhat isolated and tension relaxed.[2]

But it mounted again with the approach of the campaigning season in 1773. Rumours of Russian military preparations led Sweden to mobilize troops on the Finnish border and to call on France to send a fleet to the Baltic, and when Britain warned against this, orders were in fact sent to Toulon to begin the arming of ships to demonstrate against the Russian fleet in the Mediterranean. Before, however, any commitments had been entered into, Russo–Swedish relations, central to the whole issue, relaxed. In March Catherine's peace negotiations with the Turks broke down, and even before news of this reached St Petersburg, Gustavus's envoy to Russia, Johan Fredrik von Nolcken, found himself well received at the Russian court, at news of which the Swedish king began to run down his military preparations; Catherine II had decided to await a more favourable opportunity to attempt to reassert Russian influence in Stockholm. That the threat to Sweden remained was evident in the secret clauses of the Russo–Danish defence alliance concluded in August which envisaged action against Sweden to restore the old constitution as soon as conditions were more favourable.[3]

Tension in the Baltic, however, remained at a low level for the remainder of the decade. Russia finally made peace with the Turks at Küchük Kainardji in 1774, but this left the tsarina with many problems and temptations in the south. She also had to cope with the aftermath of the great Cossack rebellion led by Emilian Pugachov. For his part, Gustavus III was engaged in an extensive reform programme and for the time being supported the pacific policy favoured by his chancellor Ulrik Scheffer. The new conservative regime in Denmark had no foreign ambitions. And Frederick II's policy in Brandenburg–Prussia continued to be essentially pacific and defensive; he was much concerned during these years with the ambitions of the young co-ruler of the

Habsburg dominions, Emperor Joseph II. These constituted much more of a threat to Prussia than did any ambitions which might be entertained by Gustavus III, especially as Joseph II drew closer to the tsarina.[4]

This new move in Russian foreign policy away from Prussia towards Austria reflected the growing influence over the tsarina of Grigori Potemkin and the waning of Panin's star. In September 1781 the latter was replaced as chief adviser on foreign affairs by Alexander Bezborodko. He never exercised Panin's power and influence.[5]

Sweden's relations with both Denmark and Russia remained strained for some time after the coup. This forced Gustavus to rely heavily on his alliance with France for both diplomatic support and subsidies with which to create a military machine more effective than the one he had inherited. At the beginning of his reign he had no more than twenty-six ships of the line, of which only seven were immediately usable, and four seaworthy frigates with which to face the navies of Denmark and Russia; only three new warships had been launched during the fifteen years before the coup.[6]

And although a defence committee was set up in 1774, only slow progress was made in this sphere before the 1780s. Financial problems long limited Gustavus's options in foreign policy. His eventual aim had to be to break the links between his neighbours by weaning one away from the other, and in making a choice, Russia appeared to be the most promising target. He had inherited a deep antagonism towards and distrust of Denmark because of its policy towards the house of Holstein–Gottorp. And in Copenhagen the new foreign minister, Andreas Peter Bernstorff, nephew of J. H. E. Bernstorff, had little interest in a close association with Sweden at the risk of Denmark's Russian alliance. Gustavus made several approaches to Catherine in the early 1770s, but it was not until 1777 that he overcame French opposition to a meeting with the tsarina. This brought no immediate agreement; Catherine still refused even to recognize the new constitution. But it did result in a regular correspondence between the two monarchs.[7]

At the end of the decade the Swedish king found himself faced at home by increasing opposition, both to specific reforms like the state monopoly on home distilling introduced in an attempt to solve the persistent financial problem, and to his increasingly autocratic style of government, which alienated many of his former supporters, especially among the nobility. His original advisers began to be replaced by younger, less cautious men, who did little to restrain his growing desire to cut a dash on the international stage. A success abroad might also dampen criticism at home. His dislike of Denmark (which a loveless marriage to a Danish princess had done nothing to discourage) led him to revive ancient Swedish designs on Norway and to cultivate yet closer relations with the tsarina, whose neutrality at least must be assured in the event of a Swedo–Danish war.[8]

Much of his reforming enthusiasm was now directed towards his army and navy. On land a regular reserve was created, and in Finland the fortress of Sveaborg was completed and mobile units formed on the eastern borderlands. With the assistance of the designer Fredrik Henrik af Chapman, the son of an English naval officer who had in the 1760s worked with Ehrensvärd on the army's fleet in Finland, and under the able direction of Admiral Henrik af Trolle, was created an impressive high seas and army fleet, vital arms with which to face either Denmark or Russia. No fewer than eleven ships of the line and ten large frigates were built in the first half of the 1780s. No true galleys were built after the 1740s, but af Chapman had designed for Ehrensvärd in the 1760s three new types of small heavily armed vessel to co-operate with the army on the Finnish coast, each named after a Finnish province.[9]

The outbreak of war between Britain and France as a result of the War of American Independence led, as in the past, to co-operation between neutrals to protect their shipping. On this occasion, however, the lead was taken by Russia, which provided King Gustavus with a welcome opportunity to draw nearer to the tsarina, while in Denmark Bernstorff's reactions were hesitant for fear of offending Britain; as early as February 1779 an agreement was made between Russia and Sweden to the exclusion of Denmark. Denmark did, however, join the Armed Neutrality League formed by Catherine the following year with Sweden and Prussia. Bernstorff's conclusion almost immediately of a separate convention on contraband with Britain was deeply resented in St Petersburg and led to his fall from power in November.[10]

Bernstorff's fall did bring an improvement in Russo–Danish relations, but an opportunity for action seemed to present itself to Gustavus in 1783 when Catherine's occupation of the Crimea seemed to presage a Russo–Turkish war. Plans were rapidly evolved for a lightning strike against Denmark with the object of securing Norway. The motive was to be an attack on a Swedish frigate in the Sound. Catherine, disturbed by troop movements in Finland, invited the king to meet her at Fredrikshamn on the Russo–Finnish border at the end of June and beginning of July, which provided him with an opportunity to test her possible reactions to the Danish adventure. What exactly transpired at this meeting is not clear, but the Swedish king certainly did not obtain any firm agreement from Catherine. He had already been warned by his military adviser General Johan Christopher Toll and by Admiral Trolle against opening a campaign so late in the year, and in view of the failure of the expected Russo–Turkish war to materialize, he reluctantly decided to postpone the attack for twelve months. Military preparations went ahead, but implementation would have to depend on developments outside Sweden.[11]

To conceal his intentions, Gustavus set off in September on a European tour which took him as far south as Naples. The acceptance by the Turks of Russia's annexation of the Crimea in January 1784 persuaded him to order a temporary halt in military preparations, but it was not until April, when he was clearly informed by Catherine of her intention to fulfil her treaty obligations in the event of an attack on Denmark and by France of its refusal to give its support, that he finally abandoned the enterprise altogether. The tsarina's offer of a triple alliance to include Sweden and Denmark suggested her opposition to the very principles on which Gustavus's policy had been based. To accept such an offer would deprive him of all room to manoeuvre.[12]

While he never wholly abandoned his plans for a war with Denmark, the Swedish king turned more and more to thoughts of using a future diversion of Russian resources to strike at St Petersburg and force Catherine to disgorge at least the gains made by Russia at Sweden's expense since the Great Northern War earlier in the century, possibly even some of Peter I's conquests. Even while in Italy in 1783 Gustavus had contacted the Young Pretender in Florence, possibly in the belief that he could persuade the latter to grant him the succession to the headship of the Order of Teutonic Knights, who had retained a claim to Livonia. And in 1786 the Swedish minister in St Petersburg was instructed to investigate reports of unrest among the nobility and burghers of Livonia and Kurland after Catherine had undermined the privileges which had been guaranteed to them after they had become Russian subjects in 1721. The minister confirmed such reports, though his successor Nolcken in 1787 discounted the hope of revolt which might lead to a peasant rebellion against their masters.[13]

Relations between Sweden and Russia became increasingly strained; the Russian envoy in Stockholm negotiated with the Swedish opposition, while Catherine encouraged the small Finnish separatist party inspired by Göran Sprengtporten. Sprengtporten had been one of Gustavus's most enthusiastic supporters at the time of the coup in 1772, but he had become disillusioned with the king, and in 1786 entered Russian service and came to enjoy considerable influence at the Russian court. At the same time Gustavus's principal ally France grew disturbingly close to the latter.[14]

In August 1787 war broke out again between Russia and the Sultan, which drew the bulk of Catherine's army far from the Baltic. During a dramatic descent on the Danish court in Copenhagen in November, Gustavus failed to persuade A. P. Bernstorff, who had returned to power in 1784, to conclude an alliance which did not include Russia, and the new Prussian king, Frederick William II, was equally unwilling to promise his neutrality, let alone his active participation in a war against Russia. The Swedish king did, however, have reason to hope for British and Turkish subsidies and, on this slight basis, he secured a decision in the royal Council in April 1788 for the navy to seize control of the Gulf of Finland and for an amphibious landing to be made by the bulk of the Swedish forces at Oranienbaum in the vicinity of St Petersburg, which was defended only by some 18,000 troops. This was to be combined with an attack across the Finnish border against Fredrikshamn. Hopes of a rebellion in Livonia either by the nobility if their privileges were confirmed or by the peasantry might well have encouraged the enterprise, but an alternative plan for the main attack to be made through Livonia was rejected. This was partly because it would have given the Russians time to prepare the defence of St Petersburg, partly because it was still hoped that Prussia might be enticed into the war and Livonia would then be its obvious sphere of operations. Gustavus also possibly feared the consequences of a peasant uprising, which was also anticipated by the local Russian commander.[15]

Preparations for such an enterprise could not be kept wholly secret, and in March Russian mobilization began in the Baltic regions and warnings were sent from St Petersburg to Copenhagen. But the bulk of the tsarina's land forces were concentrated against the Turks, and even a large part of the main fleet was equipped to sail for the Mediterranean.[16]

In spite of having failed to secure support for his enterprise from any power and in face of a threat by Denmark to fulfil her treaty obligations to Russia in the event of a Swedish attack, Gustavus sailed for Finland in the middle of June and on the 28th came a border incident at Puumala to justify the declaration of war which followed. As the price of peace the tsarina was to surrender all those areas of Finland won by Russia in 1721 and 1743.[17]

The preparations for the campaign had been made with considerably more efficiency than for Sweden's previous eighteenth-century military enterprises, but the commanders of both the high seas and army fleets had warned the king that further time was needed to implement vital reforms, and at sea the war began ominously in July with an indecisive naval engagement off Hogland, near Borgå on the Finnish coast. The king's brother, Charles, duke of Södermanland, commanding a fleet of fifteen ships of the line and five frigates (somewhat over half the total number of Swedish ships) encountered a Russian force of seventeen battleships and seven frigates. After a fierce engagement in which each side had taken one of the other's ships, the action was broken off; the Swedes failed to re-engage because of shortage of ammunition. They were then blockaded in Helsinki Roads, whither they had retired for repairs. If Gustavus had waited until the Russian squadron had left for the Mediterranean he might have secured command of the sea with little difficulty.[18]

As it was, it was the Russians who had gained the initiative. The amphibious operation, which was to have been conducted by 15,000 men led by the king himself, had to be abandoned. The land attack was no more successful. Poorly led and impeded by bad weather, it was blocked at the gates of Fredrikshamn. And while there was considerable unrest among the Livonian peasantry, the nobility remained loyal to the tsarina.[19] Denmark mobilized to fulfil her treaty obligations to Russia. Such setbacks led even Gustavus to consider peace negotiations and revealed latent discontent within the Swedish officer corps with a war which many considered the king had begun unconstitutionally and whose purpose was unclear. At the Swedish HQ at Anjala in August a large party of officers called on Gustavus to make peace and assemble the Estates, while a small body of Finnish separatists sent one of their number to St Petersburg with a request to the tsarina (the 'Liikala Note') to restore peace and good relations on the basis of the status quo. This act of treason was backed by a majority of the remaining officers. Consequently the campaign came to a humiliating halt.[20]

Catherine responded with a demand to withdraw Swedish troops from Russian territory and call a Finnish Diet. Encouraged by Sprengtporten and his allies in Finland, she hoped, as Elizabeth had done, to create an independent Finland under Russian 'protection'.[21]

From this low point, however, matters began to move in Gustavus's favour. A Danish attack launched with little enthusiasm from Norway in the direction of Gothenburg in November enabled Gustavus to rally the Swedish population against the traditional enemy as well as against the mutinous nobles and to introduce in the Diet, which he was able to call on his own terms at the end of the year, amendments to the constitution which gave him well-nigh absolute power. The last limits on his conduct of foreign policy were removed. Pressure from Britain and Prussia, allied since 1787 in the Triple Alliance with the United Provinces of the Netherlands and equally concerned to limit Russian gains, brought about an armistice on the western front in October and a Danish withdrawal from Swedish soil the following month. The armistice was extended for six months.[22]

Having regained the initiative, Gustavus managed to hold the front in Finland in 1789, though the army fleet suffered a serious defeat at Svensksund, which could have been turned into a disaster had the Russian galley fleet pressed home its advantage. Prussia, hoping for territorial gains in a general redrawing of the map, offered its mediation, but Gustavus refused to petition for peace, and Catherine failed to get further support from Prussia beyond a small loan. At least Denmark declared itself neutral after the expiry of the armistice.[23]

In June 1790, after an unsuccessful attack by the Swedish army fleet on the Russian galley fleet, the Swedish combined fleets with the king on board were blockaded by the Russian fleet in Viborg bay. In breaking out, seven battleships and three frigates were lost and the king himself nearly captured. The main fleet retired to Sveaborg, but the army fleet secured on 9 July, at the second battle of Svensksund, the greatest of modern Swedish naval victories in which a third of the Russian archipelago fleet was destroyed for the loss of only six small ships. At the same time Sweden's diplomatic position was strengthened by the conclusion of an alliance between Poland and Prussia in March.[24]

The new Prussian king's chief minister, Count E. F. Hertzberg, had evolved a 'grand plan' of territorial exchange by which Poland would surrender Danzig and Thorn to Prussia and gain compensation in Galicia, which Austria had won by the First Partition. Gustavus had encouraged such ambitions at the time of abortive alliance negotiations on the eve of the war, and later put pressure on the Poles to agree. Hertzberg envisaged his plan being accomplished by diplomatic means, but his master, King Frederick William, favoured war against Russia in alliance with Poland. To this the Poles, who were at the same time approached by Russia with an offer of an alliance directed against Prussia, finally agreed. They then opened negotiations with the Swedes and the Turks. An extension of the war in the Baltic seemed highly likely at this stage.[25]

But Gustavus could get no firm commitments from Prussia, who was drawing towards Austria because of events in France. The Swedish king was also increasingly perturbed by these and wished to have his hands free to lead a crusade to release the French royal family from the toils their revolutionary subjects were trying to place on them. In these circumstances he agreed to conclude peace at Värälä a month after Svensksund. This resulted in no territorial changes, but Russia did recognize the new Swedish constitution and failed to renew the treaties of Nystad and Åbo, thus implicitly abandoning its claims to interfere in Sweden's internal affairs.[26]

Catherine was equally ready for peace. She was also concerned by events in France, but largely because of the relief which they promised from French pressure in eastern Europe. She had failed to conclude the Turkish war and was threatened at the same time by the loss of her Austrian ally and by the Prusso-Polish entente.[27]

She had for some time been concerned by developments in Poland, which was slipping from Russia's grasp since the opening of the Great Diet in October 1788 and which had declared itself a confederation (in which the *liberum veto* could not be used) in order to put through the programme of reforms so necessary if the country was to play an independent part in European affairs. Prussia offered its support. As has been seen, Gustavus III also sought to take advantage of the state of Polish affairs. After the end of the war he even talked of putting himself forward as a candidate to the Polish throne in succession to King Stanislas, though it is difficult to know how seriously he considered this. The proposal was treated by many Poles with scepticism as the Swedish king drew rapidly closer to the Russian empress in search of a firmer alliance than he had found hitherto, a *rapprochement* which ended with the conclusion of a defensive alliance between the two at Drottningholm in October 1791. Six months before this the Poles had offered their crown to the Elector of Saxony.[28]

Epilogue

THE BALTIC IN THE REVOLUTIONARY AND NAPOLEONIC WARS (1790–1815)

The Russo–Swedish war had come to an end in 1790 partly because both powers wished to have their hands free to deal with the consequences of the fall of absolute government in France the year before. Gustavus III dreamed of heading a European crusade on behalf of Monarchy against Revolution (from which he also hoped to harvest both prestige and more tangible results). Catherine II, while she agreed to assist Gustavus in this enterprise and in October 1791 made with him an eight-year defensive alliance, was principally interested, having concluded peace with Turkey on favourable terms, in expoiting the weakened influence of France in eastern Europe to pursue her designs in Poland.[1]

Gustavus III's assassination in 1792 as the result of a plot by disgruntled nobles put an end to any plans for Sweden's participation in a crusade against revolutionary France; its place was taken by Austria and Prussia. The regency for Gustavus's son Gustav IV, headed by his uncle Charles, for a time indeed leaned towards the French republic.[2]

Prussia concluded in March 1790 an alliance with the Polish republic promising 18,000 troops in the event of an attack on the latter in exchange for the promise of Danzig and Thorn. But King Frederick William then lost interest in the cause of Polish reform which had been making some progress under King Stanislas-Augustus and which seemed to have triumphed in the four year *Sejm* of 1788–91. When Catherine II, having lost patience and alarmed by the independence being shown by her satellite, ordered the invasion of the country in May, Frederick William not only refused to send any assistance against her but dispatched troops to help crush Polish resistance. With some reluctance, Catherine recognized the need for a fresh partition and secured an agreement with Prussia, who finally gained Danzig and Thorn, an agreement which the Poles were then bullied into accepting in July and September 1793. Two years later, after a Polish national revolt under Tadeusz Kosciuszko had been crushed, the Third Partition, in which Austria was again involved, marked the end of the Polish Commonwealth. Kurland, which had enjoyed a precarious independence under members of the Wettin house since 1759, acknowledged Russian sovereignty and was incorporated into Livonia.[3] The policy of neutrality pursued by Prussia after withdrawing from the initial campaign against France by the treaty of Basle in 1795 helped to keep war away from the Baltic for the remainder of the century.

As in previous European conflicts involving Britain and France from which the Scandinavian powers were excluded, in the early years of the wars with Revolutionary France, Denmark and Sweden were brought together in defence of their trade with western Europe, and in March 1794 concluded an agreement which declared the Baltic a neutral sea. Continued intervention outside the Baltic led to the formation of convoys in 1798. After a number of clashes between Danish escorts and British warships, however, in 1800 a British squadron was sent to Copenhagen. The Danes responded by abandoning convoys. But at the end of the same year they joined, with Sweden, the new Armed Neutrality League formed by Tsar Paul.[4]

In response, early in 1801 the British sent a fleet under the command of Admiral Sir Hyde Parker to Copenhagen Roads. The Russian fleet was unable to leave its ice-bound harbour to assist the Danes. The Swedish fleet was unable to come to the Danes' assistance because of contrary winds. The latter put up a spirited resistance on 2 April 1801, but had to surrender after Nelson, Parker's second-in-command, threatened to burn the ships he had captured. Denmark consequently left the League and in May evacuated Hamburg and Lübeck which it had occupied before the arrival of the British. The Swedes were saved from a similar humiliation by the assassination of Tsar Paul and the accession of his son Alexander, who abandoned the League altogether.[5]

Relations between Sweden and Russia had become strained as a result of the leanings towards France shown by the regency for Gustavus IV. A Franco–Swedish subsidy alliance was finally concluded in September 1795. But this was cancelled by France within a year, and with the end of the regency negotiations were entered into for a marriage between King Gustavus and the tsarina's grand-daughter. These also, however, were eventually abandoned because of the couple's irreconcilable religious differences.[6]

By a series of treaties in 1804 and 1805 Gustavus IV took his country into the Third Coalition against France largely for personal reasons. The effective demise of the Holy Roman Empire with the Napoleonic territorial settlement in Germany about the same time led Brandenburg–Prussia, whose relations with Sweden had cooled as Russian and Swedish troops gathered in Pomerania, to propose the establishment of a Nordic Union to include Denmark, Sweden, Mecklenburg, Holstein and Lübeck. None of the invited powers showed much enthusiasm for the project, and soon afterwards war broke out between Prussia and France. French power established itself on the southern Baltic coastline after the defeat of Prussia at the battle of Jena in October 1806. Lübeck fell in November, and both Schleswig–Holstein and Swedish Pomerania were directly threatened.[7]

At the beginning of 1807 the French invaded Swedish Pomerania, but in April agreed to an armistice. Russia negotiated an agreement between Prussia and Sweden by which each side was to supply troops for a counterattack. But the defeat suffered by the Russians at Friedland in June was followed next month by the agreement between the French and Russian emperors at Tilsit on the Vistula by which continental Europe was to all intents and purposes divided between them. The lands Prussia was allowed to retain at the peace were occupied by French troops, and the Prussian court withdrew to Königsberg. Eight thousand British troops had been sent into the Baltic to help in the defence of Swedish Pomerania, but these were soon withdrawn westward for a more urgent operation in Denmark, and Pomerania was abandoned to the French; in September the remainder of the Swedish garrison was withdrawn to Sweden.[8]

The British troops were in fact used in an assault on Copenhagen. The Dano–Norwegian fleet of eighteen line of battleships and sixteen frigates would be a valuable addition to Franco–Spanish naval power after Trafalgar, and from Britain's point of view must not be allowed to fall into enemy hands. The behaviour of Denmark had for some time led to growing concern in London, and it was finally decided in the month of Tilsit (though in ignorance of the final outcome of the meeting) to put pressure on the Danes to surrender their fleet for the duration of the war and to rely on British protection against French reprisals. To back up the demand, in July 1807 a fleet was again sent to the Sound, with 20,000 troops who were to be joined by those withdrawn from Pomerania.[9]

The Danish government, headed by Crown Prince Frederik acting as regent for his sick father, Christian VII, was faced with the choice of giving way and facing a French occupation of Jutland, against which the British could do nothing to protect it, or defiance and war with Britain. In spite of the fact that the main Danish army of 20,000 men was stationed in the duchies with Prince Frederik, it chose the latter. As a result, the Danes suffered a three-night-long bombardment of their capital, which caused much damage and loss of life, and the seizure of their fleet. Frederik could do little except to throw in his lot with France, then reaching the height of its power on the continent, and to agree to implement the Continental System.[10]

King Gustavus was equally adamant in the face of Tsar Alexander I's demands that Sweden leave the coalition and join the Continental System. Russian troops consequently began an invasion of Finland in February 1808. The Swedish plan of defence depended largely on the holding of the fortress of Sveaborg, while the main army withdrew into the interior of the country and prepared for a counterattack. Sveaborg was, however, surrendered after offering only token resistance; its commander, Admiral Carl Olof Cronstedt, was overcome by his subordinates' conviction that the war with Russia would inevitably be lost. With Sveaborg the Finnish army's fleet of over a hundred units fell into Russian hands giving them a decided superiority in the archipelagoes of the Baltic.[11] A Swedish counter-attack was nevertheless launched in the spring and enjoyed some initial success, but eventually Russian numbers told, and by the end of the year the whole country had to be evacuated.[12]

Meanwhile Scania was threatened by a Franco-Spanish-Danish army gathered on Fyn under the command of Napoleon's brother-in-law, Marshal Jean-Baptiste Bernadotte. A British contingent under General Moore was sent to Gothenburg to aid the Swedes, but no agreement could be made with Gustavus as to how it was to be used, and it never even landed on Swedish soil.

The threat from the south was in any case soon removed. A British squadron under Admiral Sir James Saumarez joined a squadron of the Swedish high seas fleet to establish command of the sealanes into the Baltic, and when news came of the Spanish uprising against the French, many from the large contingent of Spanish troops in Bernadotte's force deserted to the British ships sailing the Great Belt.[13]

The Swedes were less lucky with their Russian foes, and when the king insisted on planning a further campaign, he was in March deposed by noble conspirators in favour of his uncle Charles, who agreed to a new constitution and a ministry which opened peace negotiations with the Russians at Fredrikshamn. These resulted in peace in September after a vain attempt had been made to influence it by an amphibious operation behind the Russian front on the coast of Norrland. By the peace, the whole of Finland and a strip of Sweden proper at the northern end of the Gulf of Bothnia were surrendered to the tsar; in spite of the efforts of the Swedish negotiators, the Åland Islands also had to be abandoned. Peace between Sweden and Denmark followed in December and between Sweden and France in January 1810.[14]

Tsar Alexander did not absorb Finland into the Russian Empire but chose to rule it as grand duke with the powers enjoyed by a Swedish king under the constitutional changes made by Gustavus III in 1789. Existing Finnish laws were recognized as valid and the Lutheran church protected. A governor-general (after the first one, always a Russian) represented the tsar in the country, but internal affairs were left in the hands of a Council (later a Senate) made up of Finns. Russian troops were stationed in Finland, but the garrison was small.[15]

King Charles XIII was childless, and the choice of an heir to the Swedish throne took up much of the energies of his regime immediately after its establishment. The choice eventually fell on Marshal Bernadotte, who had led the French army which had occupied Swedish Pomerania (now restored) as well, as has been seen, of the army gathered to invade from Denmark. It was hoped that through him French support might be gained for the recovery of Finland. Bernadotte, who arrived in Sweden in October 1810 and adopted the name of Charles John on his reception into the Lutheran church, immediately stamped his personality on the administration and took over responsibility for foreign policy. He anticipated a breach between Napoleon and Alexander and the eventual collapse of the French Empire. In view of this, he aimed to accept the loss of Finland and use Russian support to secure from Denmark the strategically more attractive Norway. If Denmark agreed to abandon the French alliance, it would be given compensation in Germany, the map of which was in a state of flux after the dissolution of the Holy Roman Empire. Napoleon played into Charles John's hands. Discontented with Sweden's lax implementation of the Continental System, he ordered the reoccupation of Pomerania at the beginning of 1812. This enabled Bernadotte to swing the Council behind his plan for an alliance with Russia.[16]

In Denmark, Frederik, now king, stubbornly refused to abandon France against the wishes of his advisers. Plans were consequently drawn up for a joint Russo–Swedish attack on Zealand which, together with Norway and Bornholm, was to be Sweden's prize with compensation found for Denmark elsewhere. But this action had to be postponed because of the French invasion of the tsar's domains.[17]

After Napoleon's Russian débâcle, Sweden was assigned the task of holding Denmark in check from its base in Pomerania. But Charles John himself was given command of the main allied army in north Germany, of which only a fifth was made up of Swedish troops. After participating in the decisive battle of Leipzig, he marched northwards, against the wishes of his allies, to force the Danes to make peace, which, faced by overwhelming force, they did at Kiel in January 1814. Loyally supported by Tsar Alexander, Charles John gained Norway in exchange for Swedish Pomerania and Rügen and monetary compensation. But Denmark never effectively took charge of these. At the Congress of Vienna it was compelled to surrender them to Prussia in exchange for the duchy of Saxe–Lauenburg south of Holstein.[18]

The Napoleonic upheaval had resulted in the strengthening of Russia's and Prussia's position on the Baltic, though it remained difficult to envisage the latter as a Baltic power. Denmark was permanently weakened and seemingly Sweden also. The former's loss of Norway and of its fleet, and the disastrous economic consequences of the war, from which it recovered only slowly, deprived it of the significance which it still enjoyed in the eighteenth century. But the case of Sweden is rather more complex. The loss of its German possessions,[19] from which it had derived little economic benefit and which, as has been seen, had more than once drawn it into a conflict in which none of its vital interests were involved, can in fact be seen as a positive gain. On the other hand, the independent spirit of the Norwegians, which secured for them an even greater degree of autonomy under their king in Stockholm than was granted to the Finns by their absolute grand duke in St Petersburg, meant that the acquisition of Norway was a mixed blessing and could never compensate for the loss of Finland, bound to Sweden for so many centuries. Yet the breaking of such ties across the Gulf of Bothnia did hold out hopes of more peaceful and fruitful relations between Sweden and its great neighbour to the east than in the past and assisted in ensuring Sweden's neutrality in all European conflicts from that day to this. That a large number of Swedes took long to be convinced of these benefits accounts for some of the tensions which affected the Baltic world for half a century after the Congress of Vienna.[20]

Postlude

THE BALTIC IN THE NINETEENTH AND TWENTIETH CENTURIES

The political map of the Baltic area was thus considerably changed by the Napoleonic Wars, although the balance of power in it was largely confirmed.

While Sweden's loss of Finland in 1809 may have benefited it in the long run, the loss was felt deeply by many and left in certain circles a lust for revenge and anti-Russian sentiments which were to surface in the middle of the century, and which led to hopes as late as the 1860s to use, as in the past, Russian embarrassment to regain Finland with the support of one or more of the great powers.

For Russia, the Baltic was throughout the nineteenth century of secondary importance compared with the Balkans and Asia. Its attention was directed towards it whenever there was a threat of war with Britain, for whom it provided the readiest access to the enemy. Although its position in Europe as a whole was seriously weakened by the Crimean War, its status in the Baltic was, however, not seriously challenged until the formation of a German battle fleet at the end of the nineteenth century and the victories scored in the east by Germany in the First World War.[1]

Charles John came to the throne of Sweden as Charles XIV in 1818 and continued his '1812 policy' of friendship with the Russia of Tsar Alexander I and Nicholas I. His more liberal son Oscar I, who succeeded him in 1844, had more sympathy for his father's critics, and Russo–Swedish relations consequently cooled. On the outbreak of the Crimean War an Anglo–French squadron sailed into the Baltic and burned shipyards and timber stores on the east coast of Finland and the Åland Islands, where the fortress of Bomarsund was also destroyed. In 1855 an Anglo-French squadron bombarded Sveaborg and Sweden concluded an agreement with Britain and France (the November treaty) which King Oscar at least regarded as a first step towards his country's entry into the war and the possible regaining of Finland.[2] Peace, however, came four months later before Sweden's neutrality had been infringed. One of the terms of the peace treaty was that the Åland Islands should be demilitarized. Plans for the reunion of Sweden and Finland surfaced for the last time in 1863 when King Charles XV hoped to get the support of the French Emperor Napoleon III at the time of the Polish revolt in that year.[3]

The rising tide of German nationalism already threatened Denmark's position in the Duchies in the 1840s and led to a bid for independence by the German-speaking population in Slesvig and Holstein in 1848. These claims were backed by liberals in Germany itself and by Prussia, but as the tide of liberalism on the continent ebbed, the rebels found themselves increasingly isolated. Prussia made peace with Denmark under strong pressure from Russia, where Tsar Nicholas I was strongly opposed to any disturbance of the status quo from which he could derive no benefit, and in 1850 the great powers guaranteed the existing relationship between the kingdom of Denmark and the Duchies; they were to remain under the Danish crown, but Slesvig, with its large Danish element, was not to be allowed the closer relationship with the kingdom desired by Danish liberals.[4]

Both fear of Russia and fear of Germany formed large elements in the movement for closer political and cultural ties between Denmark, Norway and Sweden known as Pan-Scandinavianism which emerged in the 1840s. While strongly supported within Danish and Swedish intellectual and academic circles, it never enjoyed widespread popular support and was never adopted as official policy by any government, although in Sweden Kings Oscar I (1844–59) and Charles XV (1859–72) regarded it with some favour. The Danes were indeed misled into believing that they would enjoy more than merely moral suppport from their Scandinavian neighbours in the event of a clash with Germany. When, however, Prussia and Austria declared war in 1864 in protest against Denmark's unilateral union of Slesvig with the kingdom in breach of international agreements, no significant help was forthcoming from Sweden–Norway. Political Scandinavianism consequently collapsed, although collaboration between the monarchies in other spheres grew in the course of the later nineteenth century.

The outcome of the Second Schleswig–Holstein War was a drastic diminution of Denmark's territory with the loss of the Duchies to Prussia and Austria, an event in many ways as traumatic for the loser as the acquisition of Finland by Russia some sixty years earlier, and with no prospect of compensation. Concurrently it strengthened Prussia in the Baltic area, particularly after its defeat of Austria in 1866 and subsequent absorption of Holstein as well as Slesvig. The grand duchies of Mecklenburg–Schwerin and Mecklenburg–Strelitz and the 'free city' of Lübeck retained their autonomous status within the North German Confederation formed under Prussian leadership in 1867, and within the German Empire founded four years later, but they had long lost any significance in international affairs.[5]

Kiel in Holstein provided the new German Empire with a potentially significant naval base in the Baltic, but it was not until the 1890s that a German navy rivalling that of Russia finally emerged. On the outbreak of war in 1914 Germany compelled the Danes to mine the Belts to prevent the entry of a British fleet into the Baltic, but Britain had no plans for a naval campaign in the Baltic and took no retaliatory action.[6]

Russia's subsequent military failures brought about a threat of German domination thoroughout the area; the treaty of Brest Litovsk in 1918 gave Germany complete control of the southern coastline as far as the Gulf of Finland. And the assistance given by a German expeditionary force to the White army in the Finnish Civil War and proposals that a German prince be elected to the throne of a Finnish kingdom suggested that the country, which had declared its independence from Russia in November 1917, had become a German satellite.[7]

The danger was averted only by the collapse of the German Empire at the end of 1918. But while civil war raged in Russia, the Anglo–French interventionist forces operated from Archangel close to the Finno–Russian border, the new Estonian, Latvian and Lithuanian republics struggled to assert their independence, and the Poles fought to secure acceptable boundaries with the Soviet Union, the situation in the eastern Baltic remained extremely fluid. Not until 1920 were relations between Finland and the Soviet Union regularized, and they were far from cordial during the whole inter-war period. Russia's hold on the Baltic was now confined to the area around Leningrad, and Germany's position was pushed westward with the recreation of the 'Polish Corridor' between East Prussia and the remainder of Germany and the granting to Danzig of the status of a free city under the aegis of the League of Nations.

In many ways the Baltic returned to the situation of the middle of the sixteenth century with no power enjoying domination and the south-eastern region a potential flashpoint. With the revival of German naval power after the creation of the Third Reich, recognized by the Anglo–German Naval Agreement of 1936, a new situation arose. Nevertheless the smaller Baltic powers – Denmark, Sweden, Finland, the Baltic republics and Poland – could take comfort from the balance created by the antagonism between the Soviet Union and the fanatically anti-bolshevik Nazi Germany. This balance was shattered by the pact between the two concluded in August 1939 and the division of a prostrate Poland between them after the German victory in the following month. This was soon followed by military agreements between Russia and the Baltic states which turned them into little better than satellites with Soviet garrisons. Finland escaped their fate, but was compelled to surrender territory at the end of its heroic struggle in the Winter War of 1939/40, which gave the Soviet Union control of the Gulf of Finland. After this, Finland moved rapidly into the German sphere of influence in the hope of receiving German protection against further Soviet pressure and of revenge against its eastern neighbour.

Germany's occupation of Denmark and Norway in April 1940 and the answering occupation of the Baltic states by Russia in June left Sweden as the only Baltic country enjoying any degree of independence, and even Sweden was compelled by the terms of the so-called 'Transit Agreements' to allow German troops and war *matériel* to pass along its railways to and from Norway. The German attack on the Soviet Union in July 1941 brought the rapid occupation of the whole of Russia's Baltic coastline. Finland's attack on the Soviet Union at the same time, as Germany's 'co-belligerent', made the Baltic by the end of 1941 virtually a German lake. Not since the seventeenth century had one power enjoyed such a stranglehold on the area. This situation did not change until 1944, when Russian forces broke through to the Baltic on a broad front and compelled the Finns to conclude an armistice which enabled the Soviet Union to occupy a base at Porkkala near Helsinki.

The return of peace found the boundaries of Soviet power

pushed as far west as the Vistula. Through its control of Poland and the eastern zone of Germany (soon to become the German Democratic Republic) they were indeed pushed as far as the Oder. The dreams of Peter the Great, when he established his troops in Mecklenburg during the Great Northern War, seemed to have been finally realized. To the north of the Gulf of Finland, although the Porkkala base was abandoned in 1956, Russia had little to fear from a country bound to it by subtle ties through the 1948 Treaty of Friendship, even if fiercely jealous of its independence. While Sweden maintained a strictly neutral stance amidst the growing international tension of the immediate post-war years, the entry of Denmark into NATO in 1949 after the failure of plans for a Nordic defence pact increased the likelihood that the Baltic would be drawn into any armed conflict between the great powers.

The dissolution of the Warsaw Pact, the unification of Germany and the re-establishment of the independence of Estonia, Latvia and Lithuania have opened a new phase in Baltic politics. There is hardly any prospect of a struggle for power between the existing Baltic states. This ended with the Second World War. While, however, an economically powerful Germany retains its Baltic coastline and a potentially powerful Russian Republic has its principal outlets to the west on the sea, this will remain a significant area in European and indeed in world affairs.

NOTES AND REFERENCES

PREFACE

1 Stewart Oakley, 'War in the Baltic, 1550–1790', in Jeremy Black (ed.) *The Origins of War in Early Modern Europe* (Edinburgh, 1987).
2 Stewart Oakley, *William III and the Northern Crowns during the Nine Years War, 1689–1697* (New York and London, 1987).

INTRODUCTION

1 Adam Szelągowski, *Der Kampf um die Ostsee (1544–1621)* (Munich, 1916), 7, 18.
2 Szelągowski, 19, 36: Nils Ahnlund, 'Dominium maris Baltici', in his *Tradition och historia* (Stockholm, 1956), 116–17.

1 SETTING THE SCENE

1 The area of the Mediterranean is 2,496,000 km², of the Baltic 422,000 km².
2 Eirik Hornborg, *Kampen om Östersjön till slutet av segelfartygens tidevarv* (Stockholm, 1945), 2.
3 The German form *Funen* is often used in English. I have preferred the Danish form throughout.
4 This a convenient term employed in the Germanic languages to describe the area of the south-eastern Baltic now occupied by the republics of Estonia, Latvia and Lithuania.
5 Most Finnish towns have a Finnish and a Swedish form (e.g. Helsinki/ Helsingfors). Most English-speaking readers will (with the exception of Helsinki) be more familiar with the Swedish form (e.g. Nystad rather than Uusikaupunki). I have indicated both forms when the name is first introduced.
6 i.e. about 274,000 km².
7 Dietrich Schäfer, 'Der Kampf um die Ostsee im 16. und 17. Jahrhunderte', *Historische Zeitschrift* 83 (1899), 423–4.
8 Hornborg, 2; R. M. Hatton, 'Russia and the Baltic', in Jarus Hunczak

(ed.) *Russian Imperialism from Ivan the Great to the Revolution* (New Brunswick, 1974), 106.

9 Hornborg, 3, 6; Szelągowski, 46–7.

10 Hornborg, 4.

11 Ibid., 8.

12 North-western Finland or Ostrobothnia (Österbotten/Pohjanmaa) was in the sixteenth century often thought of as part of Sweden rather than of Finland (Hornborg, 96).

13 Hornborg, 10.

14 Ibid., 115; David Kirby, *Northern Europe in the Early Modern Period: The Baltic World 1492–1772* (London and New York, 1990), 25.

15 Alfred Bilmanis, *A History of Latvia* (Westport, 1951), 115; Thomas Esper, 'Russia and the Baltic 1494–1558', *Slavic Review* 25 (1966), 469–70; Hatton (1974), 108–10; Robert J. Kerner, *The Urge to the Sea: The Course of Russian History* (New York, 1942), 42; W. Kirchner, *The Rise of the Baltic Question* (Newark, N.J., 1954), 89–90; George Vernadsky, *A History of Russia vol. 5: The Tsardom of Muscovy 1547–1682*, Part I (New Haven and London, 1969), 65.

16 Bilmanis (1951), 111–14; Kirby, 25–6, 68; Kirchner (1954), 1, 5–11, 16–20.

17 Kirchner (1954), 33; Stanislaw Kutrzeba, 'Dantzig et la Pologne à travers les siècles', in *Pirmā Baltijas vēsturnieku konference Rigā, 16–20 viii 1937* (Riga, 1938), 293–4; P. Skwarczynski, 'Poland and Lithuania', in R. B. Wernham (ed.) *New Cambridge Modern History III: The Counter-Reformation and Price Revolution 1559–1610* (Cambridge, 1968), 381; Szelągowski, 26.

2 THE BALTIC WORLD IN THE MIDDLE OF THE SIXTEENTH CENTURY

1 Hornborg, 95–6; Kirby, 98; Michael Roberts, *Gustavus Adolphus: A History of Sweden 1611–1632*, Vol. I (1611–1626) (London, 1953), 317–18; ibid., Vol. II (1626–1632) (London, 1958), 28–30, 32–3, 38–42, 44–66.

2 Wilhelm Tham, *Den svenska utrikespolitikens historia I: 2 1560–1648* (Stockholm, 1960), 9; Roberts (1953), 284–5.

3 Walter Leitsch, 'Russo–Polish confrontation', in Jarus Hunczak (ed.) *Russian Imperialism from Ivan the Great to the Revolution* (New Brunswick, 1974), 138; Norman Davies, *God's Playground: A History of Poland I: Origins to 1795* (Oxford, 1981), 330.

4 Hornborg, 95; Kirby, 42–3; Oakley (1987), 51–2.

5 R. R. Betts, 'Constitutional development and political thought in Eastern Europe', in G. R. Elton (ed.) *New Cambridge Modern History: II The Reformation 1520–59* (Cambridge, 1965), 464, 466; Kirby, 50.

6 Hornborg, 105–6; Gunnar Mickwitz, 'Handelsverbindungen der spät-hänsischen Zeit', in *Pirmā Baltijas vēsturnieku konference Rigā, 16–20 viii 1937* (Riga, 1938), 377–9; Schäfer, 433; Tham, 13.

7 Erich Donnert, *Der Livländische Ordensritterstaat und Russland: Der*

livländische Krieg und die Baltische Frage in der europäischen Politik 1558–1583 (Berlin, 1963); Kirchner (1954), 61–4; Szelągowski, 53.

8 Kirchner (1954), 95; Leitsch, 139; Szelągowski, 53.

9 J. L. I. Fennell, 'Russia 1462–1583', in G. R. Elton (ed.) *New Cambridge Modern History II: The Reformation 1520–1559* (Cambridge, 1965), 551–3.

10 Kazimierz Lepszy, 'Die Bedeutung der polnischen Kriegsmarin im XVI Jahrhunderte', in *Pirmā Baltijas vēsturnieku konference Rigā, 16–20 viii 1937* (Riga, 1938), 368–70; Szelągowski, 38, 44–8.

11 Hornborg, 98–9; Gunner Lind, 'Rigets sværd: Krig og krigsvæsen under Christian IV', in Svend Ellehøj (ed.) *Christian IVs Verden* (Copenhagen, 1988), 102, 109; Otto Lybeck, *Öresund i Nordens Historie: en marinpolitisk studie* (Malmö, 1943), 85; Otto Röhlk, 'Der Einfluss der Seemacht auf Dänemarks Geschichte', *Historische Zeitschrift* 165 (1941–2), 7–8. The Danish and Swedish navies were probably the largest in Europe at this time.

12 Kirby, 137–9; Lind, 100; Roberts (1958), 190–1.

13 M. S. Anderson, *Peter the Great* (London, 1978), 27; Kirchner, (1954), 31; Walther Mediger, *Moskaus Weg nach Europa* (Brunswick, 1952), 5; W. F. Reddaway *et al.*, *The Cambridge History of Poland: From the Origins to Sobieski (to 1696)* (Cambridge, 1950), 432.

14 Władisław Czaplinski, 'Le problème baltique aux xvie et xviie siècles', in *Congrès international des sciences historiques. XIe Congrès. Rapports I* (Stockholm, 1960), 27; Michael Roberts, *The Early Vasas* (Cambridge, 1968), 152.

15 Ibid., 152, 156.

16 M. Handelsmann, 'La politique polonaise sur la Baltique aux xviii et xix siècles', in *Pirmā Baltijas vēsturnieku konference Rigā, 16–20 viii 1937* (Riga, 1938), 510.

17 Hatton (1974), 111; Hornborg, 115–16; Roberts (1968), 155–6.

18 Davies, 147; Hatton (1974), 106; Henry J. Huttenbach, 'The origins of Russian Imperialism', in Jarus Hunczak (ed.) *Russian Imperialism from Ivan the Great to the Revolution* (New Brunswick, 1974), 20, 35–6; Kerner, 1–5, 25, 33, 41, 44; Klaus Zernack, *Studien zu den schwedisch–russischen Beziehungen in der 2. Hälfte der 17 Jahrhunderts I: Die diplomatischen Beziehungen zwischen Schweden und Moskau von 1675 bis 1689* (Giessen, 1958), 26.

19 Bilmanis (1951), 119; Alfred Bilmanis, 'The struggle for domination of the Baltic: an historical aspect of the Baltic problem', *Journal of Central European Affairs* V (1945), 127; Donnert, 40–1; Esper, 473; Hatton (1974), 112; Huttenbach, 30, 35–7; Kirchner (1954), 90–1, 96–7; Ladislas Konopczynski, 'Le problème baltique dans l'histoire moderne', *Revue historique* 162 (1929), 310; Szelągowski, 53; Vernadsky, 85; Reinhard Wittram, *Baltische Geschichte. Die Ostseelande: Livland, Estland, Kurland 1180–1918* (Munich, 1954), 66.

20 Czaplinski, 29, 31; Donnert, 221–6; Kirchner (1954), 201; Leitsch, 139; Roberts (1968), 163.

21 Bilmanis (1951), 119–20; Bilmanis (1945), 128; Davies, 146–7; O. Halecki, 'Les Jagellions et la Livonie', in *Pirmā Baltijas vēsturnieku*

konference Rigā, 16–20 viii 1937 (Riga, 1938), 348; Kirchner (1954), 35–7, 92–3, 198–9, 203–4; Reddaway, 352; Szelągowski, 54–5; Wittram (1954), 64, 66.

22 Bilmanis (1951), 120–1; Bilmanis (1945), 129; Donnert, 40, 43; Kirchner (1954), 38, 205–6; Szelągowski, 55; Vernadsky, 95; Wittram (1954), 66–7.

23 Bilmanis (1951), 121; Bilmanis (1945), 129; Donnert, 39, 43; Hatton (1974), 112; Hornborg, 116, 120; Huttenbach, 37; Kirchner (1954), 38–9, 100–3; Reddaway, 353; Roberts (1968), 56–7; Vernadsky, 96; Wittram (1954), 67–8.

24 Huttenbach, 37–8; Kirchner (1954), 101; Vernadsky, 87–8, 90, 95.

25 Artur Attman, *The Struggle for Baltic Markets: Powers in Conflict 1558–1618* (Acta Regiae Societatis Scientarum et Litterarum Gothburgensis: Humaniora 14; Gothenburg, 1979), 7–8; Bilmanis (1945), 120; Szelągowski, 22; Tham, 13–14.

26 Hornborg, 8–9; Lybeck, 83–4; Roberts (1953), 6–7; Schäfer, 429; Szelągowski, 24–5.

27 Attman, 8; Kirby, 125–6; Roberts (1968), 155, 158.

28 Attman, 56, 63, 75, 208–14; Hatton (1974), 130; Huttenbach, 25; Roberts (1968), 155.

29 Bilmanis (1951), 121–2, 130; Konopczynski, 307–8.

30 Bilmanis (1951), 122; Bilmanis (1945), 130; Donnert, 32, 106–9, 151–2, 160; Kirchner (1954), 44–5, 76–7; Wittram (1954), 70.

31 Donnert, 45, 175; Kirchner (1954), 129; Roberts (1968), 163–4.

32 Bilmanis (1951), 124; Bilmanis (1945), 124; Czaplinski, 28; Troels Dahlerup, 'Christian IVs udenrigspolitik set i lyset af de første oldenborgeres dynastipolitik', in Svend Ellehøj (ed.) *Christian IVs Verden* (Copenhagen, 1988), 48; Donnert, 176–81; Helge Gamrath and E. Ladewig Pedersen, *Danmarks Historie B.2: Tiden 1340–1648 (Andet Halvbind 1556–1648)* (Copenhagen, 1980), 445, 447; Kirchner (1954), 132, 137–8; W. Kirchner, 'A milestone in European history: the Danish–Russian treaty of 1562', *Slavonic and East European Review* XXXII (1944), 41–2; Tham, 15.

33 Donnert, 177–8; Gamrath and Petersen, 446; Charles E. Hill, *The Danish Sound Dues and the Command of the Baltic* (Durham, N.C. 1926), 59–60; Kirchner (1954), 140, 142–3; Tham, 16.

34 Bilmanis (1951), 122–3; Bilmanis (1945), 132; Donnert, 47; Kirchner, 134, 207, 208–9; Reddaway, 354; Roberts (1968), 162; Tham, 15; Wittram (1954), 69–70.

35 Bilmanis (1951), 122; Donnert, 202–5; Kirchner (1954), 162–3, 165; Roberts (1968), 165; Tham, 16–17.

36 Czaplinski, 28; Kirchner (1954), 132, 167; Roberts (1968), 167; Tham, 17–18.

37 Donnert, 48, 206–7, 209–11; Hornborg, 120–1; Kirchner (1954), 70, 173–5; Roberts (1968), 202; Heribert Seitz and Erik Rosengren, *Sveriges freder och fördrag 1524–1905* (Stockholm, 1944), 13; Tham, 21–4; Wittram (1954), 70.

3 THE STRUGGLE FOR LIVONIA (1558–95)

1 Czaplinski, 30; Martin Gerhardt and Walther Hubatsch, *Deutschland und Skandinavien im Wandel der Jahrhunderte* (Bonn, 1977), 169; Kirchner (1954), 3.

2 Donnert, 44; Kirchner (1954), 93–4, 104–6; Leitsch, 140; Vernadsky, 96; Wittram (1954), 68.

3 Donnert, 48; Kirchner (1954), 107–8; Vernadsky, 98–9; Wittram (1954), 68.

4 Kirby, 112; Vernadsky, 101–2.

5 Bilmanis (1945), 132–4; Bilmanis (1951), 125–6; Kirchner (1954), 178, 216; Reddaway, 354; Tham, 26; Vernadsky, 99; Wittram (1954), 70.

6 Bilmanis (1945), 131–2, 134; Bilmanis (1951), 125–7, 138; Donnert, 48; Kirchner (1954), 110–11, 218–19, 225; Reddaway, 355; Tham, 26–7; Wittram (1954), 71.

7 Bilmanis (1945), 136; Bilmanis (1951), 137–8; Donnert, 229; Kirchner (1954), 109, 180–1, 223; Roberts (1968), 209–10; Tham, 27–9; Vernadsky, 99.

8 Attman, 47–53, 78; Czaplinski, 31; Donnert, 168; Gamrath and Petersen, 444, 447; Gerhardt and Hubatsch, 170; Hornborg, 121; Lybeck, 85; Roberts (1968), 203; Schäfer, 431; Tham, 23–4, 29–30.

9 Donnert, 185–7; Kirchner (1954), 110, 144, 146–9; Kirchner (1944) 43–6; Roberts (1968), 205.

10 R. C. Anderson, *Naval Wars in the Baltic 1522–1850* (London, 1910), 4–5; Kirchner (1954), 145, 223; Lybeck, 88; Roberts (1968), 207, 211–12; Tham, 34–7.

11 Gamrath and Petersen, 448; Hill, 64–5; Hornborg, 121–2; Lybeck, 89–91; Roberts (1968), 216–17.

12 Gamrath and Petersen, 448–9; Lybeck, 92; Roberts (1968), 217.

13 Bilmanis (1945), 134; Bilmanis (1951), 139–40; Kirchner (1954), 227–8; Reddaway, 356; Roberts (1968), 250, 252; Szelągowski, 60–1; Tham, 46–7; Wittram (1954), 78.

14 Donnert, 169; Gamrath and Petersen, 449–50; Hill, 67–8; Kirchner (1954), 50–1, 72–4, 150–1; Roberts (1968), 252–3; Seitz and Rosengren, 13–15; Tham, 49–50; Wittram (1954), 74.

15 Kirchner (1954), 55–6, 151, 193; Roberts (1968), 257; Tham, 70–2.

16 Kirby, 118.

17 Bilmanis (1945), 137; Bilmanis (1951), 139; Donnert, 212; Kirchner (1954), 184–7; Roberts (1968), 235–6, 255–6; Tham, 38–40, 47.

18 Bilmanis (1951), 138, 142; Jan Dąbrowski, 'Baltische Handelspolitik Polens und Litauens im XIV–XVI Jahrhunderte', in *Pirmā Baltijas vēsturnieku konference Rigā, 16–20 viii 1937* (Riga, 1938); Donnert, 50–2, 212, 234–6, 242; Kirchner (1954), 109, 184; Roberts (1968), 233, 256; Vernadsky, 104–5, 107, 113–14, 126.

19 Bilmanis (1945), 137; Donnert, 183–5; Kirchner (1954), 113; Vernadsky, 122.

20 Bilmanis (1945), 137–8; Bilmanis (1951), 142–3; Donnert, 52–4, 56; Hornborg, 139; Kirchner, 116–17; Roberts (1968), 256; Vernadsky, 122, 126, 128, 130–1, 133; Wittram (1954), 74.

21 Bilmanis (1951), 141; Donnert, 238; Reddaway, 358–65; Vernadsky, 118.
22 Bilmanis (1945), 138; Bilmanis (1951), 143–4; H. Jablonowski, 'Poland–Lithuania 1609–48', in J. P. Cooper (ed.) *New Cambridge Modern History IV: The Decline of Spain and the Thirty Years War 1610–48/59* (Cambridge, 1970), 585–6; Kirby, 103.
23 Bilmanis (1945), 139; Bilmanis (1951), 144–5; Reddaway, 375–7.
24 Bilmanis (1951), 145; Donnert, 60; Kutrzeba, 295, 320; Reddaway, 375–7, 379–80; Roberts (1968), 263; Skwarczynski, 384, 397; Szelągowski, 64–5, 71–2, 75–6, 82.
25 Kirchner (1954), 120.
26 Fennell, 554–7.
27 Donnert, 58–9; Hornborg, 139–40; Kirchner (1954), 21–2, 94, 116, 120; Reddaway, 381; Roberts (1968), 258–9; Vernadsky, 147–9, 150; Wittram (1954), 75–6.
28 Bilmanis (1945), 139; Bilmanis (1951), 145–6; Donnert, 51, 59–60; Kirchner (1954), 119, 194–5; Reddaway, 383–4; Roberts (1968), 259, 263; Vernadsky, 135, 153–4, 156, 160; Wittram (1954), 76.
29 Hornborg, 141–3; Roberts (1968), 260–1, 263; Szelągowski, 93–4; Tham, 53–4; Vernadsky, 165–6.
30 Bilmanis (1945), 134, 140; Bilmanis (1951), 146–7, 149–50; Donnert, 61, 248; Kirchner (1954), 121, 231–3; Leitsch, 142; Reddaway, 382, 385–6; Roberts (1968), 263–4; Vernadsky, 163–5.
31 Donnert, 62; Kirchner (1954), 122, 196; Seitz and Rosengren, 15; Tham, 55; Vernadsky, 166.
32 Attman, 114–28; Donnert, 62; Fennel, 561; Tham, 55–6.
33 Bilmanis (1945), 139–40; Bilmanis (1951), 146; Dahlerup, 49; Donnert, 195–6; Gamrath and Petersen, 448–9, 451; Kirchner (1954), 152–6. Piltene was eventually incorporated into Kurland by the 'great duke' Jakob in 1661.
34 Vernadsky, 184, 188–9.
35 Kazimierz Lepszy, 'The Union of the crowns between Poland and Sweden in 1587', in *Poland at the XIth International Congress of Historical Sciences in Stockholm* (Warsaw, 1960), 168; Szelągowski, 89; Vernadsky, 199–200.
36 Lepszy (1960), 157, 161–2.
37 Ibid., 156–7, 162; Roberts (1968), 269; Szelągowski, 100–1; Tham, 63–5.
38 Lepszy (1960), 162–70, 178; Reddaway, 453; Roberts (1968), 270–1; Szelągowski, 111–14.
39 Hornborg, 145–7; Szelągowski, 138–40.
40 Hatton (1974), 113–14; Roberts (1968), 271; Seitz and Rosengren, 15–16; Tham, 56–8; Vernadsky, 199.

4 THE TIME OF TROUBLES (1595–1617/21)

1 The decision to move the Polish court to Warsaw was taken in 1596 (Davies, 310).
2 Czaplinski, 39; Szelągowski, 165–6.

3 Stanislaw Herbst, 'Der livländische Krieg 1600–1602', in *Pirmā Baltijas vēsturnieku konference Rigā, 16–20 viii 1937* (Riga, 1938), 383; Lybeck, 97; Reddaway, 477; Roberts (1968), 399; Tham, 101; Wittram (1954), 84.

4 Herbst, 384–7; Reddaway, 477–8; Roberts (1968), 400, 402; Szelągoswki, 151–2, 161, 172; Wittram (1954), 85.

5 Herbst, 389; Reddaway, 478; Roberts (1968), 402–3; Szelągowski, 161, 172; Wittram (1954), 86.

6 Reddaway, 463–4, 478; Roberts (1968), 403; Skwarczynski, 387–8; Szelągowski, 175–6.

7 Ingvar Andersson, 'Sweden and the Baltic', in R. B. Wernham (ed.) *New Cambridge Modern History III: The Counter-Reformation and Price-Revolution 1559–1610* (Cambridge, 1968), 418; Leitsch, 144; Roberts (1968), 397; Tham, 103; Vernadsky, 205–6, 211–12.

8 Kirby, 120; Reddaway, 464; Roberts (1968), 452, Vernadsky, 222.

9 Roberts (1968), 452; Tham, 104–5; Vernadsky, 228–31, 233–6, 240–1.

10 I. Andersson, 419; Reddaway, 465; Roberts (1968), 453–4; Tham, 106–7; Vernadsky, 245–6.

11 I. Andersson, 419; Kirby, 121; Reddaway, 465–6; Roberts (1968), 454–5; Tham, 107; Vernadsky, 247–8, 252.

12 Jablonowski (1970), 594; Leitsch, 144–5; Reddaway, 466–8; Roberts (1968), 455; Seitz and Rosengren, 19; Tham, 107–9; Vernadsky, 252–3, 255–6, 264–5.

13 Hill, 62, 69–70, 73; Kirby, 99–100; Gamrath and Petersen, 449; Sven Ulric Palme, *Sverige och Danmark 1596–1611* (Uppsala, 1942), 51–60.

14 Kirby, 144; Roberts (1968), 446; Szelągowski, 136, 144.

15 Kirby, 138, 140; Lind, 109, 113.

16 Hatton (1974), 114; Hill, 81–3; Lybeck, 98; Palme, 74–8; Georg von Rauch, 'Zur Geschichte des schwedischen Dominium Maris Baltici', *Die Welt als Geschichte* 12 (1952), 134; Roberts (1968), 447–8; Tham, 89–90.

17 Gamrath and Petersen, 489; Roberts (1968), 447, 450–1; Szelągowski, 177–9; Tham, 92–4.

18 Gamrath and Petersen, 489; Palme, 207 *et seq.*; Roberts (1968) 456–7; Tham, 95.

19 R. C. Anderson, 29–32; Hornborg, 148–51; Lybeck, 99–100; Roberts (1968), 457–8.

20 Kirby, 133; Axel Norberg, *Polen i svensk politik 1617–26* (Stockholm, 1974), 114; Tham, 144–5.

21 Tham, 96.

22 Kirby, 147; Roberts (1958), 2, 43–6, 55–7; Michael Roberts, *The Swedish Imperial Experience 1560–1718* (Cambridge, 1979), 43.

23 Sven-Erik Åström, 'The Swedish economy and Sweden's role as a great power 1632–1697', in Michael Roberts (ed.) *Sweden's Age of Greatness 1632–1718* (London, 1973), 65–7; Kirby, 149; Roberts (1958), 28–30, 32–3; Roberts (1970a), 394; Roberts (1979), 49.

24 Roberts (1958), 781–9; Szelągowski, 184.

25 I. Andersson, 423; Vernadsky, 275, 277, 285.

26 Jablonowski (1970), 594–5; J. L. H. Keep, 'Russia 1613–45', in J. P.

Cooper (ed.) *New Cambridge Modern History IV: The Decline of Spain and the Thirty Years War 1610–48/59* (Cambridge, 1970), 602–3; Reddaway, 466–8; Szelągowski, 188; Tham, 109; Vernadsky, 257–61.

27 Keep, 605; Vernadsky, 286.

28 R. C. Anderson, 34–5; Hornborg, 151; Lybeck, 101–2.

29 Hill, 85–6; Lybeck, 103; Seitz and Rosengren, 19–20.

30 Keep, 604–5; Seitz and Rosengren, 20–1; Szelągowski, 191, 217; Tham, 110, 112–13; Vernadsky, 286–8.

31 Hatton (1974), 115–16.

32 Kerner, 47–52.

33 Czaplinski, 39.

34 Norberg, 37–46; Szelągowski, 208–11; Tham, 102.

35 R. C. Anderson, 35–6; Jablonowski (1970), 595; Norberg, 40–1; Szelągowski, 213–16, 225; Tham, 115; Vernadsky, 290.

36 Gerhardt and Hubatsch, 173; Hill, 88; Schäfer, 437; Szelągowski, 198–9; Tham, 97–8, 119–20.

5 THE BALTIC DURING THE THIRTY YEARS WAR (1618/21–48)

1 Norberg, 47–8, 53–65, 72, 75, 281; Reddaway, 472, 479; Szelągowski, 228–30; Leo Tandrup, *Mod triumf eller tragedie* (Aarhus, 1979), 534; Tham, 115, 120, 123–6.

2 Bilmanis (1951), 182–3; Kurt Forstreuter, *Preussen und Russland von den Anfängen des Deutschen Ordens bis zu Peter dem Grossen* (Göttinger Bausteine zur Geschichtswissenschaft Bd.23, Gottingen, 1955), 151; Gerhardt and Hubatsch, 174; Otto Hintze, *Die Hohenzollern und ihr Werk* (Berlin, 1915), 163, 166; Norberg, 35, 64, 101; Reddaway, 472; Szelągowski, 166–7, 222–3, 248–52; Tham, 132–3.

3 Forstreuter, 152–3; Hintze, 163; Jablonowski (1970), 600; Skwarczynski, 396.

4 Jablonowski (1970), 595, 599; Keep, 605; Leitsch, 145; Norberg, 62, 77–80, 112, 119, 122–3; Reddaway, 469; Roberts (1970a), 388, 390; Tham, 116–17; Vernadsky, 291; Erik Zeeh, 'Gustav Adolf und die Belagerung Rigas im Jahre 1621', in *Pirmā Baltijas vēsturnieku konference Rigā, 16–20 viii 1937* (Riga, 1938), 402–3.

5 Norberg, 126; Szelągowski, 260–2; Zeeh, 404–7.

6 Bilmanis (1951), 164; Norberg, 87, 127–30, 149–50, 244, 282–3; Roberts (1953), 209–10, 212; Szelągowski, 264–5.

7 Dąbrowski, 291; Norberg, 136, 158–62, 282–3; Geoffrey Parker (ed.) *The Thirty Years War* (London, 1984), 70; Reddaway, 480; Roberts (1953), 214; Szelągowski, 267–70.

8 Norberg, 147–8, 162–3, 186–7; Reddaway, 480; Roberts (1953), 215; Tham, 117–19.

9 Czaplinski, 41; Jablonowski (1970), 599; Norberg, 123, 175; Reddaway, 473; Roberts (1953), 202, 212–13, 216–20.

10 Norberg, 137; Parker, 63; E. Ladewig Petersen, 'Defence, war and finance: Christian IV and the Council of the Realm 1596–1629', *Scandi-*

navian Journal of History 7 (1982), 281; Roberts (1953), 197; Szelągowski, 256.

11 Parker, 161–4.

12 Dahlerup, 58; Parker, 63; Roberts (1953), 198–9; Tandrup (1979), 538; Leo Tandrup, 'Når to trættes, så ler den tredje: Christian IVs og rigsrådets forhold til det tyske Rige og især Sverige', in Svend Ellehøj (ed.) *Christian IVs Verden* (Copenhagen, 1988), 82.

13 Lind, 114–15; E. Ladewig Petersen, 'The Danish Intermezzo', in Geoffrey Parker (ed.) *The Thirty Years War* (London, 1984), 72; Petersen (1982), 294–5; Tandrup (1979), 531–2.

14 John Casimir was the husband of Gustavus's half-sister Catherine.

15 Norberg, 90–5, 189, 193; Parker, 69; Roberts (1953), 188, 193; Tham, 118, 129–31.

16 Gerhardt and Hubatsch, 177; Hill, 93; Lybeck, 106; Norberg, 168, 195, 214–19; Parker, 70, 74; Roberts (1953), 224–7, 229–32, 237–41; Tandrup (1979), 537, 539; Tham, 136–9.

17 Hill, 94–5; Norberg, 240; Lybeck, 106; Roberts (1953), 232–3, 241–5; Tham, 139–42.

18 Gamrath and Petersen, 494; Kirby, 146, 198; Petersen (1982), 282, 296; Petersen (1984), 72; Tandrup (1979), 535–6, 543.

19 Gamrath and Petersen, 494; Norberg, 260; Petersen (1984), 74–5; Roberts (1953), 241–2.

20 Petersen (1984), 75–8.

21 Gerhard Benecke, 'The practice of absolutism II: 1626–1629', in Geoffrey Parker (ed.) *The Thirty Years War* (London, 1984), 99; Roberts (1958), 345–7; Tham, 187–8.

22 Hintze, 169–70; Parker, 62, 115; Petersen (1984), 79; Roberts (1958), 339.

23 Kirby, 170–1; Norberg, 268.

24 Bilmanis (1951), 164; Norberg, 228, 241, 283; Reddaway, 481–2; Roberts (1953), 245–8; Tham, 160.

25 Bilmanis (1951), 164; Norberg, 168, 178–81, 189, 243; Reddaway, 481–2; Roberts (1953), 252–3; Roberts (1958), 248, 312–13.

26 Kirby, 201; Norberg, 274–7; Roberts (1958), 320–7; Tandrup (1988), 83; Tham, 160–1.

27 Roberts (1953), 173–4; Tandrup (1988), 83.

28 Gerhardt and Hubatsch, 182; Hill, 95; Hornborg, 177–9; Lybeck, 107, 111; Roberts (1958), 336–7, 355–6; Tham, 180–1, 187–8.

29 Parker, 121; Petersen (1984), 79; Tandrup (1988), 64–9; Tham, 183.

30 Petersen (1984), 79–80; Roberts (1958), 373–6, 387.

31 Czaplinski, 41; Hornborg, 176–7; Lepszy (1938), 370; Norberg, 279; Reddaway, 473–4, 484; Roberts (1958), 284.

32 Czaplinski, 44; Jablonowski (1970), 599; Parker, 121; Reddaway, 474, 485; Roberts (1958), 248, 342–3.

33 Jablonowski (1970), 600; Lybeck, 107; Parker, 122–3; Reddaway, 474, 486; Roberts (1958), 344–5; Szelągowski, 24; Tham, 165–70; 172; Wittram (1954), 87.

34 Roberts (1958), 353–4, 403–4, 412–13; Tham, 190–4, 197–9.

35 Roberts (1958), 418–25; Michael Roberts, 'The political objectives of

Gustav Adolf in Germany 1630–2', in his *Essays in Swedish History* (London, 1967), 82–6; Parker, 123.

36 Kirby, 174; Roberts (1958), 420–1; Roberts (1979), 36–7.
37 Lybeck, 112; Roberts (1958), 409, 411–12; Tham, 175–8, 194–7.
38 Kirby, 135, 172; Roberts (1979), 68–70; Tham, 158–9.
39 Michael Roberts, *Gustavus Adolphus and the Rise of Sweden* (London, 1973), 85–9; Tham, 148–51.
40 Roberts (1958), 198 *et seq.*; Michael Roberts, 'Gustav Adolf and the art of war', in his *Essays in Swedish History* (London, 1967), 64–71; Roberts (1970a), 396–7.
41 R. C. Anderson, 44; Lybeck, 113; Roberts (1958), 416–17, 441–9, 454–6; Roberts (1970a), 399; Tham, 162, 164–5, 203–8.
42 Gerhardt and Hubatsch, 181; Hintze, 169, 171–2; Parker, 116–18.
43 Roberts (1958), 426–7, 435–40.
44 Parker, 124; Roberts (1958), 464–9; Seitz and Rosengren, 26–7; Tham, 213.
45 Hintze, 172–3; Parker, 125; Roberts (1958), 446, 469–72, 481, 483, 490–2, 496; Tham, 209–10.
46 Hintze, 173; Roberts (1958), 528 *et seq.*; Tham, 220–7.
47 Kirby, 175–6; Parker, 130–1.
48 Parker, 135; Michael Roberts, 'The Swedish dilemma', in Geoffrey Parker (ed.) *The Thirty Years War* (London, 1984), 156; Michael Roberts, 'Oxenstierna in Germany 1633–1636', in his *From Oxenstierna to Charles XII: Four Studies* (Cambridge, 1991), 21, 23, 30–1; Tham, 234–8.
49 Hintze, 174–6; Parker, 163; Roberts (1984), 157, 160; Roberts (1991), 42; Tham, 247, 252–4.
50 Parker, 133; Roberts (1984), 159; Roberts (1991), 28, 39–40, 43–7; Tham, 248–50, 262–4.
51 Huttenbach, 38–9; Keep, 606, 608–9; Georg von Rauch, 'Moskau und die europäischen Mächte des 17. Jahrhunderts', *Historische Zeitschrift* 178 (1954), 30; Tham, 215–16; Vernadsky, 313, 336, 346.
52 Leitsch, 146; Reddaway, 489; Tham, 233; Vernadsky, 374.
53 Huttenbach, 38–9; Jablonowski (1970), 595; Keep, 610–11; Leitsch, 146; Reddaway, 489; Vernadsky, 349–53.
54 Czaplinski, 44; Parker, 141; Reddaway, 486–7, 491–2; Seitz and Rosengren, 29–30; Tham, 260–2.
55 Parker, 167; Roberts (1970a), 401; Roberts (1984), 160; Tham, 269–71, 280.
56 Kirby, 199; Petersen (1984), 80–1; Tandrup (1988), 88–9.
57 Hill, 113–15, 121–6; Lybeck, 112; Gamreth and Petersen, 523–4, 526–7; Roberts (1970a), 402–3.
58 Czaplinski, 45–6; Lybeck, 114; Reddaway, 495, 498–500; Tham, 274, 303–4, 310, 318.
59 Gamrath and Petersen, 524–5; Hill, 102; Roberts (1970a), 402; Tandrup (1988), 92.
60 Gamrath and Petersen, 525–6; Hill, 131–4; Roberts (1970a), 399, 402–3; Tandrup (1988), 92; Tham, 319–25.
61 Gamrath and Petersen, 527; Lybeck, 116, 119, Tham, 325.

62 Hornborg, 169–72; Lind, 110; Lybeck, 108.
63 R. C. Anderson, 48–60; Hill, 136–9; Hornborg, 184–9; Lybeck, 116–19; Tandrup (1988), 93–4.
64 R. C. Anderson, 61–9; Gamrath and Petersen, 528; Hill, 142; Hornborg, 191–7; Lybeck, 121.
65 Gamrath and Petersen, 528; Hill, 142–50; Roberts (1970), 405–6; Seitz and Rosengren, 31–2; Tham, 328–38.
66 Parker, 183; Seitz and Rosengren, 32, 34–6, 39.
67 Tandrup (1979), 530–2.
68 Hintze, 181, 183–6; Parker, 167, 183.

6 THE FIRST GREAT NORTHERN WAR (1648–67)

1 Ahnlund, 114; Tandrup (1979), 114.
2 Sven Lundkvist, 'The experience of empire: Sweden as a Great Power', in Michael Roberts (ed.) *Sweden's Age of Greatness 1632–1718* (London, 1973), 39, 42–6, 49–51; Jerker Rosén, 'Statsledning och provinspolitik under Sveriges stormaktstid: En författningshistorisk skiss', *Scandia* (1946), 227–46.
3 Nils Edén, 'Grunderna för Karl X Gustafs anfall på Polen', *Historisk Tidskrift* (Stockholm), 26 (1906), 8; Georg Landberg, *Den svenska utrikespolitikens historia I:3 1648–1697* (Stockholm, 1952), 11, 51; Roberts (1970a), 404.
4 Muscovy began to be referred to commonly as 'Russia' in the second half of the seventeenth century, and the tsar's dominions will henceforth be referred to as such.
5 Kirby, 200–1.
6 Sven Ingeman Olofsson, *Efter Westfaliska Freden. Sveriges Yttre Politik 1650–1654* (Kungl. Vitterhets Hist. och Antikvitets Akademiens Handlingar: Historiska serie 4; Stockholm, 1957), 3–4; Michael Roberts, 'Karl X and the great parenthesis: a reconstruction', *Karolinska Förbundets Årsbok* (1989), 64; Jerker Rosén, 'Scandinavia and the Baltic', in F. L. Carsten (ed.) *New Cambridge Modern History V: The Ascendancy of France 1648/59–88* (Cambridge, 1961), 520; Zernack, 37–8.
7 Gerhardt and Hubatsch, 203; Hintze, 190–1; Landberg, 65–6; Olofsson, 75; Parker, 189; Roberts (1970a), 407.
8 F. L. Carsten, 'The rise of Brandenburg', in F. L. Carsten (ed.) *New Cambridge Modern History V: The Ascendancy of France 1648/59–88* (Cambridge, 1961), 546; Hintze, 205–7.
9 Rosén (1961), 523.
10 Kirby, 10; Tham, 360.
11 Carsten (1961), 549–50; Hintze, 207–9.
12 Edén, 6–7; Jablonowski (1970), 587–8.
13 Philip Longworth, *Alexis: Tsar of all the Russias* (London, 1984), 26–8; Werner Philipp, 'Russia: the beginnings of westernization', in F. L. Carsten (ed.) *New Cambridge Modern History V: The Ascendancy of France 1648/59–88* (Cambridge, 1961), 577–8, 581–2.
14 Olofsson, 2, 17, 19, 184–5, 228, 311–15, 320–7; Roberts (1989), 63.
15 Landberg, 81–2, 87; Rosén (1961), 521.

16 Bilmanis (1951), 187–8; Edén, 30–4; Landberg, 13–14; Leitsch, 147; Odén, 108; Reddaway, 519; Roberts (1989), 69–70.

17 Edén, 11–12, 27–37, 41–5; Landberg, 75, 82; Reddaway, 519; Vernadsky, 502.

18 Landberg, 89–90; Lybeck, 127; Roberts (1989), 62, 95–7.

19 Konopczynski, 319–20; Landberg, 92; Rauch (1954), 35; Reddaway, 519–21.

20 Forstreuter, 160–1; Gerhardt and Hubatsch, 217–18; Hintze, 193; Landberg, 94; Reddaway, 521–2; Seitz and Rosengren, 40–1; Vernadsky, 502.

21 Quoted in Hatton (1974), 128.

22 Hatton (1974), 117; Leitsch, 148; Longworth, 114–16; Philipp, 574; Reddaway, 552; Vernadsky, 503–4; Wittram (1954), 88.

23 Gerhardt and Hubatsch, 218; Hintze, 193–4; Landberg, 96; Reddaway, 522; Seitz and Rosengren, 41.

24 Forstreuter, 161; Hintze, 195; H. Jablonowski, 'Poland to the death of John Sobieski', in F. L. Carsten (ed.) *New Cambridge Modern History V: The Ascendancy of France 1648/59–88* (Cambridge, 1961), 567; Landberg, 97–8; Philipp, 574; Reddaway, 522–3; Seitz and Rosengren, 42–3.

25 Hill, 149–51, 153–6; Lybeck, 125; Roberts (1970a), 406; Tham, 355–7.

26 R. C. Anderson, 74–5; Finn Asgaard, *Kampen om Östersjön på Carl X Gustafs tid* (Carl X Gustaf Studier 6; Stockholm, 1974), 493–4; Hill, 159, 161–2; Landberg, 90; Lybeck, 125, 127.

27 Landberg, 101–4; Lybeck, 128; Reddaway, 523.

28 R. C. Anderson, 76–8; Asgaard, 495; Hornborg, 201–3; Lybeck, 128; Röhlk, 12–13.

29 Hill, 165–7; Kirby, 189–90; Lybeck, 130, 132; Birgitta Odén, 'Karl X Gustaf och det andra danska kriget', *Scandia* 27 (1961), 77; Seitz and Rosengren, 43–4.

30 Forstreuter, 162–3; Gerhardt and Hubatsch, 221; Hintze, 196–7; Reddaway, 524.

31 Hill, 166–8; Odén, 64–5, 72–3, 77–80, 95–9, 110–18.

32 R. C. Anderson, 80–1; Hill, 168–9; Kirby, 190; Odén, 53–4, 57–9, 99, 121, 131–2.

33 R. C. Anderson, 81–5; Asgaard, 496–7; Gerhardt and Hubatsch, 222; Hill, 169–70; Hintze, 198–9; Hornborg, 204–8.

34 R. C. Anderson, 85–6; Hill, 170; Hornborg, 209; Lybeck, 135.

35 R. C. Anderson, 87–98; Asgaard, 497–9; Hintze, 199; Hornborg, 211–12; Landberg, 119; Lybeck, 136.

36 Asgaard, 498–500; Hill, 174–84; Lybeck, 137; Seitz and Rosengren, 50–2.

37 Carsten (1961), 546–7; Hintze, 199–200, 212–17; Seitz and Rosengren, 48–50.

38 Bilmanis (1951), 191; Jablonowski (1961), 568; Landberg, 116, 119–21; Heinz Mathiesen, 'Herzog Jakob von Kurland und seine Politik', in *Pirmā Baltijas vēsturnieku konference Rīgā, 16–20 viii 1937* (Riga, 1938), 433; Reddaway, 525; Wittram (1954), 88, 116.

39 Davies, 343, 466–9; Jablonowski (1961), 568–9; Leitsch, 148; Longworth, 137, 175–6, 181–2; Reddaway, 526–9; Vernadsky, 525–7.

40 Hatton (1974), 117; Philipp, 575; Seitz and Rosengren, 52–3; Vernadsky, 525; Wittram (1954), 88; Zernack, 40–6.

7 THE LATER SEVENTEENTH CENTURY (1667–1700)

1 Landberg, 123–4; Zernack, 39.
2 Hintze, 211–13; Kazimierz Piwarski, 'Das baltische Problem in der öffentlichen Meinung in Polen im XVII. Jahrhundert', in *Pirmā Baltijas vēsturnieku konference Rigā, 16–20 viii* 1937 (Riga, 1938), 489.
3 Davies, 287–91, 346; Josef Gierowski and Andrzy Kaminski, 'The eclipse of Poland', in J. S. Bromley (ed.) *New Cambridge Modern History VI: The Rise of Great Britain and Russia 1688–1725* (Cambridge, 1970), 681–3, 687; Jablonowski (1961), 570; Piwarski, 489–90.
4 Hatton (1974), 118; Leitsch, 151; Roberts (1989), 108.
5 Andrew Lossky, *Louis XIV, William III and the Baltic Crisis of 1683* (University of California Publications in History vol. 49; Berkeley and Los Angeles, 1954), viii–ix, 1–2.
6 Landberg, 130, 132.
7 Longworth, 207–8; Zernack, 49.
8 Hill, 184–6; Landberg, 133–4; Rosén (1961), 527–8.
9 Hill, 187; Landberg, 141–2; Rosén (1961), 528.
10 Landberg, 18–19; Rosén, 28–9; Göran Rystad, 'Magnus Gabriel de la Gardie', in Michael Roberts (ed.) *Sweden's Age of Greatness 1632–1718* (London, 1973), 213–14.
11 Kirby, 192; Rosén (1961), 528; Zernack, 51.
12 Landberg, 170–3; Rystad, 214–15; Seitz and Rosengren, 56–7.
13 Carsten (1961), 552; F. L. Carsten, *The Origins of Prussia* (Oxford, 1954), 270; Hintze, 221, 225–8; Landberg, 177.
14 Gerhardt and Hubatsch, 223; Hintze, 229, 231; Landberg, 185–8; Claude Nordmann, *Grandeur et liberté de la Suède 1660–1792* (Paris-Louvain, 1971), 66–7.
15 Gerhardt and Hubatsch, 224; Hintze, 232–4; Landberg, 189.
16 J. A. Fridericia, review of Otto Vaupell's *Rigskansler Grev Griffenfeld* (in *Historisk Tidskrift* (Copenhagen), 5.Række: 4), 457 *et seq.*; Landberg, 166, 182–4; Lybeck, 142.
17 Gerhardt and Hubatsch, 224; Hill, 192–3; Landberg, 189–90; Lybeck, 142, 144, 147; Röhlk, 14.
18 Hornborg, 212–13; Landberg, 192.
19 R. C. Anderson, 107–14, 123–4; Gerhardt and Hubatsch, 223–5; Hill, 193; Hornborg, 215–20, 233; Lybeck, 144; Nordmann (1971), 68; Röhlk, 14.
20 R. C. Anderson, 116–22; Hornborg, 221–2; Lybeck, 144–7; Nordmann (1971), 68–9.
21 Ragnar Hoffstedt, *Sveriges utrikespolitik under krigsåren 1675–1679* (Uppsala, 1943), 320–36; Gerhardt and Hubatsch, 225; Hintze, 236–8; Landberg, 201–2; Lybeck, 150; Seitz and Rosengren, 59–66.
22 Hill, 195; Kirby, 218–19; Landberg, 204–7; Lossky, 3–4; Nordmann (1971), 70; Rosen, 530; Åke Stille, *Studier över Bengt Oxenstiernas politi-*

ska system och Sveriges förbindelser med Danmark och Holstein–Gottorp 1689–1692 (Uppsala, 1947), 35–8.

23 Oakley (1987a), 33; Rosén (1961), 531, 538; Stille, 38–9.

24 Landberg, 16, 213–14; Lossky, 3; Nordmann (1971), 104; Oakley (1987a), 29; Karl-Olof Rudelius, *Sveriges utrikespolitik 1681–1684: Från garantitraktaten till stilleståndet i Regensburg* (Uppsala, 1942), 12–15; Rosén (1961), 538, Stille, 39–40.

25 Landberg, 220; Lossky, 4; Oakley (1987a), 30; Rosén (1961), 539; Rudelius, 16–28, 42–8.

26 Hill, 197; Hintze, 239–40; Landberg, 214–15, 222, 225; Lossky, 5, 9, 12–13; Rudelius, 61–7.

27 Landberg, 216; Lossky, 3; Nordmann (1971), 82–3; Rudelius, 73–7.

28 Åström, 71–2; Oscar Bjurling, 'Swedish shipping and British–Dutch competition during the 1670s and 1680s', *Economy and History* XIII (1971), 24–6; Kirby, 229–32, 242, 321; Nordmann (1971), 53, 76–80, 97–8, 102–3.

29 Alf Åberg, 'The Swedish army, from Lutzen to Narva', in Michael Roberts (ed.) *Sweden's Age of Greatness* (London, 1973), 268–72; R. M. Hatton, *Charles XII of Sweden* (London, 1968), 113–14; Nordmann (1971), 87–91; J. W. Stoye, 'Soldiers and civilians', in J. S. Bromley (ed.) *New Cambridge Modern History VI: The Rise of Great Britain and Russia 1688–1725* (Cambridge, 1970), 771.

30 Hornborg, 227–30, 232; Lybeck, 153–6; Nordmann (1971), 91–2.

31 Rosen (1961), 533.

32 J. S. Bromley and A. N. Ryan, 'Navies', in J. S. Bromley (ed.) *New Cambridge Modern History VI: The Rise of Great Britain and Russia 1688–1725* (Cambridge, 1970), 805; Hornborg, 230–1; Lybeck, 156; Röhlk assesses the strength of the Danish fleet at the end of the century as thirty-three ships of the line, nine frigates and thirty smaller vessels (15).

33 Hill, 197–8; Hintze, 241–2; Landberg, 222, 225; Lossky, 6–9, 24; Rudelius, 158–86.

34 R. C. Anderson, 129–30; Landberg, 226; Lossky, 13–17, 24–9; Rudelius, 205–22, 256–8.

35 Hintze, 241–2; Landberg, 226–7; Lossky, 18–21, 34–5, 43; Rudelius, 222–6.

36 Hintze, 243; Landberg, 226; Lossky, x, 1, 22, 43.

37 Landberg, 229–31; Oakley (1987a), 54; Rosén (1961), 539–40; Stille, 43.

38 Gerhardt and Hubatsch, 226; Hintze, 248–50; Rosén (1961), 540.

39 Landberg, 231–2, 235–9; Lybeck, 158; Oakley (1987a), 55, 61–9; Rosén (1961), 540–1; Stille, 44–7.

40 R. C. Anderson, 131; Landberg, 239.

41 Ibid., 243, 246–7, 240; Nordmann (1971), 108–9; Oakley (1987a), 77–88, 100–5, 130–7, 164–7, 200–2; Stille, 82–93, 201–9.

42 Hatton (1968), 102; Landberg, 252–3, 256–9; Lybeck, 160; Oakley (1987a), 286–90, 295–301.

43 Landberg, 255, 259–60; Oakley (1987a), 304–10.

44 Kirby, 224–5; Landberg, 258; Nordmann (1971), 111; Rosén (1961), 537; Wittram (1954), 100.
45 Forstreuter, 170; Hatton (1974), 118; L. R. Lewitter, 'Russia, Poland and the Baltic 1697–1720', *Historical Journal* 11 (1968), 4–5; Longworth, 207–8; Mediger (1952), 136; Rauch (1954), 40; Reinhard Wittram, *Peter I Czar und Kaiser*, I–II (Göttingen, 1964), I, 32–3.
46 M. S. Anderson (1978), 83; Longworth, 241–2; Mediger (1952), 6; Philipp, 577–9; Wittram (1964), I, 48–51.
47 M. S. Anderson (1978), 40–2; Gierowski and Kaminski, 692; Hatton (1974), 119; Huttenbach, 41–2; Leitsch, 151; Walther Mediger, 'Russland und die Ostsee im 18.Jahrhunderte', *Jahrbuch für Geschichte Osteuropas* NF16 (1968), 90; Wittram (1964), 129–30.
48 Hatton (1968), 106; Kirby, 225; Wittram (1954), 101–3.
49 Hatton (1968), 106–7; R. M. Hatton, 'Charles XII and the Great Northern War', in J. S. Bromley (ed.) *New Cambridge Modern History VI: The Rise of Great Britain and Russia 1688–1725* (Cambridge, 1970), 119; Mediger (1952), 7–8; Wittram (1954), 200, 203–11, 214–15.
50 Davies, 476–89, 480, 487, 491; Jablonowski (1961), 569; Lewitter, (1968), 5; Piwarski, 490–1; Reddaway, 543–4.
51 Gierowski and Kaminski, 687, 692; Hatton (1968), 104, 106–7; Hatton (1974), 119–20; Lewitter (1968), 10; Lybeck, 160; Wittram (1954), 215–17.
52 Forstreuter, 179–82; Gerhardt and Hubatsch, 229; Gierowski and Kaminski, 689–90; Erich Hassinger, *Brandenburg–Preussen, Schweden und Russland 1700–1713* (Veröffentlichungen des Osteuropa-instituts München II; Munich, 1953), 32–5, 46.

8 CHARLES XII, PETER THE GREAT AND THE END OF SWEDISH DOMINANCE (1700–21)

1 Bromley and Ryan, 805; Stoye, 773 and n.1.
2 Hatton (1968), 117–19; Hatton (1970), 653–4; Lybeck, 164; Wittram (1954), 104.
3 R. C. Anderson, 133–6; Hatton (1968), 112–13, 132–7; Hornborg, 237; Lybeck, 162–3; Röhlk, 16; Seitz and Rosengren, 71–2.
4 Gerhardt and Hubatsch, 230; Gierowski and Kaminski, 693; Hatton (1968), 117, 144–5; Hatton (1970), 655.
5 M. S. Anderson (1978), 52; Hassinger, 44; Hatton (1968), 149–54; Hatton (1970), 655; Nordmann (1971), 152–3; Wittram (1964), 229–41.
6 Gierowski and Kaminski, 693–4; Hatton (1968), 157–69, 171, 174, 177–8; Hatton (1970), 656; Nordmann (1971), 154–5.
7 Gierowski and Kaminski, 695; Hatton (1968), 178–83; Hatton (1970), 655; Nordmann (1971), 155.
8 Davies, 497; Gierowski and Kaminski, 687, 696–9; Hatton (1968), 183–5, 192, 195–9, 202–4; Hatton (1970), 659; V. D. Koroljok, 'Der Eintritt der Rzeczpospolita in den Nordische Krieg', in Johannes Kalisch and Josef Gierowski (eds) *Um die Polnische Krone: Sachsen und Polen während des Nordischen Krieges 1700–21* (Berlin, 1962), 133–53; Leitsch,

153; Lewitter (1968), 32; Nordmann (1971), 155–7; Seitz and Rosengren, 172–3.

9 Davies, 497; Gierowski and Kaminski, 700; Hassinger, 188, 217–18; Hatton (1968), 203, 205–6, 212–14; Koroljuk, 158–9; Nordmann (1971), 158–9; Seitz and Rosengren, 73–5.

10 M. S. Anderson (1978), 54, 84–5; M. S. Anderson, 'Russia under Peter the Great', in J. S. Bromley (ed.) *New Cambridge Modern History VI: The Rise of Great Britain and Russia 1688–1725* (Cambridge, 1970), 720; Hatton (1974), 120, 122; Kerner, 52–3; Nordmann (1971), 156–7; Wittram (1954), 105; Wittram (1964), I, 253–64; ibid., II, 8–9.

11 M. S. Anderson (1970), 722; R. C. Anderson, 139–40; Bromley, 806; Wittram (1964), II, 21–2.

12 M. S. Anderson (1978), 57; Hassinger, 188, 202–5; Hatton (1968), 233, 247–8; Nordmann (1971), 162; Roger Roux, 'Politique exterieur de Pierre le Grand', *Revue d'histoire diplomatique* 17 (1903), 190–1.

13 Hatton, (1968), 233, 253–6, 275, 279–81, 297–306; Nordmann (1971), 163–71; Wittram (1964), 295, 297–9, 307–20.

14 Hatton (1968), 328; Hatton (1970), 627; Lybeck, 166–7.

15 M. S. Anderson (1978), 61; Gierowski and Kaminski, 708; Hatton (1968), 325; Leitsch, 153; Lewitter (1968), 13; Wittram (1964), I, 324–5.

16 J. F. Chance, *George I and the Northern War* (London, 1909), 12–19; Gerhardt and Hubatsch, 233–4; Hatton (1968), 327, 330; Mediger (1952), 10–11; Nordmann (1971), 173–4.

17 Chance, 29–30; Gerhardt and Hubatsch, 234; Hatton (1968), 334; Hatton (1970), 671; Hatton (1974), 121; Lybeck, 168–9; Claude J. Nordmann, *La crise du nord au début du xviiie siècle* (Paris, 1962), 2–3; Nordmann (1971), 175–8; Wittram (1954), 106.

18 R. C. Anderson, 152–4; Chance, 32–3, 39; Gerhardt and Hubatsch, 234; Hatton (1968), 352–3, 361–2, 366–7; Hatton (1970), 671; Hornborg, 255–6; Lybeck, 169; Nordmann (1971), 178.

19 Chance, 68–73; Gerhardt and Hubatsch, 234; Hatton (1968), 369; Hintze, 276–7; Mediger, 19; Nordmann (1962), 17; Wittram (1964), I, 255.

20 Gerhardt and Hubatsch, 231; Gierowski and Kaminski, 694; Hassinger, 59–61 *et passim*; Hintze, 262–3, 272–5.

21 M. S. Anderson (1970), 735; Gerhardt and Hubatsch, 232–3; Hassinger, 120–1, 209–24, 262–74; Hatton (1968), 352.

22 Hassinger, 278–80.

23 Kirby, 308; Hatton (1968), 370–8; Nordmann (1971), 178, 183; Wittram (1964), I, 330–5, 337–44; ibid., II, 244–5.

24 R. C. Anderson, 158–61; Hornborg, 267–9, 271–2; Nordmann (1962), 2, 32–3.

25 Gerhardt and Hubatsch, 235; Hatton (1968), 402–3; Hatton (1970), 674; Hintze, 277; Nordmann (1962), 17, 27.

26 R. C. Anderson, 164; Chance, 65–7, 82–92; Gerhardt and Hubatsch, 235; Hatton (1968), 399–400, 403–7; Mediger 17–19; John J. Murray, *George I, The Baltic and the Whig Split* (London, 1969), 101–4, 161–3, 179–89; Nordmann (1962), 26; Nordmann (1971), 186–7, 189–90, 192.

27 R. C. Anderson, 174–6; Chance, 110–12, 120–33; Hornborg, 276;

Hatton (1970), 676; Raymond E. Lindgren, 'A projected invasion of Sweden, 1716', *Huntington Library Quarterly* VII (1944), 225–43; Lybeck, 173–4; Mediger (1952), 31–2; Murray (1962), 226–33, 263–9; John J. Murray, 'Scania and the end of the Northern Alliance (1716)', *Journal of Modern History* XVI (1944), 86–91; Nordmann (1962), 60; Nordmann (1971), 192–3; Wittram (1964), II, 272–3, 282–3, 286–91.

28 Hans Bagger, 'The role of the Baltic in Russian foreign policy 1721–1773' (unpublished conference paper, 1991), 8–9; Chance, 106–9, 224–5; Hatton (1974), 122–3; Mediger (1952), 25, 27–8, 30–2, 34–5, 39–40; Mediger (1968), 93–4; Murray (1969), 224–5; Nordmann (1962), 60, 102–7, 200.

29 Hatton (1968), 329–30; Kirby, 315–16; Nordmann (1962), 18, 123; Nordmann (1971), 175, 179–80.

30 Hatton (1968), 342–6, 348–401, 436–9; Kirby, 310, 316–17; Nordmann (1962), 19, 31–2, 128–31; Nordmann (1971), 194–8, 201–4.

31 Chance, 158–84; Hatton (1968), 416–21; Kirby, 310; Murray (1969), 289–317; Nordmann (1962), 23, 39, 65–91; Nordmann (1971), 198–200.

32 Chance, 240–51, 325–8; Hatton (1968), 451–62, 475; Mediger (1952), 36; Nordmann (1962), 113–14, 154–6, 183; Nordmann (1971), 200–1, 204–5.

33 Hatton (1968), 465–8, 478–91; Nordmann (1971), 206–7.

34 Chance, 370–9, 394–7; Hatton (1968), 511–12; Lybeck, 178; Mediger (1952), 44–5; Nordmann (1962), 222–6; Nordmann (1971), 217–21; Michael Roberts, *The Age of Liberty: Sweden 1719–1772* (Cambridge, 1986), 11; Seitz and Rosengren, 75–6, 79–80.

35 R. C. Anderson, 195–8, 200; Chance, 335, 355–9; Hornborg, 281–3; Mediger (1952), 44, 47–8; Nordmann (1962), 211; Nordmann (1971), 220.

36 R. C. Anderson, 201–5; Chance, 427–9, 445; Hornborg, 285–9; Mediger (1952), 48–51; Nordmann (1962), 233–5, 238; Nordmann (1971), 223–4; Roberts (1986), 12; Wittram (1964), II, 420–1, 437–44, 449–56.

37 Hatton (1968), 456–8; Nordmann (1962), 158; Wittram (1964), II, 336–41.

38 Hatton (1970), 677; Nordmann (1962), 239; Nordmann (1971), 224–5; Roberts (1986), 12; Seitz and Rosengren, 80–1. No formal peace treaty between Sweden and Poland was signed at the end of the Great Northern War. Russia took it upon itself to mediate between them as part of the Nystad settlement, but neither Sweden nor Poland wished to allow this amount of Russian influence in their affairs, and the state of war between them was consequently not brought to an end until declarations made in Stockholm and Warsaw in September 1732 (Hatton (1970), 678; Seitz and Rosengren, 89–90).

39 Hatton (1968), 247–9, 514–16.

40 Ibid., 516–17; Kirby, 314, 318–20; Lundkvist, 57.

9 A NEW BALANCE (1721–51)

1 Joh. Rich. Danielson, *Die Nordische Frage in den Jahren 1746–1751* (Helsinki, 1888), 3–4.

2 Hornborg, 424; Konopczynski, 317.

3 Mediger (1952), 597–604, 615–17; Mediger (1968), 99.

4 Otto Brandt, 'Das Problem der Ruhe des Nordens im 18. Jahrhunderte', *Historische Zeitschrift* 140 (1929), 550–1; Edvard Holm, *Danmark–Norges Historie fra den Store Nordiske Krigs Slutning til Rigernes Adskillelse I–VII (1720–1814)*, I (Copenhagen, 1891–1901), 31–3, 64–5.

5 Erik Amburger, *Russland und Schweden 1762–1772* (Berlin, 1934), 25–6; Olof Jägerskiöld, *Den svenska utrikespolitikens historia II: 2 1721–1792* (Stockholm, 1957), 23–5; Nordmann (1971), 231–2; Roberts (1986), 40–1.

6 Danielson, 13–14; Jägerskiöld, 44–5.

7 M. S. Anderson (1978), 26–7, 125–6, 128, 132; Philipp, 586; Wittram (1964), II, 105–17.

8 Hintze, 282, 284–6.

9 Bagger (1991), 12.

10 R. M. Hatton, 'Scandinavia and the Baltic', in J. O. Lindsay (ed.) *New Cambridge Modern History VII: The Old Regime 1713–63* (Cambridge, 1957), 346; Holm, I, 12–15; Kirby, 318.

11 Hans Bagger, *Russlands alliancepolitik efter freden i Nystad* (Københavns Universitets Slaviske Institut. Studier 4; Copenhagen, 1974), 99–106; Ole Feldbæk, *Danmarks Historie Bd.4 Tiden 1730–1814* (Copenhagen, 1982), 261; Hatton (1957), 347; Hatton (1974), 129; Holm, I, 18–26; Mediger (1968), 95; Romuald Misiunas, 'The Baltic question after Nystad', *Baltic History* (Columbus, Ohio, 1974), 73–4.

12 Amburger, 26; Bagger (1974), 129–32; Bagger (1991), 12; H. Arnold Barton, 'Russia and the problem of Sweden–Finland, 1721–1809', *East European Quarterly* V (1971–2), 435; Hatton (1957), 347, 355; Jägerskiöld, 50–60; Lybeck, 180; Misiunas, 76–7; Seitz and Rosengren, 87.

13 Amburger, 27; Hatton (1957), 355; Jägerskiöld, 48–51, 64–5, 70–1; Nordmann (1971), 232–3, 236–7.

14 Bagger (1974), 134–6, 166–71; Roux, 212.

15 Bagger (1974), 27–49, 77–9, 223–35; Bagger (1991), 4, 6, 10, 12–14, 16.

16 Amburger, 27–8; Hatton (1957), 356; Jägerskiöld, 70–1, 77–81.

17 Bagger (1974), 240–50; Bagger (1991), 16; Feldbæk, 261–2; Hatton (1957), 347; Holm, I, 169–76; Nordmann (1971), 248–50; Seitz and Rosengren, 87–8.

18 M. S. Anderson (1970), 722; M. S. Anderson (1978), 89; Hornborg, 304; Mediger (1968), 98.

19 Bagger (1991), 30–1.

20 Anna had in 1710 married Duke Frederick William of Kurland and after his death the following year administered the duchy on behalf of her absent uncle-in-law, the childless Duke Ferdinand. The latter died in 1737, and on coming to the Russian throne Anna forced the Kurland nobility to elect her favourite Count Ernst Johann Bühren as his successor, thus making of the duchy a Russian satellite (Bagger (1991), 7, 19; Hatton (1974), 123; Misiunas, 73; Wittram (1954), 120–1).

21 Bagger (1991), 18; Mediger (1952), 140–7; Michael G. Müller, *Polen*

zwischen Preussen und Russland (Einzelveröffentlichungen der Historischen Kommission zu Berlin beim Friedrich Meinicke Institut der Freien Universitat Berlin, Bd.40; Berlin, 1984), 47–9.

22 Davies, 500, 502–4; Hatton (1974), 123; Mediger (1952), 82–3; Müller, 7, 9–11, 14–15, 22–3.

23 Davies, 500–1; Leitsch, 154–5; Misiunas, 75; Müller, 42.

24 Amburger, 28–9; Davies, 504; Hatton (1957), 357; Jägerskiöld, 106–8, 121–3; Nordmann (1971), 251–2; Roberts (1986), 34–5; Seitz and Rosengren, 90–1.

25 Jägerskiöld, 126–9; Mediger (1952), 86–7; Nordmann (1971), 252–3; Roberts (1986), 35.

26 Amburger, 30; Holm, *Ib.*II (Copenhagen, 1894), 127–30; Jägerskiöld, 130–8; Nordmann (1971), 254–5; Roberts (1986), 35; Seitz and Rosengren, 93.

27 Mediger (1952), 166–8, 514–15; Müller, 48–9, 74.

28 Mediger (1952), 168–9.

29 Amburger, 30; Barton (1971–2), 438; Jägerskiöld, 140–2, 144; Lybeck, 181; Nordmann (1971), 255–6; Roberts (1986), 24, 36.

30 Barton (1971–2), 438–9; Jägerskiöld, 142–3, 146–8; Nordmann (1971), 255–6; Roberts (1986), 23–4.

31 Barton (1971–2), 439; Danielson, 30–1; Jägerskiöld, 148–9; Mediger (1952), 105, 176–8, 188–90, 195.

32 Jägerskiöld, 150; Mediger (1952), 189, 197–200; Müller, 61–2.

33 Barton (1971–2), 438–9; Danielson, 15, 22–3, 28–9, 31–4; Kirby, 328–9; Mediger (1952), 212–13; Nordmann (1971), 257.

34 Barton (1971–2), 439–40; Danielson, 35–42, 49–50; Hatton (1957), 359; Mediger (1952), 200; Nordmann (1971), 256–7.

35 Barton (1971–2), 440–1; Danielson, 54–6; Hatton (1957), 359–60; Holm, II, 191–5; Jägerskiöld, 155–7; Mediger (1952), 213–17.

36 He was appointed Grand Chancellor in 1744.

37 Danielson, 56; Mediger (1952), 208, 211–12, 217; Misiunas, 72; Müller, 58–60.

38 Danielson, 58–9; Hatton (1957), 348, 360–1; Jägerskiöld, 156–60; Richard Lodge, 'The treaty of Åbo and the Swedish Succession', *English Historical Review* XLIII (1928), 540 *et seq.*; Mediger (1952), 213–15, 217–19; Nordmann (1971), 257–9; Seitz and Rosengren, 94–6.

39 Feldbæk, 257, 262–4; Hatton (1957), 347; Holm, II, 41–54, 60–3; Jägerskiöld, 98–9; Lybeck, 181.

40 R. C. Anderson, 220–1; Barton (1971–2), 441; Danielson, 79; Feldbæk, 263–4; Hatton (1957), 347–8, 361; Holm, II, 131–2, 181–7, 219–31; Jägerskiöld, 162–3; Lybeck, 181–2; Mediger (1952), 219–20; Nordmann (1971), 260.

41 Feldbæk, 265; Hatton (1957), 361; Holm, II, 233–40; Jägerskiöld, 164.

42 Amburger, 32; Danielson, 68; Hatton (1957), 361; Jägerskiöld, 165–8; Mediger (1952), 304; Nordmann (1971), 260; Roberts (1986), 39; Seitz and Rosengren, 97.

43 Barton (1971–2), 442; Danielson, 95–6, 101, 112–13, 118, 124, 188; Jägerskiöld, 170; Nordmann (1971), 261.

44 Danielson, 132, 212, 230; Jägerskiöld, 173; Mediger (1952), 304–6; Roberts (1986), 38; Seitz and Rosengren, 97–8.
45 Danielson, 156, 159.
46 Danielson, 261–3, 283, 286; Holm, III:1 (Copenhagen, 1897), 32–6, 39–45; Mediger (1952), 308–13.
47 Danielson, 278, 292, 294–8, 332; Holm, III:1, 68–9; Mediger (1952), 312–17.
48 Danielson, 230–40, 288, 307, 316; Hintze, 341; Mediger (1952), 308, 549–50.
49 Amburger, 35; Barton (1971–2), 443; Danielson, 323–4, 328–9, 357–64, 371–3, 397, 497; Hatton (1957), 349, 362; Holm, III:1, 60–77; Jägerskiöld, 178–82; Mediger (1952), 317; Roberts (1986), 40; Seitz and Rosengren, 99.
50 Danielson, 89–90; Hatton (1957), 349.

10 MID-CENTURY CRISES (1750–72)

1 Lybeck, 182; Jägerskiöld, 180–1; Seitz and Rosengren, 100.
2 Danielson, 440.
3 Müller, 57–8.
4 Brandt, 556–7; Holm, III:1, 130–6; Michael Roberts, 'Great Britain, Denmark and Russia, 1763–1770', in Ragnhild Hatton and M. S. Anderson (eds) *Studies in Diplomatic History: Essays in Memory of David Bayne Horn* (London, 1970), 238–40.
5 Amburger, 36, 38; Holm, III:1, 179–80; Jägerskiöld, 195; Lybeck, 182; Nordmann (1971), 263.
6 Hatton (1957), 349.
7 Hintze, 358–60; Mediger (1952), 474–6, 572–3.
8 Kirby, 334; Mediger (1952), 618–22; Mediger (1968), 100–1.
9 Mediger (1952), 675–6; Mediger (1968), 100.
10 Hintze, 361–4.
11 Hornborg, 309, 311–12; Jägerskiöld, 20–1, 202–4; Lybeck, 182; Nordmann (1971), 264; Roberts (1986), 21.
12 Amburger, 38; Hatton (1957), 363; Jägerskiöld, 197–8; Nordmann (1971), 262–4; Roberts (1986), 44.
13 Jägerskiöld, 199–202; Lybeck, 183; Roberts (1986), 43–4; Seitz and Rosengren, 102–3.
14 Gerhardt and Hubatsch, 278–9; Hornborg, 310.
15 R. C. Anderson, 228–9; Amburger, 43–4, 49; Gerhardt and Hubatsch, 278–80; Hatton (1957), 363; Hornborg, 310; Jägerskiöld, 204, 214–16; Nordmann (1971), 266–7.
16 Hintze, 371; Mediger (1952), 682–6, 688.
17 Hatton (1957), 349; Holm, III:1, 292–3; Mediger (1962), 689; Sergei M. Soloviev, *History of Russia Vol. 42: A New Empress* (ed. Nicholas Lupinin; Gulf Breeze, 1990), 20–30, 33.
18 Amburger, 38–40; Holm, III:1, 250–5; Jägerskiöld, 205–6.
19 Amburger, 47, 50–3, 57–8; Barton (1971–2), 444; Hatton (1957), 349; Soloviev (1990), 47–8.
20 Amburger, 53–4, 58–60; Feldbæk, 267; Gerhardt and Hubatsch, 237;

Hatton (1957), 349–50; Holm, III:1, 302; Jägerskiöld, 216; Seitz and Rosengren, 104–5; Soloviev (1990), 30–2.

21 Amburger, 74; Brandt, 558; Hatton (1957), 350; Isobel de Madariaga, *Russia in the Age of Catherine the Great* (London, 1981), 188–9; Soloviev (1990), 148–9.

22 Amburger, 22, 61–2, 72–3, 84–6, 88–9, 109–10; Brandt, 560; Feldbæk, 268; D. M. Griffiths, 'The rise and fall of the Northern System', *Canadian–American Slavic Studies* IV (1970), 551, 553; Holm, III:1, 315–17, 331–41; Madariaga, 192; Roberts (1970b), 240–1.

23 Amburger, 87; Bagger (1991), 22–3; Griffiths, 553; Hatton (1957), 350; Holm, III:1, 341–3; Madariaga, 192.

24 Danielson, 442; Feldbæk, 269–71; Holm, III:1, 365–6.

25 Amburger, 77, 79; Gerhardt and Hubatsch, 281; Griffiths, 554; Hintze, 387; Jägerskiöld, 221; Lybeck, 184; Madariaga, 190; Roberts (1986), 47.

26 Amburger, 70–3, 117, 122, 186; Jägerskiöld, 229–30; Nordmann (1971), 272–8.

27 Amburger, 184–5, 188–91, 193, 208–11, 213; Barton (1971–2), 445–6; Danielson, 443; Feldbæk, 269; Gerhardt and Hubatsch, 281–2; Holm, IV:1 (Copenhagen, 1902), 114–39; Jägerskiöld, 234, 236; Lybeck, 184; Madariaga, 216–18; Roberts (1970b), 262–3.

28 Amburger, 264–6, 285; Barton (1971–2), 446; Jägerskiöld, 238; Erik Lönnroth, *Den stora rollen: konung Gustaf III spelad av honom själv* (Stockholm, 1986), 36–50; Nordmann (1971), 280–4; Claude Nordmann, *Gustave III; un démocrate couronné* (Lille, 1986), 36–43; Stewart Oakley, 'Gustavus III of Sweden', in *Studies in History and Politics/ Etudes d'histoire et de politique* IV (Lennoxville, 1985), 71–4; Roberts (1986), 198–207.

29 Davies, 517–20; Herbert H. Kaplan, *The First Partition of Poland* (New York and London, 1962), 47–105; L. R. Lewitter, 'The Partitions of Poland', in A. Goodwin (ed.) *New Cambridge Modern History VIII: The American and French Revolutions 1763–93* (Cambridge, 1965), 337–40; Madariaga, 191, 196–204; Mediger (1952), 690.

30 Amburger, 197–8, 228–9, 251; Sv. Cedergreen Bech, *Struensee og hans tid* (Copenhagen, 1972), 226–7; Holm, IV:1, 235–40, 277–80; Holm, IV:2 (Copenhagen, 1902), 183–7, 328–46, 382–423; Madariaga, 218.

31 Davies, 514–15; Kaplan, 28; Lewitter (1965), 334–5; Madariaga, 189; Mediger (1952), 689–90; Mediger (1968), 101.

32 Hintze, 388–9; Kaplan, 20–1, 140–3.

33 Davies, 520–3; Hintze, 389; Kaplan, 147–8, 157, 159; Madariaga, 224.

11 THE AGE OF GUSTAVUS III (1772–90)

1 Jägerskiöld, 241–9; Nordmann (1971), 336–7; Nordmann (1986), 57–8; C. T. Odhner, *Sveriges politiska historia under konung Gustaf III:s regering 1.del 1771–1778* (Stockholm, 1885), 240–6.

2 Gerhardt and Hubatsch, 282–3; Jägerskiöld, 260–3; Lönnroth (1986), 66, 68; Nordmann (1986), 61–70; Odhner (1885), 174–81; 190–8;

NOTES AND REFERENCES

Michael Roberts, 'Great Britain and the Swedish Revolution, 1772-3', in his *Essays in Swedish History* (London, 1967a), 295-304.

3 Barton (1971-2), 447; Holm, V (Copenhagen, 1906), 172-3; Jägerskiöld, 264-7; Lönnroth (1986), 69; Madariaga, 228, 231; Nordmann (1986), 70-5; Odhner (1885), 218-35; Roberts (1967a), 310-21; Sergei M. Soloviev, *History of Russia*, vol. 48 (ed. George E. Munro, Gulf Breeze, 1991), 152-6.

4 Madariaga, 235, 384.

5 Griffiths, 558-60; Madariaga, 384-6.

6 Hornborg, 311; Jägerskiöld, 269-70; Nordmann (1986), 96; Odhner (1885), 474-8; Roberts (1989), 25.

7 Barton (1971-2), 447; Holm, V, 275-85; Jägerskiöld, 271-2; Lönnroth (1986), 69; Nordmann (1971), 347; Nordmann (1986), 122; Stewart Oakley, 'Gustavus III's plans for war with Denmark in 1783-1784', in Ragnhild Hatton and M. S. Anderson (eds) *Studies in Diplomatic History: Essays in Memory of David Bayne Horn* (London, 1970), 268-70; Odhner (1885), 281, 340-4.

8 Jägerskiöld, 249-50, 275-6, 278-80; Nordmann (1971), 371-2; Nordmann (1986), 139-40; Oakley (1985), 77-8; Odhner, II (1896), 1-27.

9 Hornborg, 313-17; Jägerskiöld, 249-50, 275; Nordmann (1971), 348-9; Nordmann (1986), 94-9; Odhner (1896), 97-101.

10 Feldbæk, 279-80; Holm, V, 294-8, 316-38; Jägerskiöld, 281-6; Lönnroth (1986), 71-2; Nordmann (1971), 364-7; Nordmann (1986), 124-31.

11 Jägerskiöld, 289-92; Lönnroth (1986), 84-94; Nordmann (1986), 153-4; Oakley (1970), 271-8; Odhner (1896), 229-31, 235-55.

12 Jägerskiöld, 292-5; Lönnroth (1986), 96-102; Nordmann (1971), 381-2; Nordmann (1986), 155-6; Oakley (1970), 278-85; Odhner (1896), 258-93.

13 H. Arnold Barton, 'Gustav III of Sweden and the East Baltic, 1771-1792', *Journal of Baltic Studies* 7 (1976), 14; Lönnroth (1986), 110-12; Nordmann (1986), 156-7, 219-20; Rauch (1952), 143; Odhner (1896), 276-8.

14 Jägerskiöld, 300, 302-3.

15 Barton (1976), 15-16, 24-5; Barton (1971-2), 447; Erik Ludvig Birck, *General Tolls krigsplan år 1788. Dess utförande och sammanbrott* (Svenska Litteratursällskapet i Finland CCXCVI; Helsingfors, 1944), 49-62; Feldbæk, 271-2; Jägerskiöld, 307-12; Lönnroth (1986), 126, 146-52; Erik Lönnroth, 'Gustavus III of Sweden: the final years. A political portrait', *Scandinavica* 6 (1967), 18; Nordmann (1971), 383-5; Nordmann (1986), 158-61; 163; Rauch (1952), 143.

16 Jägerskiöld, 314; Lönnroth (1986), 159.

17 Jägerskiöld, 315-16; Lönnroth (1986), 164-5; Nordmann (1986), 162.

18 Barton (1971-2), 448; Birck, 156 *et seq.*; Hornborg, 320-5; Jägerskiöld, 318-19; Lönnroth (1986), 152, 166-70; Lönnroth (1967) 21; Madariaga, 400-1; Nordmann (1986), 161, 163-4.

19 Barton (1976), 15-16; Jägerskiöld, 318-19; Madariaga, 402; Rauch (1952), 143.

20 Barton (1971–2), 449; Jägerskiöld, 317–20; Madariaga, 402; Nordmann (1971), 385–8; Nordmann (1986), 164–8.
21 Feldbæk, 272; Jägerskiöld, 321–5, 328; Madariaga, 402–3; Nordmann (1971), 386–7.
22 Barton (1971–2), 449–50; Holm, VI:1 (Copenhagen, 1907), 292–300; Hornborg, 329–37; Jägerskiöld, 326–7, 329–31; Lönnroth (1986), 185–91, 194–200; Madariaga, 398; Nordmann (1971), 388–90; Nordmann (1986), 168–71, 175–85.
23 Barton (1971–2), 450; Holm, VI:1, 306–8; Hornborg, 348–59, 316–72; Lönnroth (1986), 209, 216–18; Madariaga, 413; Nordmann (1986), 172, 189–91.
24 Lönnroth (1986), 229–36; Nordmann (1986), 232.
25 Barton (1976), 19–21; Hintze, 414–15; Jägerskiöld, 309; Madariaga, 398–400, 405, 411.
26 Jägerskiöld, 335–6; Lönnroth (1986), 237–40; Nordmann (1971), 492; Nordmann (1986), 232–3; Seitz and Rosengren, 113–15.
27 Barton (1976), 21.
28 Barton (1976), 19–26; Jägerskiöld, 338; Lewitter (1965), 351; Lönnroth (1986), 256; Nordmann (1986), 220, 234; Seitz and Rosengren, 115–16.

EPILOGUE

1 Barton (1986), 192–5; Jägerskiöld, 337, 340–7; Madariaga, 427–8; Seitz and Rosengren, 115–16.
2 Barton (1986), 226.
3 Davies, 528–30, 535–42; Leitsch, 161–2; Lewitter (1965), 352–9; Madariaga, 422–7, 428–38, 444–51; Wittram (1954), 122–4.
4 R. C. Anderson, 301–2; Barton (1986), 226–7, 248–9, 250–1; T. K. Derry, 'Scandinavia', in C. W. Crawley (ed.) *New Cambridge Modern History IX: War and Peace in an Age of Upheaval 1793–1830* (Cambridge, 1965), 484.
5 R. C. Anderson, 303–11; Barton (1986), 251–3; Derry, 484–5; Feldbæk, 284; Gerhardt and Hubatsch, 285–6.
6 Barton (1986), 226, 249–50; Sten Carlsson, *Gustaf IV Adolf* (Stockholm, 1946), 61–7; Seitz and Rosengren, 116–17.
7 Barton (1986), 267–70; Derry, 485; Gerhardt and Hubatsch, 291; Seitz and Rosengren, 119–20.
8 Barton (1986), 270–1; Gerhardt and Hubatsch, 291.
9 R. C. Anderson, 315; Barton (1986), 272–3, 275–6; Derry, 486; Feldbæk, 294.
10 R. C. Anderson, 315–19; Barton (1986), 276–8; Feldbæk, 295, 302.
11 Barton (1986), 278–9; Derry, 487; Hornborg, 390–1.
12 Barton, (1986), 279–80.
13 R. C. Anderson, 326; Barton (1986), 280–1; Hornborg, 391; Feldbæk, 302.
14 R. C. Anderson, 341; Barton (1986), 282–4, 292; Derry, 487; Hornborg, 404; Seitz and Rosengren, 122–7.
15 Barton (1986), 300–2.
16 Ibid., 290–2, 306–7, 311–20; Derry, 488–9.

17 Barton (1986), 320; Feldbæk, 304–5.
18 Barton (1986), 323–4, 336–8, 355–6; Derry, 490; Feldbæk, 305; Seitz and Rosengren, 132–3, 138–9.
19 Wismar was pawned to the duke of Mecklenburg–Schwerin for 100 years in 1803. In 1903 the Swedish crown surrendered all its rights to the city (Barton (1986), 240; Seitz and Rosengren, 118–19, 156).
20 Barton (1986), 361–2.

POSTLUDE

1 Mediger (1968), 103; C. F. Palmstierna, 'Schweden und Russland im 19. Jahrhundert', in *Pirmā Baltijas vēsturnieku konference, Rigā 16–20 viii 1937* (Riga, 1938), 520–2; A. J. P. Taylor, *The Struggle for Mastery in Europe 1848–1918* (Oxford, 1954), 153.
2 G. Andersson, 'The Scandinavian area and the Crimean War in the Baltic', *Scandinavian Studies* XLI (1969), 263–75; Hatton (1974), 126; Hornborg, 415–16, 418–19; Palmstierna, 524; Taylor, 138.
3 Handelsmann, 515; Hatton (1974), 127; Taylor, 138.
4 J. P. T. Bury, 'Nationalities and nationalism', in J. P. T. Bury (ed.) *New Cambridge Modern History X: The Zenith of European Power 1830–1870* (Cambridge, 1960), 219–20; Taylor, 12–16, 36–40.
5 Danzig, after a brief period of semi-independence under Napoleon, was successfully reclaimed by Prussia at the Congress of Vienna (Kutrzeba, 297).
6 T. K. Derry, *A History of Scandinavia* (London, 1979), 304.
7 Handelsmann, 509.

BIBLIOGRAPHY

Alf Åberg, 'The Swedish army, from Lutzen to Narva', in Michael Roberts (ed.) *Sweden's Age of Greatness* (London, 1973).

Nils Ahnlund, 'Dominium maris Baltici', in *Tradition och historia* (Stockholm, 1956).

Erik Amburger, *Russland und Schweden 1762–1772. Katharina II die schwedische Verfassung und die Ruhe des Nordens* (Berlin, 1934).

M. S. Anderson, 'Russia under Peter the Great', in J. S. Bromley (ed.) *New Cambridge Modern History VI: The Rise of Great Britain and Russia 1688–1725* (Cambridge, 1970).

——*Peter the Great* (London, 1978).

R. C. Anderson, *Naval Wars in the Baltic 1522–1850* (London, 1910).

G. Andersson, 'The Scandinavian area and the Crimean War in the Baltic', *Scandinavian Studies* XLI (1969).

I. Andersson, 'Sweden and the Baltic', in R. B. Wernham (ed.) *New Cambridge Modern History III: The Counter-Reformation and Price-Revolution 1559–1610* (Cambridge, 1968).

Finn Asgaard, *Kampen om Östersjön på Carl X Gustafs tid* (Carl X Gustafs Studier 6; Stockholm, 1974).

Sven-Erik Åström, 'The Swedish economy and Sweden's role as a great power', in Michael Roberts (ed.) *Sweden's Age of Greatness 1632–1718* (London, 1973).

Artur Attman, *The Struggle for Baltic Markets: Powers in Conflict 1558–1618* (Acta Regiae Societatis Scientiarum et Litterarum Gothburgensis: Humaniora 14; Gothenburg, 1979).

Hans Bagger, *Russlands alliancepolitik efter freden i Nystad* (Københavns Universitets Slaviske Institut. Studier 4; Copenhagen, 1974).

——'The role of the Baltic in Russian foreign policy 1721–1773' (unpublished conference paper, 1991).

H. Arnold Barton, 'Russia and the problem of Sweden–Finland, 1721–1809', *East European Quarterly* V (Boulder, Color., 1971–2).

——'Gustav III of Sweden and the East Baltic, 1771–1792', *Journal of Baltic Studies* 7 (1976).

——*Scandinavia in the Revolutionary Era 1760–1815* (Minneapolis, 1986).

Gerhard Benecke, 'The practice of absolutism II: 1626–1629', in Geoffrey Parker (ed.) *The Thirty Years War* (London, 1984).

R. R. Betts, 'Constitutional development and political thought in Eastern Europe', in G. R. Elton (ed.) *New Cambridge Modern History II: The Reformation 1520–59* (Cambridge, 1965).

Alfred Bilmanis, 'The struggle for domination of the Baltic: an historical aspect of the Baltic problem', *Journal of Central European Affairs* V (1945).

——*A History of Latvia* (Westport, 1951).

Erik Ludvig Birck, *General Tolls krigsplan år 1788. Dess utförande och sammanbrott* (Svenska Litteratursällskapet i Finland CCXCVI; Helsingfors, 1944).

Oscar Bjurling, 'Swedish shipping and British–Dutch competition during the 1670s and 1680s', *Economy and History* XIII (1971).

Otto Brandt, 'Das Problem der Ruhe des Nordens im 18. Jahrhunderte', *Historische Zeitschrift* 140 (1929).

J. S. Bromley and A. N. Ryan, 'Navies', in J. S. Bromley (ed.) *New Cambridge Modern History VI: The Rise of Great Britain and Russia 1688–1725* (Cambridge, 1970).

J. P. T. Bury, 'Nationalities and nationalism', in J. P. T. Bury (ed.) *New Cambridge Modern History X: The Zenith of European Power 1830–1870* (Cambridge, 1960).

Sten Carlsson, *Gustaf IV Adolf* (Stockholm, 1946).

F. L. Carsten, *The Origins of Prussia* (Oxford, 1954).

——'The rise of Brandenburg', in F. L. Carsten (ed.) *New Cambridge Modern History V: The Ascendancy of France 1648/59–1688* (Cambridge, 1961).

Sv. Cedergreen Bech, *Struensee og hans tid* (Copenhagen, 1972).

J. F. Chance, *George I and the Northern War* (London, 1909).

Władisław Czaplinski, 'Le problème baltique aux xvie et xviie siècles' *Congrès international des sciences historiques. XIe Congrès. Rapports I* (Stockholm, 1960).

Jan Dąbrowski, 'Baltische Handelspolitik Polens und Litauens im XIV–XVI Jahrhunderte', in *Pirmā Baltijas vēsturnieku konference Rigā, 16–20 viii 1937* (Riga, 1938).

Troels Dahlerup, 'Christian IVs udenrigspolitik set i lyset af de første oldenborgeres dynastipolitik', in Svend Ellehøj (ed.) *Christian IVs Verden* (Copenhagen, 1988).

Joh. Rich. Danielson, *Die Nordische Frage in den Jahren 1746–1751* (Helsinki, 1888).

Norman Davies, *God's Playground: A History of Poland I: Origins to 1795* (Oxford, 1981).

T. K. Derry, 'Scandinavia', in C. W. Crawley (ed.) *New Cambridge Modern History IX: War and Peace in an Age of Upheaval 1793–1830* (Cambridge, 1965).

——*A History of Scandinavia* (London, 1979).

Erich Donnert, *Der Livländische Ordensritterstaat und Russland: Der livländische Krieg und die Baltische Frage in der europäischen Politik 1558–1583* (Berlin, 1963).

Nils Edén, 'Grunderna för Karl X Gustafs anfall på Polen', *Historisk Tidskrift* (Stockholm), 26 (1906).

Thomas Esper, 'Russia and the Baltic 1494–1558', *Slavic Review* 25 (1966).

Birger Fahlborg, 'Sverige på fredskongressen i Nymegen 1676–1678', *Historisk Tidskrift* (Stockholm) 64 (1944).

Ole Feldbæk, *Danmarks Historie Bd.4 Tiden 1730–1814* (Copenhagen, 1982).

J. L. I. Fennell, 'Russia 1462–1583', in G. R. Elton (ed.) *New Cambridge Modern History II: The Reformation 1520–1559* (Cambridge, 1965).

Kurt Forstreuter, *Preussen und Russland von den Anfängen des Deutschen Ordens bis zu Peter dem Grossen* (Göttinger Bausteine zur Geschichtswissenschaft Bd. 23, Göttingen, 1955).

J. A. Fridericia, rev. of Otto Vaupell's *Rigskansler Grev Griffenfeld* in *Historisk Tidskrift* (Copenhagen) 5: 4.

Helge Gamrath and E. Ladewig Petersen, *Danmarks Historie B.2: Tiden 1340–1648 (Andet Halvband 1559–1648)* (Copenhagen, 1980).

Martin Gerhardt and Walther Hubatsch, *Deutschland und Skandinavien im Wandel der Jahrhunderte* (Bonn, 1977).

Josef Gierowski and Andrzy Kaminski, 'The eclipse of Poland', in J. S. Bromley (ed.) *New Cambridge Modern History VI: The Rise of Great Britain and Russia 1688–1725* (Cambridge, 1970).

D. M. Griffiths, 'The rise and fall of the Northern System', *Canadian–American Slavic Studies* IV (1970).

O. Halecki, 'Les Jagellions et la Livonie', in *Pirmā Baltijas vēsturnieku konference Rigā, 16–20 viii 1937* (Riga, 1938).

M. Handelsmann, 'La politique polonaise sur la Baltique aux xviii. et xix. siècles', in *Pirmā Baltijas vēsturnieku konference Rigā, 16–20 viii 1937* (Riga, 1938).

Erich Hassinger, *Brandenburg–Preussen, Schweden und Russland 1700–1713* (Veröffentlichungen des Osteuropa-instituts München II; Munich, 1953).

R. M. Hatton, 'Scandinavia and the Baltic', in J. O. Lindsay (ed.) *New Cambridge Modern History VII: The Old Regime 1713–63* (Cambridge, 1957).

——*Charles XII of Sweden* (London, 1968).

——'Charles XII and the Great Northern War', in J. S. Bromley (ed.) *New Cambridge Modern History VI: The Rise of Great Britain and Russia 1688–1725* (Cambridge, 1970).

——'Russia and the Baltic', in Jarus Hunczak (ed.) *Russian Imperialism from Ivan the Great to the Revolution* (New Brunswick, 1974).

Stanislaw Herbst, 'Der livländische Krieg 1600–1602', in *Pirmā Baltijas vēsturnieku konference Rigā, 16–20 viii 1937* (Riga, 1938).

Charles E. Hill, *The Danish Sound Dues and the Command of the Baltic* (Durham, N.C., 1926).

Otto Hintze, *Die Hohenzollern und ihr Werk* (Berlin, 1915).

Ragnar Hoffstedt, *Sveriges utrikespolitik under krigsåren 1675–1679* (Uppsala, 1943).

BIBLIOGRAPHY

Edvard Holm, *Danmark–Norges Historie fra den Store Nordiske Krigs Slutning til Rigernes Adskillelse (1720–1814)*, I–VII (Copenhagen, 1891–1901).

Eirik Hornborg, *Kampen om Östersjön till slutet av segelfartygens tidevarv* (Stockholm, 1945).

Jarus Hunczak (ed.) *Russian Imperialism from Ivan the Great to the Revolution* (New Brunswick, 1974).

Henry J. Huttenbach, 'The origins of Russian Imperialism' (in Hunczak, op. cit.).

H. Jablonowski, 'Poland to the death of John Sobieski', in F. L. Carsten (ed.) *New Cambridge Modern History V: The Ascendancy of France 1648/ 59–88* (Cambridge, 1961).

————'Poland–Lithuania 1609–48', in J. P. Cooper (ed.) *New Cambridge Modern History IV: The Decline of Spain and the Thirty Years War 1610–48/59* (Cambridge, 1970).

Olof Jägerskiöld, *Den svenska utrikespolitikens historia II: 2 1721–1792* (Stockholm, 1957).

Herbert H. Kaplan, *The First Partition of Poland* (New York and London, 1962).

J. L. H. Keep, 'Russia 1613–45', in J. P. Cooper (ed.) *New Cambridge Modern History IV: The Decline of Spain and the Thirty Years War 1610–48/59* (Cambridge, 1970).

Robert J. Kerner, *The Urge to the Sea: The Course of Russian History* (New York, 1942).

David Kirby, *Northern Europe in the Early Modern Period: The Baltic World 1492–1772* (London and New York, 1990).

W. Kirchner 'A milestone in European history: the Danish–Russian treaty of 1562', *Slavonic and East European Review* XXXII (1944).

————*The Rise of the Baltic Question* (Newark, N.J., 1954).

Ladislas Konopczynski, 'Le problème baltique dans l'histoire moderne', *Revue historique* 162 (1929).

V. D. Koroljuk, 'Der Eintritt der Rzeczpospolita in den Nordische Krieg', in Johannes Kalisch and Josef Gierowski (eds) *Um die Polnische Krone: Sachsen und Polen während des Nordischen Krieges 1700–21* (Berlin, 1962).

Stanislaw Kutrzeba, 'Dantzig et la Pologne à travers les siècles', in *Pirmā Baltijas vēsturnieku konference Rigā, 16–20 viii 1937* (Riga, 1938).

Georg Landberg, *Den svenska utrikespolitikens historia I:3 1648–1697* (Stockholm, 1952).

Walter Leitsch, 'Russo–Polish confrontation' (in Hunczak, op. cit.).

Kazimierz Lepszy, 'Die Bedeutung der polnischen Kriegsmarin im XVI Jahrhunderte', in *Pirmā Baltijas vēsturnieku konference Rigā 16–20 viii 1937* (Riga, 1938).

————'The union of the crowns between Poland and Sweden in 1587', in *Poland at the XIth International Congress of Historical Sciences in Stockholm* (Warsaw, 1960).

L. R. Lewitter, 'The Partitions of Poland', in A. Goodwin (ed.) *New Cambridge Modern History VIII: The American and French Revolutions 1763–93* (Cambridge, 1965).

———'Russia, Poland and the Baltic 1697–1720', *Historical Journal* 11 (1968).

Gunner Lind, 'Rigets sværd: Krig og krigsvæsen under Christian IV', in Svend Ellehøj (ed.) *Christian IVs Verden* (Copenhagen, 1988).

Raymond E. Lindgren, 'A projected invasion of Sweden, 1716', *Huntington Library Quarterly* VII (1944).

Richard Lodge, 'The treaty of Åbo and the Swedish Succession', *English Historical Review* XLIII (1928).

Philip Longworth, *Alexis: Tsar of all the Russians* (London, 1984).

Erik Lönnroth, 'Gustavus III of Sweden: the final years. A political portrait', *Scandinavica* VI (1967).

———*Den stora rollen: Konung Gustaf III spelad av honom själv* (Stockholm, 1986).

Andrew Lossky, *Louis XIV, William III and the Baltic Crisis of 1683* (University of California Publications in History vol. 49; Berkeley and Los Angeles, 1954).

Sven Lundkvist, 'The experience of empire: Sweden as a Great Power', in Michael Roberts (ed.) *Sweden's Age of Greatness 1632–1718* (London, 1973).

Otto Lybeck, *Öresund i Nordens Historie: en marinpolitisk studie* (Malmö, 1943).

Isobel de Madariaga, *Russia in the Age of Catherine the Great* (London, 1981).

Marian Malowist, 'Riga und Dantzig vom Ausbruch des dreissigjährigen Krieges bis zum Ende des XVII. Jahrhundert', in *Pirmā Baltijas vēsturnieku konference Rigā 16–20 viii 1937* (Riga, 1938).

Heinz Mathiesen, 'Herzog Jakob von Kurland und seine Politik', in *Pirmā Baltijas vēsturnieku konference Rigā, 16–20 viii 1937* (Riga, 1938).

Walther Mediger, *Moskaus Weg nach Europa* (Brunswick, 1952).

———'Russland und die Ostsee im 18. Jahrhunderte', *Jahrbuch für Geschichte Osteuropas* NF16 (1968).

Gunnar Mickwitz, 'Handelsverbindungen der späthänsischen Zeit', in *Pirmā Baltijas vēsturnieku konference Rigā, 16–20 viii 1937* (Riga, 1938).

Romuald J. Misiunas, 'The Baltic question after Nystad', *Baltic History* (Columbus, Ohio, 1974).

Michael G. Müller, *Polen zwischen Preussen und Russland* (Einzelveröffentlichungen der Historischen Kommission zu Berlin beim Friedrich Meinicke Institut der Freien Universitat Berlin, Bd. 40; Berlin, 1984).

John J. Murray, 'Scania and the end of the Northern Alliance (1716)', *Journal of Modern History* XVI (1944).

———*George I, the Baltic and the Whig Split* (London, 1969).

Bodo Nischan, 'On the edge of the abyss' (in Parker, op. cit.).

Axel Norberg, *Polen i svensk politik 1617–26* (Stockholm, 1974).

Claude J. Nordmann, *La crise du nord au début du xviiie siècle* (Paris, 1962).

———*Grandeur et liberté de la Suède 1660–1792* (Paris–Louvain, 1971).

———*Gustave III: un démocrate couronné* (Lille, 1986).

Stewart Oakley, 'Gustavus III's plans for war with Denmark in 1783–1784', in Ragnhild Hatton and M. S. Anderson (eds) *Studies in*

Diplomatic History: Essays in Memory of David Bayne Horn (London, 1970).

——'Gustavus III of Sweden', in *Studies in History and Politics/Etudes d'histoire et de politique* IV (Lennoxville, 1985).

——*William III and the Northern Crowns during the Nine Years War 1689–1697* (New York and London, 1987a).

——'War in the Baltic, 1550–1790', in Jeremy Black (ed.) *The Origins of War in Early Modern Europe* (Edinburgh, 1987b).

Birgitta Odén, 'Karl X Gustaf och det andra danska kriget', *Scandia* 27 (1961).

C. T. Odhner, *Sveriges politiska historia under konung Gustaf III:s regering*, I–III (1885–1905).

Sven Ingeman Olofsson, *Efter Westfaliska Freden. Sveriges Yttre Politik 1650–1654* (Kungl. Vitterhets Hist. och Antikvitets Akademiens Handlingar: Historiska serie 4; Stockholm, 1957).

Sven Ulric Palme, *Sverige och Danmark 1596–1611* (Uppsala, 1942).

C. F. Palmstierna, 'Schweden und Russland im 19. Jahrhundert', in *Pirmā Baltijas vēsturnieku konference Rigā, 16–20 viii 1937* (Riga, 1938).

Geoffrey Parker (ed.) *The Thirty Years War* (London, 1984).

E. Ladewig Petersen, 'Defence, war and finance: Christian IV and the Council of the Realm 1596–1629', *Scandinavian Journal of History* 7 (1982).

——'The Danish Intermezzo' (in Parker, op. cit.).

Werner Philipp, 'Russia: the beginnings of westernization', in F. L. Carsten (ed.) *New Cambridge Modern History V: The Ascendancy of France 1648/59–88* (Cambridge, 1961).

Kazimierz Piwarski, 'Das baltische Problem in der öffentlichen Meinung in Polen im XVII. Jahrhundert', in *Pirmā Baltijas vēsturnieku konference Rigā, 16–20 viii 1937* (Riga, 1938).

Georg von Rauch, 'Moskau und die europäischen Mächte des 17. Jahrhunderts', *Historische Zeitschrift* 178 (1954).

——'Zur Geschichte des schwedischen Dominium Maris Baltici', *Die Welt als Geschichte* 12 (1952).

W. F. Reddaway et al. (eds) *The Cambridge History of Poland: From the Origins to Sobieski (to 1696)* (Cambridge, 1950).

Michael Roberts, *Gustavus Adolphus: A History of Sweden 1611–1632*, Vol. I (1611–1626) (London, 1953); Vol. II (1626–1632) (London, 1958).

——'Great Britain and the Swedish Revolution, 1772–3', in Michael Roberts, *Essays in Swedish History* (London, 1967a).

——'Gustav Adolf and the art of war', in Michael Roberts, *Essays in Swedish History* (London, 1967b).

——'The political objectives of Gustav Adolf in Germany 1630–2', in Michael Roberts, *Essays in Swedish History* (London, 1967c).

——*The Early Vasas* (Cambridge, 1968).

——'Sweden and the Baltic 1611–54', in J. P. Cooper (ed.) *New Cambridge Modern History IV: The Decline of Spain and the Thirty Years War 1610–48/59* (Cambridge, 1970a).

——'Great Britain, Denmark and Russia 1763–1770', in Ragnhild

Hatton and M. S. Anderson (eds) *Studies in Diplomatic History: Essays in Memory of David Bayne Horn* (London, 1970b).
——*Gustavus Adolphus and the Rise of Sweden* (London, 1973).
——*The Swedish Imperial Experience 1560–1718* (Cambridge, 1979).
——*British Diplomacy and Swedish Politics 1758–1773* (London, 1980).
——'The Swedish dilemma', (in Parker, op. cit.).
——*The Age of Liberty: Sweden 1719–1772* (Cambridge, 1986).
——'Karl X and the great parenthesis: a reconsideration', *Karolinska Förbundets Årsbok* (1989).
——'Oxenstierna in Germany 1633–1636', in Michael Roberts, *From Oxenstierna to Charles XII: Four Studies* (Cambridge, 1991).
Otto Röhlk, 'Der Einfluss der Seemacht auf Dänemarks Geschichte', *Historische Zeitschrift* 165 (1941–2).
Jerker Rosén, 'Statsledning och provinspolitik under Sveriges stormaktstid: En författningshistorisk skiss', *Scandia* (1946).
——'Scandinavia and the Baltic', in F. L. Carsten (ed.) *New Cambridge Modern History V: The Ascendancy of France 1648/59–88* (Cambridge, 1961).
Roger Roux, 'Politique extérieur de Pierre le Grand', *Revue d'histoire diplomatique* 17 (1903).
Karl-Olof Rudelius, *Sveriges utrikespolitik 1681–1684: Från garantitraktaten till stilleståndet i Regensburg* (Uppsala, 1942).
Göran Rystad, 'Magnus Gabriel de la Gardie', in Michael Roberts (ed.) *Sweden's Age of Greatness 1632–1718* (London, 1973).
Dietrich Schäfer, 'Der Kampf um die Ostsee im 16. und 17. Jahrhunderte', *Historische Zeitschrift* 83 (1899).
Herbert Seitz and Erik Rosengren, *Sveriges freder och fördrag 1524–1905* (Stockholm, 1944).
P. Skwarczynski, 'Poland and Lithuania', in R. B. Wernham (ed.) *New Cambridge Modern History III: The Counter-Reformation and Price Revolution 1559–1610* (Cambridge, 1968).
Sergei M. Soloviev, *History of Russia Vol. 42: A New Empress* (ed. Nicholas Lupinin; Gulf Breeze, 1990).
——*History of Russia Vol. 45: The Rule of Catherine the Great 1766–1768* (ed. William H. Hill; Gulf Breeze, 1986).
——*History of Russia Vol. 48: The Rule of Catherine the Great 1772–1774* (ed. George E. Munro; Gulf Breeze, 1991).
Åke Stille, *Studier över Bengt Oxenstiernas politiska system och Sveriges förbindelser med Danmark och Holstein–Gottorp 1689–1692* (Uppsala, 1947).
J. W. Stoye, 'Soldiers and civilians', in J. S. Bromley (ed.) *New Cambridge Modern History VI: The Rise of Great Britain and Russia 1688–1725* (Cambridge, 1970).
Adam Szelągowski, *Der Kampf um die Ostsee (1544–1621)* (Munich, 1916).
Leo Tandrup, *Mod triumf eller tragedie* (Aarhus, 1979).
——'Når to trættes, så ler den tredje: Christian IVs og rigsrådets forhold til det tyske Rige og især Sverige', in Svend Ellehøj (ed.) *Christian IVs Verden* (Copenhagen, 1988).

A. J. P. Taylor, *The Struggle for Mastery in Europe 1848–1918* (Oxford, 1954).

Wilhelm Tham, *Den svenska utrikespolitikens historia I: 2 1560–1648* (Stockholm, 1960).

George Vernadsky, *A History of Russia Vol. 5: The Tsardom of Moscow 1547–1682*, Part I (New Haven and London, 1969).

Walther Vogel, 'Die Ostseekämpfe 1561–1721 im Rahmen der europäischen Politik', in *Pirmā Baltijas vēsturnieku konference Rigā, 16–20 viii 1937* (Riga, 1938).

Reinhard Wittram, *Baltische Geschichte. Die Ostseelande. Livland, Estland, Kurland 1180–1918* (Munich, 1954).

——*Peter I Czar und Kaiser*, I–II (Göttingen, 1964).

Erik Zeeh, 'Gustav Adolf und die Belagerung Rigas im Jahre 1621', in *Pirmā Baltijas vēsturnieku konference Rigā, 16–20 viii 1937* (Riga, 1938).

Klaus Zernack, *Studien zu den schwedisch–russischen Beziehungen in der 2. Hälfte der 17. Jahrhunderts I: Die diplomatischen Beziehungen zwischen Schweden und Moskau von 1675 bis 1689* (Giessen, 1958).

INDEX